FAILING OUR
BRIGHTEST KIDS

THE EDUCATIONAL INNOVATIONS SERIES

The Educational Innovations series explores a wide range of current school reform efforts. Individual volumes examine entrepreneurial efforts and unorthodox approaches, highlighting reforms that have met with success and strategies that have attracted widespread attention. The series aims to disrupt the status quo and inject new ideas into contemporary education debates.

Series edited by Frederick M. Hess

Other books in this series:

FAILING OUR BRIGHTEST KIDS

The Global Challenge of Educating
High-Ability Students

Chester E. Finn, Jr.
Brandon L. Wright

HARVARD EDUCATION PRESS
CAMBRIDGE, MASSACHUSETTS

Library of Congress Control Number 2015937064
Paperback 978-1-61250-841-2
Library Edition ISBN 978-1-61250-842-9

Published by Harvard Education Press,
an imprint of the Harvard Education Publishing Group

Harvard Education Press
8 Story Street
Cambridge, MA 02138

Cover Design: Ciano Design
Cover Photo: Stuart Fox/Getty Images

The typefaces used in this book are ITC Legacy Serif and ITC Legacy Sans.

CONTENTS

PART III

Toward the Future

ACKNOWLEDGMENTS

WE LAUNCHED this ambitious investigation under the dual aegis of the Thomas B. Fordham Institute, where we primarily work, and Stanford University's Hoover Institution, where Chester Finn is a senior fellow and longtime chairman of Hoover's Koret Task Force on K–12 Education, whose distinguished members not only endorsed the research plan but also improved it in myriad ways. We benefited from additional support from the Noyce Foundation and the College Board, as well as advice from veteran education-policy scholars and participants in the field of gifted education.

Indeed, we owe huge debts of gratitude to many individuals and organizations for their assistance in making this book possible and improving its contents. None, of course, bears the faintest responsibility for our conclusions, much less for any errors, misjudgments, or misunderstandings—which are easier to make when navigating foreign lands and languages.

Special thanks are due to Hoover's John Raisian and Richard Sousa, as well as the Koret Foundation and other task force supporters, not least for enabling Chester Finn to settle into a monastic writer's life in Palo Alto for several productive months, during which Jeff Jones, Deborah Ventura, and Celeste Czeto went out of their way to make him comfortable and productive. While there, he benefited from the sage counsel of Eric Hanushek (whose pioneering analyses, undertaken with Paul Peterson and Ludger Woessmann, we repeatedly lean on in these pages) as well as William Damon, Margaret Raymond, Williamson Evers, and others on the Hoover team and Stanford faculty.

At Fordham, our home base in Washington, we've been encouraged by a great board of trustees and aided throughout by Daniela Fairchild, Gary LaBelle, Amber M. Northern, Michael J. Petrilli, Alyssa Schwenk, and Dara Zeehandelaar.

PISA experts at the OECD in Paris, particularly Andreas Schleicher, Michael Davidson, and Pablo Zoido, generously offered explanations and extra analyses, as did Andreas Oranje at the Educational Testing Service and Antonio Wendland at Harvard's Program on Education Policy and Governance.

Longtime experts on gifted education in the United States, especially Susan G. Assouline and Rena F. Subotnik, offered useful, timely feedback at key points along the way.

Above all, we could not have carried out this study without both remote and on-the-ground help in all the sites we visited and countries we examined. It's impossible to name everyone who welcomed and educated us, filled out surveys, schlepped us around, invited us into their schools and offices, submitted to interviews and follow-up queries, supplied us with reading materials, helped plan itineraries, patiently explained the idiosyncrasies of their country's education systems, and in many cases checked our early drafts for accuracy. Very special thanks go to Satoko Fukahori and Shinji Tateishi in Japan; Chwee Geok Quek in Singapore; Yewon Suh, Jiyoung Ryu, Kyungbin Park, and Seokhee Cho in South Korea; Christine Tsuei-Yuan Lai and Arthur Song in Taiwan; Kirsi Tirri and Auli Toom in Finland; Angelika Göbel, Regina Poetke, Barbara Loos, Robin Pantke, Renè Beron, Eva Stumpf, and Sylke Wischnevsky in Germany; Csilla Fuszek, Eva Gyarmathy, and Vilmos Vass in Hungary; Victor Mueller-Oppliger in Switzerland; Michael Barber, Tim Dracup, Tim Oates, Ian Fordham, Deborah Eyre, and Denise Yates in England; Joanne Foster, Paul Grogan, Barry Finlay, Dona Matthews, and Leonila Liko in Ontario; and Geoff Kinkade in Western Australia.

We also owe heartfelt thanks to our long-suffering wives, Renu Virmani and Mary Gardner, exceptional professionals in their own fields, for their encouragement, forbearance, and endurance as we churned ahead.

The Harvard Education Press, to which we were introduced by Frederick Hess, has been a pleasure to work with, especially Caroline Chauncey, Laura Cutone, Rose Ann Miller, Sumita Mukherji, and an anonymous but expert copy editor.

Our most sincere gratitude to all who helped during this project's long gestation.

Introduction

AMERICAN EDUCATION has focused in recent decades on ensuring that all children, especially those from poor and minority backgrounds, attain a minimum level of academic achievement. That is an absolutely worthy goal—and the country has made modest progress toward reaching it, particularly in the early grades.

But what about students already above that minimum? Those for whom reaching "proficiency" is no challenge? How well has the U.S. education system been serving them? How are they doing academically compared with their age-mates in other countries?

A number of studies, books, and commentaries have raised the disquieting possibility that our focus on boosting the performance of students "below the bar" has neglected girls and boys who have already cleared it; in an era committed to leaving no child behind, *these* kids are at considerable risk of languishing in classes geared toward universal but modest proficiency and taught by instructors admonished to raise the floor but under no pressure to lift the ceiling.

These are the same children who, in the words of the American Enterprise Institute's Frederick M. Hess, "may be those most likely to one day develop miraculous cures, produce inspiring works, invent technological marvels and improve the lives of all Americans."[1]

They are, in other words, an important element of the nation's human capital—and they, too, deserve an education that meets their needs, develops their potential, and maximizes their attainments. Yet far too few of these children, especially the poor and minority

1

youngsters among them, are getting that kind of education today. Our goal in this book is to persuade U.S. educators and policy makers to attend more purposefully and systematically to their schooling.

This is a steep hill to climb. Many Americans don't think these kids need special attention and are loath to divert resources in their direction. But it's a hill that others have struggled up long before we reached its foot. A full century before No Child Left Behind, some local public school systems—concerned lest the education of exceptionally able children be consigned to private schools accessible mainly to the wealthy—undertook in various ways to address the specific learning needs of such pupils. Worcester (Massachusetts) opened the first special school for gifted pupils in 1901. A decade later, the Dayton (Ohio) public schools created "The Make-Time School" in which high-ability youngsters (and those who had for some reason missed a year of formal education) could speed through the curricula of both eighth and ninth grades in a single year.[2] By 1920, many cities had made similar arrangements, though these tended to fade amid the Great Depression and the weighty, costly distractions of World War II.

The education of high-ability and high-achieving students emerged as a national concern during the 1950s in the aftermath of Sputnik—part of America's worry that its long-assumed scientific and technological prowess was being eclipsed by its chief Cold War enemy.

The National Association for Gifted Children was founded in 1954, the same year as the Supreme Court's *Brown v. Board of Education* decision. And as the country began to desegregate its schools and concern itself with educational equity, a seminal 1961 book by Carnegie Corporation president (and future Health, Education, and Welfare secretary) John W. Gardner posed the provocative question, "Can we be equal and excellent too?"[3] U.S. Education Commissioner Sidney P. Marland reported to Congress in 1972 that "Gifted and Talented children are, in fact, deprived and can suffer psychological damage and permanent impairment of their abilities to function well which is equal to or greater than the similar deprivation suffered by any other population with special needs."[4]

Then 1983 brought *A Nation at Risk*, the celebrated commission report that—echoing Sputnik-era concerns—declared that weaknesses in American primary and secondary education augured serious threats on the international front, and indeed that "[o]ur once unchallenged preeminence in commerce, industry, science, and technological innovation is being overtaken by competitors throughout the world."[5] Five years later, Congress enacted the first (and only) federal program focused on gifted students, named in honor of the late senator Jacob K. Javits (R-NY), one of the rare lawmakers to pay attention to this issue.

The topic has resurfaced in recent years, owing partly to deepening concern about America's economic competitiveness and (again) its scientific/technological leadership, partly to alarming international test score results, partly to concern that new academic standards and tests will have a homogenizing effect on school curricula and instruction, and partly to highly visible revelations that few successful students from disadvantaged backgrounds are proceeding from high school into the challenging colleges that would maximize their educational attainments and their prospects for upward mobility.

We've known for more than two decades that few students—especially poor and minority pupils—reach the "Advanced" level on the National Assessment of Educational Progress (NAEP), and that most of those trend lines are close to flat. But gifted and talented education is often viewed as an elitist enterprise that benefits mainly the daughters and sons of ambitious middle-class families, and is hence irrelevant to disadvantaged youngsters. In many places, these kids have been left to make it through school as best they can. And some—though not enough—of them have excelled there, only to encounter yet another form of neglect, this one more surprising. In fact, it made the front page of the Sunday *New York Times* in March 2013 when Stanford economist Caroline Hoxby and a colleague revealed that "Only 34 percent of high-achieving high school seniors in the bottom fourth of (sic) income distribution attended any one of the country's 238 most selective colleges."[6]

These are young people, mind you, who *succeeded* in American K–12 education despite their families' poverty, yet the system still failed to do right by them. A few other analysts and commentators, along with us, have begun to ask, How many more boys and girls with strong potential yet limited means never make it to the ranks of high achievers because they languish in the earlier grades of school?[7]

At least as concerning as the domestic data is evidence from international assessments that a number of other countries are doing better than the United States at propelling their young people, including more of those from disadvantaged circumstances, to impressive academic achievement. In 2012, twenty-seven of thirty-four countries in the Organisation for Economic Co-operation and Development (OECD) had larger percentages of their test takers score in PISA's top two tiers in mathematics than did the United States. While just 9 percent of American fifteen-year-olds reached these levels, 31 percent of Korean students and 16 percent of Canadians did so.

When we probe deeper into those data for evidence of high achievement by disadvantaged youngsters, the U.S. performance turns out to be even worse. In science, for example, PISA (Program for International Student Assessment) results indicate that just 1 percent of American fifteen-year-olds with poorly educated parents reach the high-scoring ranks, versus 5 percent in Australia, 6 percent in Germany, and 7 percent in Japan.

How do those countries do it? Is there some secret sauce for educating high-ability youngsters that other nations are sprinkling on their schools but that the United States has failed to discover or refuses to use? Are others neglecting their low achievers in favor of gifted students? Or have they figured out how to support both at once? Are they doing it for reasons of equity or economic competitiveness? Are they not plagued by worries about elitism and the diversion of resources from the "truly needy" to populations that "will do fine anyway"?

Such questions begged for answers and we resolved to seek some. Encouraged by the organizations and colleagues (and funders) identified in the acknowledgments, we embarked on visits to a dozen sites in eleven countries during 2012 and 2013, gathering insights and opinions from knowledgeable individuals in those locales, and examined other studies and data from international and domestic sources. In the pages that follow, we describe what we learned—and what we think should be done to change our own country's trajectory.

Part I reviews the twin rationales that we find most compelling for renewing America's focus on the education of high-ability youngsters; documents our present weak performance in this realm; underscores our domestic "excellence gap" whereby advantaged children are far likelier to become high achievers than are their poor and minority classmates; and examines the principal obstacles and arguments that deter us from strengthening our performance as well as some authentic dilemmas regarding how such strengthening is best done.

In part II, we explore how schools around the world educate their high-ability students and distill the main lessons that we draw from our study of them. Then in part III, we apply those lessons to the U.S. education system.

Because the topic of "gifted" education is fraught with definitional challenges—who warrants such a designation and according to what criteria—we should make our own focus clear.

We recognize that extraordinary ability and performance come in many forms, including (for example) sports and the arts. In these pages, however, we concentrate on academic or intellectual prowess, the forms of achievement measured by PISA, TIMSS, PIRLS, and NAEP. With apologies to those who contend that other forms of talent and accomplishment are just as important to the nation's future, we accept the economic and political reality that American prosperity and security over the next half century hinge more directly on intellectual ability and academic achievement.

Even within those limits, debates rage over who, exactly, qualifies as "gifted" and how to determine this. Some claim that "everyone is gifted in his or her own way and it's wrong to make distinctions." Others assert that only the kind of intellectual aptitude purportedly measured by IQ tests qualifies, and that the gifted population is therefore best defined by setting "cut scores" on such tests. Still others insist that effort and attitude always trump aptitude or ability and that it's therefore pointless, even harmful, to make any distinctions between individuals' potential to achieve great things.

There's no clear path through this thicket, which we reenter in chapters 3 and 18. But after much thought and considerable research, we reject all three of those perspectives, and find ourselves in broad agreement with such thinkers as the University of Connecticut's Joseph Renzulli, the University of Quebec's François Gagné, and the American Psychological Association's Rena Subotnik, all of whom have developed "models" of giftedness that are taken seriously in other countries (and by many gifted education specialists in the United States). Though their models differ somewhat, each considers several factors in determining which students deserve this consideration. Renzulli's "three-ring" version focuses on the intersection within an individual of "above average ability," "task commitment," and "creativity." Gagné's "differentiated model" combines "giftedness" (based on natural aptitudes) with "talent" (depicted as "outstanding mastery of systematically developed abilities, called competencies [knowledge and skills], in at least one field of human activity.") And Subotnik (often working with colleagues Paula Olszewski-Kubilius and Frank Worrell) has usefully added the element of "eminence," or outstanding achievement, in specific domains that "ought to be the chief goal of gifted education" and should influence the identification process.

Because these models are complex, relatively expensive, and involve subjective judgments about individuals, they're hard to apply to large numbers of children. That's why many educators end up relying instead on straightforward test scores—or throwing up their hands and either denying the existence of exceptional ability or insisting that it doesn't matter. We understand the challenges here, yet remain convinced that such multifactor models are the best way to think about the blend of potential and accomplishment that warrant the strongest claim on our attention. And, to repeat, we also concentrate in these pages on policies, practices, and programs that bear primarily on the education of young people whose potential and accomplishment are manifest in traditional "academic" realms.

PART I

The Challenge of Educating High-Ability Children

1

Educating Smart Kids: Why Bother?

WHY PAY SPECIAL ATTENTION to high-ability girls and boys? Won't they do fine anyway? Shouldn't we concentrate on kids with problems? Low achievers? Poor kids?

Good questions all, particularly when American education leaders (and their counterparts in most other advanced countries) are preoccupied with equalizing opportunity, closing gaps, and giving a boost to those most challenged—and when resources are chronically scarce. Yet such questions have two compelling answers. We sketched both in the introduction, but they deserve amplification.

First, the country needs these children to be highly educated in order to ensure its long-term competitiveness, security, and innovation. Frederick Hess is correct: these are the young people who hold perhaps the greatest promise for making major advances in science, technology, medicine, the humanities, and much more. The same point was framed in different words in the 1993 federal report "National Excellence: A Case for Developing America's Talent": "In order to make economic strides," the authors wrote, "America must rely upon many of its top-performing students to provide leadership—in mathematics, science, writing, politics, dance, art, business, history, health, and other human pursuits."[1]

This isn't just rhetoric. Economists don't agree on much, but almost all concur that a nation's economic vitality and growth depend heavily on the quality and productivity of its human capital and its capacity for innovation. At the forefront of creation, invention, and discovery are—nearly always—the society's cleverest, ablest, and best-educated men and women. Yes, other personal and national characteristics also loom large (such as hard work, enterprise, natural resources, stable laws, reliable banks, peace in the streets), but nothing trumps the knowledge and imagination of a country's people.[2] Whether we are picturing breakthroughs in information technology, alternative forms of energy, more efficient engines, vaccines against Ebola, ultrapowerful telescopes, or environmentally sound crop enhancers for wheat fields, we depend on smart, creative, and highly educated individuals to lead the way.

The U.S. economy is already hobbled by our shortage of such homegrown talent (and further shackled by limits on importing such people from overseas). Organizations like the Partnership for a New American Economy and U.S. Chamber of Commerce estimate that one-fourth of American science and engineering firms now face difficulty hiring the workforce they need—and forecast a shortage of 220,000 workers with STEM (science/technology/engineering/math) degrees by 2018. It's true that changing our immigration policies would ease the crunch. But what sensible nation would rely on other countries to educate and supply its highly skilled workers?[3]

This challenge extends beyond the tech world. In November 2014, the *Wall Street Journal* reported that foreign applicants (especially from India and China) are besting American candidates for admission to high-status U.S. business schools because they're doing far better on the quantitative portion of the Graduate Management Admission Test. Some leading universities are turning to country-specific scoring systems so that American applicants get compared only with fellow Americans—a sort of affirmative action scheme for people educated in our own schools and colleges! "U.S. students' raw scores on the quantitative section have remained roughly flat over the last decade," the *Journal* explained, "but their percentile ranking has fallen as more of their higher-scoring international counterparts take the exam."[4]

The problem is not that the United States lacks smart children; it's that such kids aren't getting the education they need to realize their potential. Other countries are forging ahead, while "roughly flat" accurately describes the American record. (More on this in the next chapter.)

Using international test data, economists Eric Hanushek and Ludger Woessmann estimate that a "ten percentage point increase in the share of top-performing students" within a country "is associated with 1.3 percentage points higher annual growth" of that country's economy (measured in per-capita GDP). Which is to say, if the United States propelled as many of its young people into the ranks of high achievers as, say, the Netherlands, this country would be markedly more prosperous—with faster growth, higher employment, better wages, and all that comes with these. (If 1.3 percentage points looks modest, consider that the average annual U.S. growth rate over the past forty years has been just 1.5 percent.)[5]

The second big reason to attend to the schooling of high-ability youngsters is a version of the familiar equity argument: these kids also deserve an education that meets their needs and enhances their futures, just like children with other distinctions and problems. They have their own legitimate claim on our conscience, our sense of fairness, our policy priorities, and our education budgets. What's more, many of them also face such challenges as disability, poverty, ill-educated parents, non-English-speaking homes, and tough neighborhoods. Those kids depend more than upper-middle-class youngsters on the public education system to do right by them. Some will manage to overcome the constraints of their upbringing, but many will fall by the wayside, destined by circumstances beyond their control never to realize their full potential. As Ford Foundation president Darren Walker recently remarked, "[E]ven though talent is spread evenly across America, opportunity is not."[6] That's why our failure to extend such opportunities to more high-ability kids from disadvantaged backgrounds is, as the Jack Kent Cooke Foundation team recently put it, "both unacceptable and incompatible with America's long-term prosperity."[7]

That's also why high-functioning public school systems such as that of Fairfax County, Virginia (FCPS), declare their commitment to widening opportunities for children with talent and "to providing challenging learning experiences for all learners that build on individual strengths and optimize academic potential. In order to meet the needs and develop the potential of advanced learners, FCPS provides a continuum of advanced academic services."[8]

Yet we have a long way to go before it can be said that "advanced learners" from poor circumstances are achieving anywhere near their more fortunate classmates. Today, a *random* American fifteen-year-old is four times likelier to be a top scorer on PISA math than is her lower socioeconomic age-mate. A woeful *2 percent* of Americans in the lowest SES quartile reached the uppermost PISA ranks in math, reading, or science in 2012. By contrast, in the top SES quartile, 20 percent of U.S. test takers made it to that level in math, as did 18 percent in reading and 17 percent in science.[9]

Plenty more poor kids have the ability, but lots of them lack the supports from home and family that middle-class children enjoy, and many attend schools awash in low achievement, places where all the incentives and pressures on teachers and administrators are to equip weak pupils with basic skills in reading, writing, and arithmetic. Such schools understandably invest their resources in boosting low achievers. They're also most apt to judge teachers by their success in doing that and least apt to have much to spare—energy or time, incentive or money—for students already above the proficiency bar. These might fairly be termed the kids that NCLB forgot.

We are by no means the first to flag this problem. As the authors of that 1993 report declared:

> The United States is squandering one of its most precious resources—the gifts, talents, and high interests of many of its students. . . . *This problem is especially severe among economically disadvantaged and minority students, who have access to fewer advanced educational opportunities and whose talents often go unnoticed.*[10] (Emphasis added.)

In the years since, similar alarms have been sounded time and again. In *A Nation Deceived*, published in 2004, Nicholas Colangelo, Susan G. Assouline, and Miraca Gross meticulously demonstrate how able children benefit from an accelerated education—and the damaging role of misguided education beliefs and practices in holding back such children.[11]

In a 2008 Fordham Institute publication, after analyzing NAEP data over the previous decade, Tom Loveless of the Brookings Institution cautioned:

> Gaps are narrowing because the gains of low-achieving students are outstripping those of high achievers by a factor of two or three to one. The nation has a strong interest in developing the talents of its best students to their fullest to foster the kind of growth at the top end of the achievement distribution that has been occurring at the bottom end. International comparisons of top students around the world invariably show American high-achievers falling short.[12]

In *Mind the (Other) Gap*, published in 2010, the University of Connecticut's Jonathan Plucker and colleagues again documented the widening "excellence gap" in American education, as "the economically disadvantaged, English Language Learners, and historically underprivileged minorities" have come to comprise a shrinking "proportion of students scoring at the highest levels of achievement."[13]

Two years later, in *Unlocking Emergent Talent*, Paula Olszewski-Kubilius and Jane Clarenbach of the National Association for Gifted Children wrote that, "While our nation continues to express commitment to closing the achievement gap, the proportion of low-income students performing at advanced levels on the National Assessment of Educational Progress remains shamefully low. For example, between 1998 and 2007, 2% or fewer of free and reduced lunch program-eligible students scored at the advanced level on the eighth-grade math exam compared to between 6% and 10% of non-eligible students."[14]

As noted in the introduction, Caroline Hoxby and Christopher Avery made waves in 2013 with evidence that even low-income youngsters who do exceptionally well in high school, earning excellent grades and lofty SAT or ACT scores, are far less likely than their affluent peers to wind up in high-status colleges, despite ample evidence that they could gain admission, obtain sufficient financial aid, and succeed academically. Why? Because they tend not even to apply to such colleges; nobody at home or school encourages them to do so and explains how to go about it. Nor do university "outreach" efforts manage to find many of them. Hoxby and Avery estimate that tens of thousands of high achievers from disadvantaged backgrounds are thus "missed" by the elite strata of American higher education—and these are youngsters who have succeeded in K–12 education despite all the obstacles.[15]

Plucker and colleagues returned to the "excellence gap" in October 2013 with a penetrating summary of research attesting to the K–12 system's failure to cultivate the talents of high-ability kids from disadvantaged circumstances—and bluntly stated that policy efforts to close the "minimum competency gap," important as they are ("an ethical and moral priority"), are not narrowing the excellence gap, "a unique problem that will not be solved without concerted effort."[16]

Most recently, March 2015 brought a valuable study from the Jack Kent Cooke Foundation, entitled *Equal Talents, Unequal Opportunities*, which used multiple metrics to appraise how well individual states are advancing the education of high-ability, low-income youngsters. The report's bleak conclusion: "No state received full points in either policy inputs or student outcomes, which left us unable to give any state an 'A' grade." (In fact, just six states earned student-outcome grades in the "B" range—and there were scads of D's.)[17]

One may rightly term this amply-documented situation shameful, but one ought not find it surprising. Consider the children's differing circumstances.

It's true that not all upper-middle-class kids with strong ability can count on having education-maximizing parents—some are content for their children to be well-adjusted and popular—and some youngsters themselves lack motivation. Yet the odds are hugely better that such girls and boys will get an education that does a decent job of capitalizing on their potential, beginning in their earliest months on earth. For they are all but certain to have adults in their lives who read to them, ask them questions that don't have simple answers, show them intriguing things, and take them to interesting places— adults with the knowledge and capacity to navigate our complicated education system in pursuit of suitable options for their daughters and sons, and to press for access to the best of those options. These are adults who possess resources that enable them to shift to better options when necessary, whether that means changing neighborhoods, purchasing supplemental education offerings, even sending their children to private schools.

Equally able youngsters from poor families, on the other hand, depend mainly on their local public education system to supply them with suitable learning opportunities. Many start school behind the eight ball because they haven't learned as many words or been asked to think about as many complicated things or seen as many informative places as their more-advantaged classmates. Many also enter schools that have a weak record of academic achievement and are staffed by less experienced teachers.

All of this puts at further risk those youngsters who were disadvantaged to begin with, compared with their middle-class peers, and makes it less likely that they will receive an education that nurtures their ability to the max. Able as they may be, they face a double whammy because their schools are beset by more urgent problems: poor attendance, children arriving hungry or sick, discipline challenges, language issues, and more. Such schools may also be strapped for resources—money, expert instructors, materials, and so on. Maximizing the potential of their high-ability, high-achieving pupils may be something that principals and teachers yearn to do but are simply too swamped to devote the energy and resources it requires.

Whether the children in a particular school are poor or rich, virtually all of the public-policy pressures, incentives, and accountability schemes of recent decades—whether arising from local, state, or federal sources, from private philanthropy, or from the priorities and values of educators themselves—have pushed teachers and administrators to concentrate on low achievers, those who, in the language of No Child Left Behind, are not yet "proficient" or "making adequate yearly progress" in reading or math.[18]

Helping students climb over the proficiency bar wins points and plaudits for the school, but boosting them further up the achievement ladder rarely does.[19] Schools and teachers earn few incentives or rewards for causing such youngsters to learn more. Meanwhile, plenty of these students' peers are termed "at risk"—in terms of not just prior achievement but also disabilities, immigrant status, home language, and other factors—and government (and philanthropic) funding streams, mandates, accountability systems, and special programs focus on schools' success in mitigating or compensating for such risks.

This is certainly true in the United States in the NCLB era, as that sweeping 2001 federal law focused entirely on low-achieving students. Moreover, it was recently reframed by education secretary Arne Duncan to prod states and districts to concentrate their energies and resources on the very worst schools—Duncan emphasizes the lowest-performing 5 percent—not those attended by the children with greatest potential to become academic superstars. While poorly performing schools harbor some of those kids, too, government policy effectively marginalizes them as among the (few) pupils the school does *not* have to worry about. Their low-achieving classmates get the attention. Instead of concentrating our policy energies on both boosting the entire distribution of performance *and* targeting extra help on those farthest behind, we have for years been devoted almost exclusively to the latter.

Government policy is not, however, the only driver of this focus on low achievers and troubled schools. Education discourse in the United States, as well as the preoccupations of most foundations, think tanks, pundits, and colleges of education, seems to have forgotten or repressed the grand tension that John Gardner highlighted a half-century back. Can we, in fact, "be equal and excellent too?" Despite another claxon sounded two decades later by the National Commission on Excellence in Education, the quest for excellence has all but vanished from our education priorities—and it's more thoroughly absent when such questing means paying attention to the schooling of high-ability children.

A senior faculty member at one of the country's top schools of education commented to us that the very phrase "gifted education" is a "tainted construction" among leading thinkers, policy influencers, and institutions in the field. He added that none of his faculty colleagues focus on such issues—they're much more interested in ending poverty, compensating for disability, fostering cultural pluralism, and boosting low achievement—and that his school's placement office wouldn't think of sending graduates anywhere but into the most troubled and disadvantaged settings.

Such comments match our own impressions as we ride the circuit of conferences, workshops, policy seminars, and legislative initiatives around the public education field. As a simple reality check, however, we searched for "gifted education" on the websites of the ten graduate schools of education rated most highly by *U.S. News.* That well turned out to be almost dry. We found two or three interested (if somewhat ambivalent) professors, one full-fledged graduate degree program, a couple of optional "endorsements" for special ed certification, several one-day seminars, and a summer program for kids and teachers, but little else.

Why this neglect? Briefly stated, America's failure to solve these problems arises from a mix of ideology, political correctness, flawed education theories, and disagreements over who qualifies as "gifted." Even when we agree on which children meet that definition, we divide over what to do with them. Should they be taught within "inclusive" classrooms or separately? Do they, in fact, deserve anything different at all? Some say that programs focused on such children are elitist and contend that "these kids will do fine anyway, so let's concentrate on those who are having difficulty." Others wonder what will happen to late bloomers. Still others discount talent and ability altogether, insisting that personal qualities such as "grit" are the key to high achievement. (We dig deeper into these questions in chapters 3 and 4.)

In today's culture, creating special opportunities for high-ability, high-achieving youngsters also invites allegations of discrimination. Many educators object to separating students in any way. They decry all forms of "tracking" and "grouping" as archaic and unfair. And they're not entirely wrong, considering how yesterday's tracking schemes often had a deterministic, immutable aspect that tended to permanently separate student populations and limit educational and social mobility. Any successful (and politically acceptable) approach to education in the United States in the twenty-first century must instead recognize this as a "land of opportunity" and education as a source of second chances. But that doesn't mean ignoring youngsters of exceptional ability or achievement—or assuming that everyone in fifth grade is equally adept at learning math or history, much less that they're all at the same level of achievement today.

Let's examine some evidence, both domestic and international.

2

How Is the United States Doing?

AMERICAN STUDENTS have fared poorly for decades on international tests and similar comparisons, and their results on most domestic gauges have been essentially flat, particularly in the upper grades. In this chapter, we look at both domestic and international measures, focusing on how our K–12 system is doing at the "high end," that is, producing students and graduates with the outstanding achievement that we would like all our daughters and sons to attain but that we especially need from high-ability youngsters. Wherever one comes down in the eternal debates over nature versus nurture—in this case, "giftedness" or exceptional potential in relation to pluck, drive, and persistence—the country needs more strong achievers than it's getting. Too many other countries are trouncing us. And a great many young Americans from every stratum of society would be far better off if their achievements came closer to matching their capabilities, which we believe are broadly distributed across the entire population.

We analyze test scores in the three core subjects of math, science, and reading, with particular emphasis on math. Considerable research suggests that "math skills better predict future earnings and other economic outcomes than other skills learned in high school."[1] Math also lends itself best to international comparisons because there is wide consensus about what students should learn in this subject, and because math concepts are the same regardless of the language of instruction.

The charts and graphs in this chapter are supplemented by data provided in the appendix, to which we frequently refer readers seeking deeper immersion in the numbers.

HIGH ACHIEVEMENT:
DOMESTIC DATA

On the home front, we examine high-level achievement in several ways, looking at both the present situation and recent trends. We then turn to achievement gaps and differences among high achievers by spotlighting students' race, parental education, family income, and state of residence.

The National Assessment of Educational Progress (NAEP) is our best source of achievement data within the U.S. pupil population. These tests are administered periodically to a representative sample of students in grades 4, 8, and 12, and data can be obtained for many subjects within (and sometimes outside) the curriculum. The National Assessment Governing Board classifies student scores in three achievement levels, termed "Basic," "Proficient," and "Advanced."[2] The levels are cumulative, such that a pupil who scores at the Advanced level, for example, is presumed to have mastered the expectations at the Basic and Proficient levels. Over the last eight years, approximately four-fifths of test takers have scored at (or above) the Basic level on math and reading exams, with one-third reaching at least Proficient but only one in twenty getting to Advanced.[3]

Much as Proficient on NAEP (for twelfth graders) roughly corresponds to college readiness, Advanced is a revealing benchmark for high achievers, the level we should expect exceptionally able students to reach—and that the country needs many of its young people to attain. As we show in the following discussion, it's also a level that many children in competitor countries *do* attain.

Figure 2.1 shows how students in all three grades have fared over the last two decades in reaching the Advanced level in math, reading, and science. It tells several stories.

FIGURE 2.1   Percentage of students at/above NAEP Advanced level, by subject and grade, 1990–2013

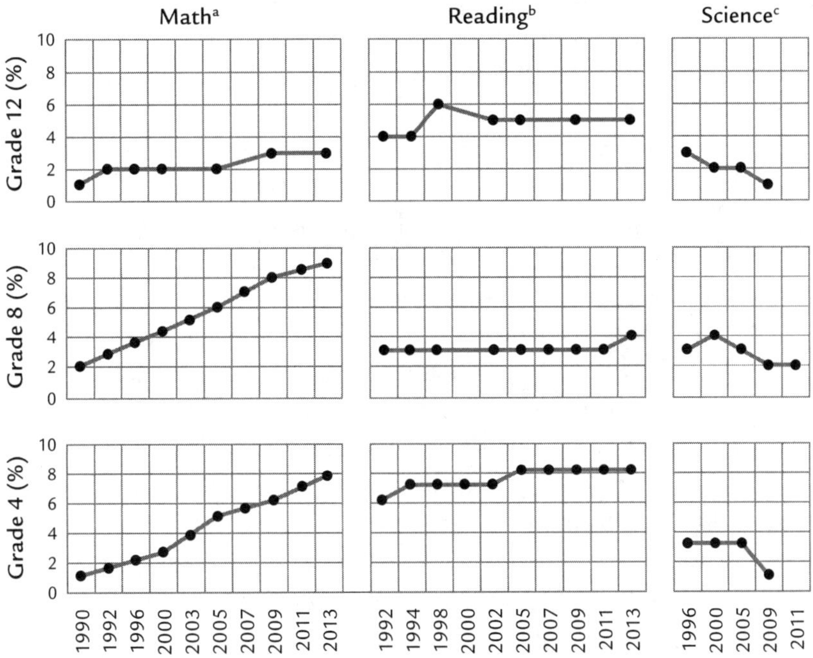

a There are three gaps in the twelfth-grade line because only fourth- and eighth-grade tests were administered in 2003, 2007, and 2011.

b In addition to the twelfth-grade gaps, there's one in eighth since only the fourth-grade test was given in 2000 and only grades 4 and 8 were tested in 2007 and 2011.

c The latest year that NAEP assessed science was 2011, and then only in eighth grade; 2009 was the latest year for fourth and twelfth graders.

First, regardless of subject, U.S. schools are doing a lamentable job of producing high achievers. The figure contains a total of nine lines, each representing a specific grade and subject. Not a single one of these lines exceeds the 10 percent mark in any year. In other words, since 1996 there has been no point when U.S. students in any of the grades tested, in any of these subjects, recorded more than nine Advanced scorers for every hundred test takers. Only three lines exceed the 5 percent mark. In science, none rises above 4 percent.

Second, most of the changes over time are discouraging. Only in fourth- and eighth-grade math do improvements deserve a bit of applause. Reading is mostly flat and science almost consistently down.

Third, look closely at twelfth grade, the final year of high school, the threshold of college, career, and adulthood. We defy you to find *any* good news there. Among 100 high school seniors, 97 fail to reach the top level in math, 95 fail to get there in reading, and a whopping 99 fail to reach that level in science. We hope you share our conviction that there are plenty more talented American kids whose potential is not being realized.

It's also revealing to compare trends among high achievers with those of low-scoring students who have been the foremost object of U.S. education concern and policy for the past two decades. In figure A.1 in the appendix, we show NAEP trends at both the 10th and 90th percentiles for grades 4 and 8. We see that both have risen since 1996 (a bit in reading, considerably more in math) and that gaps between the 10th and 90th percentiles have slightly diminished—all good news. Yet the gap-closing is a product of low scorers improving faster than high scorers. The floor is rising faster than the ceiling. One could certainly laud that development, yet a powerful case can be made that the country needs its high scorers to improve at least as much as its low scorers. If we want hard-won reforms and better schools to benefit all our children, shouldn't these lines rise in rough parallel? Can we not attend to the top at the same time as we concentrate on the bottom?

College readiness

The next step for the majority of U.S. K–12 pupils is some form of higher education—and many reformers and policy makers are convinced that every young American should be college- (and career-) ready at the conclusion of grade 12. Current data, however, show how distant that goal is. One reasonable metric is results on the ACT, a curriculum- and standards-based college-entrance exam that many students take in eleventh or (mostly) twelfth grade. It assesses four subjects: English, math, reading, and science. The ACT organization sets a benchmark for each area that corresponds to college readiness—and declares that a student who attains at least three of the four benchmarks has a solid shot at academic success during the first year of higher education. [4]

By that gauge, just 39 percent of 2014 high school graduates who took the ACT exam were prepared for college-level academics—the same as in 2013.[5] Barely a quarter of them met all four benchmarks.[6] Worse, achievement gaps were wide and persistent, as seen in table 2.1. Fifty-seven percent of Asian test takers were ready for college, as were 49 percent of whites, but only 23 percent of Hispanic and 11 percent of black students. The table also shows subject gaps, attesting to something less than well-roundedness. Sixty-four percent of test takers met the English benchmark, compared with 44 percent in reading, 43 percent in math, and 37 percent in science.

NAEP also sets college-readiness benchmarks for math and reading.[7] In 2013, 39 percent of twelfth-grade test takers reached the former and 38 percent attained the latter, both of which are very close to the ACT estimates.

Another valuable metric is the College Board's Advanced Placement (AP) program, which offers thirty-four college-level courses that students can take while still in high school.[8] In 2014, 2.3 million students—about 14 percent of all U.S. high school pupils—took 4.1

TABLE 2.1   ACT subject and achievement gaps, 2014

Achievement gaps: Percentage of test takers ready for college		Subject gaps: Percentage of test takers meeting benchmarks	
Asian	57	English	64
White	49	Reading	44
Hispanic	23	Math	43
Black	11	Science	37

Source: "The Condition of College & Career Readiness 2014: National," ACT, Inc., 2014, http://www.act.org/newsroom/data/2014/pdf/CCCR14-NationalReadinessRpt.pdf.

Note: According to ACT, students reaching each benchmark have a 50 percent chance of obtaining at least a B or a 75 percent chance of obtaining at least a C in a first-year college course in that subject. Students who meet three of four benchmarks are "ready for college."

million AP exams. These are scored from 1 to 5 (the highest). A score of 3 is generally considered to mean a student has mastered the content of an introductory-level college course in that subject.[9] Of the 4.1 million exams administered, 2.4 million—59 percent—received scores of 3 or better. In other words, about one in seven high school students—that includes ninth and tenth graders as well as juniors and seniors— tried to establish college credit via AP and fewer than three-fifths of those efforts "succeeded."

Scores again vary widely by race. Table 2.2, which is limited to high school seniors, shows the percentage of students in each racial group, the percentage of AP tests taken by each, and the group's mean score on those tests.[10] As is evident, Asian students take a great many AP exams and tend to do well on them. White students' test taking is approximately equal to their share of the twelfth-grade enrollment. But Hispanic and black students present a very different picture.[11] Bear in mind, too, that these are young people who for the most part have not only made it through high school but also made their way into Advanced Placement classrooms.

TABLE 2.2   Advanced Placement test-taking rates and exam scores for high school seniors, by race

	Percentage of students (2010–11)	Percentage of AP exams administered (2014)	Mean exam score (2014)
Asian	5.3	15.0	3.21
White	56.8	55.6	3.03
Hispanic[a]	19.8	17.0	2.42
Black	15.4	7.1	2.05

Sources: "AP Program Participation and Performance Data 2014, National Summary," College Board, accessed November 29, 2014, http://media.collegeboard.com/digitalServices/pdf/research/2014/National_Summary.xlsx; "Table 1.–Grade 12 Enrollment, by Race/Ethnicity, Gender, and State: School Years 1992–93 Through 2010–11," U.S. Department of Education, Institute of Education Sciences, National Center for Education Statistics, accessed January 29, 2014, http://nces.ed.gov/ccd/tables/ESSIN_Task5_f1.asp.

a The College Board does not use "Hispanic" as a racial category in reporting AP data. For purposes of this table, we combined figures for "Mexican American," "Puerto Rican," and "Other Hispanic," and weighted the data based on the proportion of test takers in each group.

ACHIEVEMENT GAPS:
DOMESTIC

As these data plainly show, the United States is doing a poor job of preparing young people—even college-bound young people—for university; it's doing worse at producing high scorers, a lackluster job of adding to their numbers, and a somewhat better job of boosting low scorers.

But there's more bad news: the children least apt to make it into the high end come from poor and minority backgrounds.[12]

Poverty

The standard way of relating income to school achievement is via eligibility for the federal free and reduced-price lunch (FRPL) program. In 2013, roughly half of all students who participated in NAEP were eligible for this program (though not all actually took part in it).[13]

Figure 2.2 shows the percentage of students at (or above) NAEP's Advanced level in math for grades 4, 8, and 12 from 2005 to 2013 according to eligibility for subsidized lunches.

The first message in these data—a touch of good news—is that both poor and nonpoor kids have made modest gains over time in five of the six clusters shown in the figure.

The second message, predictable yet troubling, is that poor kids don't reach the Advanced level at anything resembling the rates of nonpoor kids. In fourth grade in 2013, for example, the percentages are 2 versus 13. In eighth grade, they're 3 and 14. In twelfth grade, dismally, the percentage of poor pupils at the Advanced level rounds to 0. That's because virtually no low-income high school student got there; among nonpoor pupils, a weak 4 percent did.

The third message, worse than troubling, is that these gaps have widened with time. The proportion of high scorers among nonpoor kids has seen greater increases than among lunch-eligible students. Over these eight years, the percentages of nonpoor students at the Advanced level rose by 5, 6, and 1 point, respectively, in grades 4, 8, and 12—an average of 4 percent. For poor students, however, the numbers are 1, 2, and 0—an average of 1.

FIGURE 2.2   Percentage of students at/above NAEP Advanced level in
math, by FRPL eligibility and grade, 2005–2013

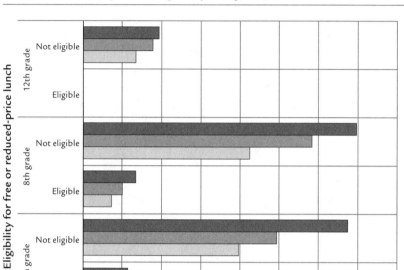

Note: Students are eligible for subsidized lunches if their household income falls below 185
percent of the federal poverty line. In 2013, that meant less than $36,131 for a family of three.

Parental education

The extent of parents' education is another way to look at disadvantage because children with better-educated parents are generally better off in a host of ways and often do better in school. Figure 2.3 looks
at math high achievers (on NAEP) according to the amount of education that their parents completed. Each category represents the highest level of education that either parent achieved, as reported by the
child—no high school diploma, a high school diploma but no college,
some college but no degree, and at least one college degree.[14] The figure compares eighth and twelfth grades over the same years (2005,
2009, 2013) that we looked at in the previous figure.

Though we see welcome gains in every eighth-grade cluster, we don't find big numbers—or differences—until we get to children whose parents had at least some college. There are woefully few high achievers with parents who never entered the ivy gates. Yet the real jump happens for youngsters with degree-holding moms and/or dads: 14 percent of their children were Advanced in eighth grade in 2013, nearly twice the national average. Twelfth grade presents a similar story. Though it contains perishingly few students at the Advanced level, the 5 percent with a degree-holding parent compares with 3 percent across the whole grade.

FIGURE 2.3   Percentage of students at/above NAEP Advanced level in math, by parents' education and grade, 2005–2013

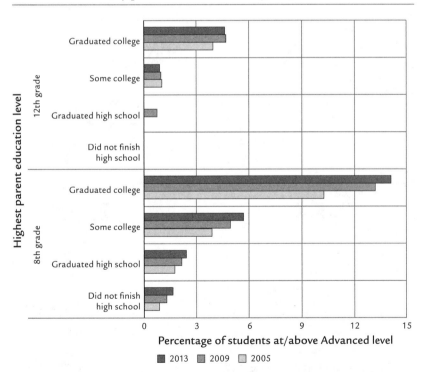

Note: Each category on the *y*-axis represents the highest level of education that either parent achieved, as reported by the test taker.

Race

Along with income, a common way to look at achievement gaps is by race or ethnicity. Those gaps have properly been a concern for many years. Here, we see (as in the AP data) that they're also conspicuous among high achievers.

Figure 2.4 shows the percentage of students in each of four major American racial-ethnic groups who scored at or above the Advanced level in math and reading in grades 4 and 8 between 2003 and 2013. Asians are the highest scorers and whites second throughout, followed by Hispanic and black students. What's most telling about these figures, however, is how *few* black and Hispanic pupils make it into the already-meager ranks of high scorers. Over the decade, across both grades and subjects, their percentages fluctuate between 0 and 3 percent.

FIGURE 2.4   Percentage of students at/above NAEP Advanced level, by subject and race, 2003–2013

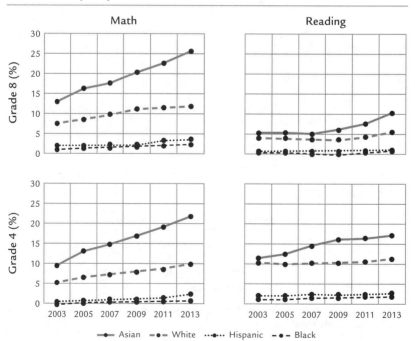

Yes, there are upward slopes in many lines and that's all to the good. But when at least 97 of every 100 Hispanic and black students are *not* reaching the Advanced level at any point in any subject, something is quite wrong.

We also examined the intersection of parent education, poverty, and race in relation to Advanced students (and display the results in figures A.2 and A.3 and table A.1 in the appendix). Unsurprisingly, the group with the highest proportion of Advanced students is Asian children not eligible for subsidized lunches who also have college-graduate parents (40 percent); the lowest proportion turns out to be among black students eligible for FRPL whose parents didn't attend college (less than 1 percent). Most arresting, however, is *how well* Asian American students do, regardless of parents' education and income. In the poorest and least educated families, a full 10 percent of Asian American pupils still reach the Advanced level. Sadly, that's higher than *any* group of black or Hispanic students, regardless of income and parent education. And it exceeds every group of white students save those who are not poor and have college-graduate parents.[15]

State differences

Sizable high-end achievement gaps exist among states, too. We looked at Massachusetts, Maryland, Nevada, and Mississippi (data are shown in figure A.4 in the appendix). On the 2013 NAEP math assessment, the proportions of Advanced students in grade 8 in these states were 18, 12, 6, and 3 percent, respectively. Viewed over time, we see that, with rare exception, the greater a state's percentage of high scorers in each test year, the larger its increase over time. In other words, the better a state is doing, the more it's also improving. For example, the percentage of Advanced students in Massachusetts rose by seven points between 2005 and 2013, while Mississippi and Nevada added just two and three points, respectively.

Racial gaps also vary by state, but differently. (See appendix figure A.5.) The scores by racial group in Massachusetts are still highest—but by far narrower margins. Hispanics actually do better in Maryland, and we see that the racial composition of a state's pupil population powerfully affects its overall performance profile. Massachusetts's overall score is higher than Maryland's in considerable part because larger segments of Maryland's pupil population are black and Hispanic.[16] A gloomier way to state it is that not even much-praised Massachusetts has been very successful at pulling minority pupils into the ranks of high scorers.

HIGH ACHIEVEMENT: INTERNATIONAL EVIDENCE

We turn next to comparisons with other nations, relying on such well-known gauges as the OECD's Program for International Student Assessment (PISA), the Trends in International Mathematics and Science Study (TIMSS), and the Progress in International Reading Literacy Study (PIRLS). Dozens of countries participate in each, and many have done so for enough years to permit trends to be compared. As you will see, the United States isn't doing well at the upper end in relation to economic-competitor countries—many of which are also geopolitical allies. Nor are we getting as many of our disadvantaged youngsters into those higher reaches as many other nations are managing.

Our study focuses on eleven countries—Australia, Canada, Finland, Germany, Hungary, Japan, Singapore, South Korea, Switzerland, Taiwan, and the United Kingdom—and in chapters 7 through 17 you will find summary data showing how each has recently fared on all of the multinational measures in which it takes part. (Chapter 6 explains this selection of countries.)

Because our focus is on high achievers, we concentrate on how many of a country's students reach the upper ranks on these metrics. PISA organizes its assessment scores into seven levels from 0 to 6, and we have defined high scorers as those reaching levels 5 and 6. On TIMSS and PIRLS, scores are split into five levels, with a high-achieving student judged to be one who reaches at least 625 on the relevant scales. We also employ that cutoff here.

Table 2.3 incorporates all three sources of data to show the percentages of high scorers in each country on the most recent round of each test and how these compare with the U.S. record.

As is immediately clear, in most cases the United States fares worse than its competitors, often by a wide margin. The extent of the

TABLE 2.3   Percentage of high scorers on PISA, TIMSS, and PIRLS

| | PISA 2012 | | | TIMSS 2011 | | | | PIRLS 2011 |
	Math	Science	Reading	Math grade 4	Math grade 8	Science grade 4	Science grade 8	Reading grade 4
United States	9	7	8	13	7	15	10	17
Australia	15	14	12	10	9	7	11	10
Canada	16	11	13	—	—	—	—	13
Finland	15	17	13	12	4	20	13	18
Germany	17	12	9	5	—	7	—	10
Hungary	9	6	6	10	8	13	9	12
Japan	24	18	18	30	27	14	18	—
Singapore	40	23	21	43	48	33	40	24
Korea	31	12	14	39	47	29	20	—
Switzerland	21	9	9	—	—	—	—	—
Taiwan	37	8	12	34	49	15	24	13
United Kingdom[a]	12	11	9	18	8	11	14	18
U.S. OECD rank[b]	28/34	21/34	19/34	4/24	8/15	3/25	7/14	3/24

Note: Throughout this chapter (and the appendix), PISA, TIMSS, and PIRLS data—including demographic data—were obtained from the National Center for Education Statistics' International Data Explorer, available at http://nces.ed.gov/surveys/international/ide. Missing data in the table indicate that a country did not participate in that test in the year indicated. Because the assessments employ different scales, the definition of "high scorer" differs. On PISA, it refers to a student who scores at level 5 or 6; on TIMSS and PIRLS, it's a student who attains a score of 625 or greater.

a We've tried throughout the book to standardize the names of countries in our sample, regardless of what others call them in various contexts. This is not always possible with regard to England because, while TIMSS and PIRLS provide data for "England," PISA data are for the "United Kingdom," which includes Wales, Scotland, and Northern Ireland; England contains about 85 percent of the UK population.

b "U.S. OECD rank" is the U.S. ranking, among all OECD countries that took part in that particular assessment, in the percentage of high scorers within the test-taking population.

difference, however, depends on the exam as well as the country— and is not always consistent. On PISA, the United States is surpassed in every subject by every country in our sample except Hungary. On TIMSS, American test takers are competitive with those in several

European and Anglophone countries, though not with Asian students. And in the fourth-grade exams, including PIRLS (which tests *only* fourth-grade reading), U.S. students are near the top of all OECD countries, even competing with the two "Asian tigers" that participated—and whose performance dwarfs ours on every other measure. This early-grade strength mirrors what we saw in the domestic data, and the fall-off by eighth grade (and age fifteen) on these international metrics underscores a major challenge that has plagued American school reformers: our inability, so far, to translate early gains into the middle grades and sustain them through high school. It's both galling and alarming to see U.S. youngsters ahead of many international peers in fourth grade but falling behind as they continue in school.

Understand, though, that these performance differences are caused in part by test differences. PISA is designed to measure the "literacy" of a country's entire fifteen-year-old population in three important skill domains. It isn't based on any particular curriculum or meant to evaluate school performance as such. TIMSS and PIRLS, on the other hand, are more like NAEP, centered on specific school grades, built around discipline-specific frameworks, roughly aligned with curricula, and intended to measure students' mastery of specific skills, knowledge, and concepts.[17]

In the analyses that follow, we again concentrate on math and we rely most heavily on PISA data. These allow us to make better comparisons with countries that the United States considers competitors, places that themselves look increasingly to PISA scores to gauge their own international standing. For example, more than half of OECD member countries (all of which take part in PISA) did not participate in the most recent eighth-grade TIMSS and nearly one-third of them skipped the fourth-grade TIMSS assessment.

Using these measures, another illuminating comparison is each country's average score for all students, examined in relation to its percentage of high scorers.

Figure 2.5 demonstrates how strongly correlated are average scores and the percentage of top scorers in almost every country: the higher a nation's average on PISA (math), the higher—usually—is the proportion of its students reaching levels 5 and 6.[18] The figure also illustrates how low the U.S. position is on both axes.

FIGURE 2.5   Average PISA math score by percentage of high scorers, 2012

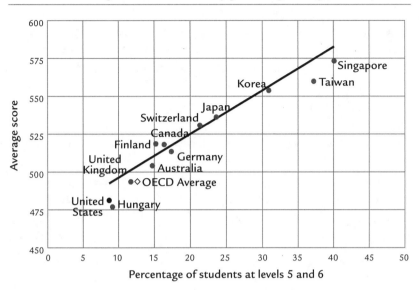

We also looked at how countries' top scorers fared on each international test over time. (We display this analysis in appendix table A.2.) Those data again affirm American strength in the early grades. Indeed, U.S. high scorers—though too few in number—have increased at a rate greater than the OECD average on all three fourth-grade exams, with TIMSS fourth-grade math being a particularly bright spot.

The data also reaffirm, however, how far American students fall by the end of middle school. (PISA takers are fifteen years old; TIMSS takers—eighth graders in the United States—are typically fourteen.) Not only is their performance weaker than that of their younger counterparts, it has actually fallen (or stayed flat) since 2003.

ACHIEVEMENT GAPS: INTERNATIONAL

We saw in the domestic data that socioeconomic status and parents' education levels tend to correlate with U.S. academic achievement. To what extent is this also the case overseas?

Socioeconomic status

The OECD has developed an Index of Economic, Social, and Cultural Status (ESCS), which enables scores to be sorted into quartiles for each country.[19] That makes it one of the few socioeconomic gauges to permit cross-national comparisons in education. Like most such gauges that use data self-reported by students, however, it's imperfect.[20] Hence we also look at high achievers through the lenses of parent education and language.

Figure 2.6 shows how many high scorers each country had (on PISA math in 2012) in its top and bottom ESCS quartiles. We see that, among the countries sampled, the United States has the lowest percentage of top-quartile kids at PISA levels 5 and 6 as well as the second-lowest proportion of low-SES students scoring at those levels, surpassing only Hungary. (Note that the scales on the *x* and *y* axes differ, due to the much greater proportions of high scorers among top-quartile students in every country.)

FIGURE 2.6   Percentage of students at levels 5 or 6, PISA math, ESCS top and bottom quartiles, 2012

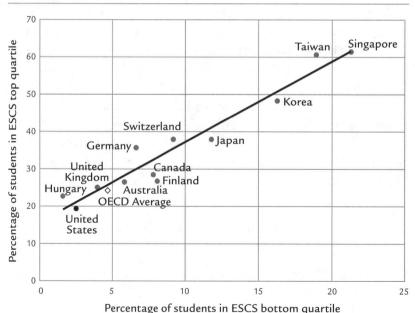

Table 2.4 compares these two groups for all three PISA subjects—math, reading, and science. For each subject, the ratio represents the percentage of children in the country's top quartile that scored at levels 5 and 6 compared to those in the bottom quartile. (See appendix table A.3 for these quartile data.) For example, the United States has a ratio of 8 to 1 on math because 19.7 percent of test takers in the top ESCS quartile reached levels 5 or 6, but just 2.4 percent from the bottom quartile got there. Which is to say, a high-SES American test taker is eight times likelier than a low-SES student to be a top scorer in math. In reading, for every disadvantaged top scorer in the United States, there are eleven in the advantaged population. In science, it's nearly 1 to 9.

No country has the one-to-one ratio that would signify total equality across the socioeconomic spectrum. In math and reading,

TABLE 2.4   Students at PISA levels 5 or 6, showing ratio of top to bottom ESCS quartiles, by subject, 2012

Math	Ratio	Reading	Ratio	Science	Ratio
Singapore	2.9:1	Japan	3.1:1	Finland	2.9:1
Korea	3.0:1	Finland	3.2:1	Japan	3.0:1
Taiwan	3.2:1	Canada	3.7:1	Canada	3.6:1
Japan	3.2:1	Korea	4.2:1	Korea	3.8:1
Finland	3.4:1	Singapore	4.5:1	Singapore	4.7:1
Canada	3.7:1	Australia	5.3:1	Australia	4.8:1
Switzerland	4.1:1	Germany	6.2:1	Germany	6.3:1
Australia	4.6:1	Taiwan	6.9:1	United Kingdom	7.5:1
Germany	5.5:1	Switzerland	7.5:1	Switzerland	8.0:1
United Kingdom	6.3:1	United Kingdom	8.5:1	**United States**	**8.8:1**
United States	**8.0:1**	**United States**	**11.1:1**	Taiwan	10.1:1
Hungary	14.8:1	Hungary	13.2:1	Hungary	18.0:1
OECD average	5.3:1	OECD average	5.9:1	OECD average	6.0:1

Note: Using the OECD's "Index of Economic, Social, and Cultural Status" (ESCS) (see note 19 for an explanation), each ratio is the percentage of high scorers in a country's top ESCS quartile divided by that percentage among test takers in its bottom ESCS quartile.

"OECD average" denotes the average ratio for all OECD countries in 2012 in each subject.

however, only Hungary has a ratio worse than ours; in science, only Hungary and Taiwan do. In other words, among these dozen nations, the United States is always in the bottom two or three. Hungary is the only other country for which that's true.

Readers may wonder whether America's significant economic inequalities are a major source of our poor ratios. We wondered, too. It's a fact that the United States has the second-highest level of income inequality among these twelve nations (exceeded only by Singapore), based on the widely used Gini coefficient.[21] But the supposition doesn't hold up very well. The Central Intelligence Agency's analysis shows that Hungary is the "most equal" country in our sample in terms of income distribution, yet it also has the worst achievement ratios in all three subjects. And the least equal country—Singapore—displays the lowest ratio in math and fifth lowest in reading and science. This flies in the face of the suggestion that income inequality may explain away our failure to get more disadvantaged youngsters into PISA's highest ranks.

Parental education

Parents' education levels are another way of looking at disadvantage, as well as a way to double-check the analysis in the previous section—worth doing because of the complexities of cross-national SES indicators.

Figure 2.7 looks at math high achievers on NAEP and PISA according to the extent of their parents' education. It relies on the analyses of Eric Hanushek, Paul Peterson, and Ludger Woessmann, who looked only at OECD member countries (thus omitting Taiwan and Singapore). The question they asked was how many students in other countries would reach NAEP's Advanced level in math, and how much the results differ by parents' education levels. They statistically linked PISA and eighth-grade NAEP results and metrics, and used PISA's three-tiered definition of parental education. (Low means neither parent has a high school diploma; moderate signifies that at least one parent has a high school diploma, but neither has a college degree; and high means at least one parent has a college degree.)[22]

The United States is in the bottom left corner, indicating that, among our sample countries, our own nation has some of the lowest

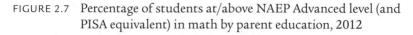

FIGURE 2.7 Percentage of students at/above NAEP Advanced level (and PISA equivalent) in math by parent education, 2012

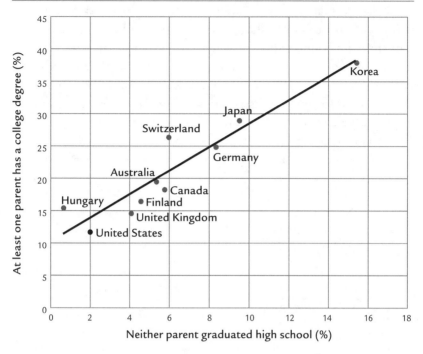

Source: Eric A. Hanushek, Paul E. Peterson, and Ludger Woessmann, "Not Just the Problem of Other People's Children: U.S. Student Performance in Global Perspective," PEPG Report 14-01, Harvard Kennedy School, Program on Education Policy and Governance and *Education Next*, May 2014.

proportions of high achievers, regardless of parent education level. Approximately 11 percent of American students whose parents are highly educated are top scorers—a figure that places us dead last among these nations. And only Hungary does worse by kids whose parents didn't finish high school. In the United States, a meager 2 percent of such youngsters reach NAEP's Advanced level.

Hanushek and his colleagues conducted this analysis only for math but provided us with the percentages of students in each PISA-participating country that fell into the three categories of parental education. This enabled us to look at reading and science high achievers on PISA according to the extent of their parents' education (but without reference to NAEP).[23]

Appendix figures A.7 and A.8 contain "scatter plots" for those two subjects, similar to figure 2.7—and show virtually the same pattern. But the combined data are best displayed as the ratios in table 2.5. Each country's ratio shows its percentage of high scorers among students with college-educated parents divided by that percentage for kids whose parents didn't graduate from high school. (See appendix table A.4 for these data.) As in table 2.4, the lower a country's ratio, the closer it is to an equal distribution of high achievers. In math, only Hungary has a ratio greater than the United States, meaning even less equality. In reading—our best subject—the U.S. ratio is fourth largest. In science, it's greatest among the eleven countries with available

TABLE 2.5   Students at PISA levels 5 or 6, ratio of those with highly educated parents to those with low-educated parents, by subject, 2012

Math	Ratio	Reading	Ratio	Science	Ratio
Korea	2.5:1	Singapore	3.2:1	Canada	3.0:1
Germany	3.0:1	Canada	3.4:1	Japan	3.3:1
Japan	3.1:1	Germany	3.5:1	Germany	3.5:1
Canada	3.2:1	Japan	3.7:1	Singapore	3.8:1
United Kingdom	3.6:1	Finland	4.2:1	Australia	3.9:1
Finland	3.6:1	Australia	4.2:1	Korea	4.1:1
Australia	3.6:1	Taiwan	4.6:1	Finland	5.3:1
Switzerland	4.4:1	Korea	5.4:1	Taiwan	5.9:1
United States	**5.9:1**	**United States**	**6.6:1**	Switzerland	6.9:1
Hungary	22.1:1	Switzerland	7.1:1	United Kingdom	10.3:1
		United Kingdom	8.7:1	**United States**	**11.5:1**
		Hungary	18.1:1		

Sources: Eric A. Hanushek, Paul E. Peterson, and Ludger Woessmann, "Not Just the Problem of Other People's Children: U.S. Student Performance in Global Perspective," PEPG Report 14-01, Harvard Kennedy School, Program on Education Policy and Governance and *Education Next*, May 2014; and "International Data Explorer," U.S. Department of Education, Institute of Education Sciences, National Center for Education Statistics, accessed November 29, 2014, http://nces.ed.gov/surveys/international/ide/.

Note: Using NAEP and PISA data, each ratio is the percentage of high scorers among those whose parents graduated from college divided by that percentage for test takers whose parents did not graduate from high school.

data. Note, too, that the same few countries tend to top each table: Germany, Canada, Japan, and Singapore or Korea.

Another way to analyze international disadvantage is to look at language. How do children fare on PISA if the language in which the test is administered in their school is not the language they speak at home? We show this analysis in the appendix (figure A.9), where we see that, with few exceptions, such a language discrepancy poses problems for students. Most such children are from immigrant families and, in the countries in our sample, many immigrant families are also poor, giving their children a double disadvantage in school. In the vast majority of cases, students are likelier to achieve high scores on PISA if their home language is the same as the language of the test, which is usually also the language of instruction in their schools.

* * *

When it comes to producing top scorers, the United States falls short of its competitors, often by wide margins. The size of the gap depends on which instrument and subject one looks at. Aside from fourth graders, however, such a gap is present and worrisome in nearly every case. Be it PISA or TIMSS or PIRLS; math, science, or reading; SES status, parent education, or the language spoken at home; America's secondary students never do better than most of our competitors— not once. And we're often at or near the bottom of the list, a deficit that deepens when we examine disadvantaged populations.

In the next several chapters, we explore some reasons for this failure.

3

How Disagreement Holds Us Back

THE MAIN REASON the United States has been faring poorly at producing high achievers is self-evident: we haven't made this a priority. But that failure arises from more than simple oversight or mere neglect. It has multiple origins, three of which we examine in this chapter—disputes over ideology, the definition of "gifted," and the identification of children who meet that definition—and four more in the next chapter.

IDEOLOGY

In the United States, as in many countries, worrying about smart kids is widely viewed as elitist and therefore unjustified, diverting resources and attention to already-fortunate youngsters. Instead, insist many politicians, academics, and interest groups, everything possible should be done for youngsters with disabilities, those who haven't yet acquired basic skills, those from troubled circumstances and neighborhoods, and those who have in various ways been discriminated against.

Think of it as a choice of priorities exacerbated by tight budgets as well as strongly held convictions, and observe that those pushing for resources to be devoted to the "truly needy" can generally summon both moral authority and the additional oomph of zealous, single-minded advocacy groups. By contrast, those who seek greater attention for high-ability youngsters are loosely organized, ill-funded, and at least slightly diffident about pressing their case. They don't want to look selfish and are probably middle class themselves; they wouldn't dare push for something as politically incorrect as "tracking"; they're nervous about children skipping grades and thereby losing friends and peers; they don't know quite how to think about late bloomers; and they have only half-answers to the suggestion that "fast learners should just help the slower kids—and everyone will benefit."

It's probably impossible to revitalize gifted education in America by tugging at heartstrings, invoking moral obligation, or appealing to liberal values. Although there is a solid "equity case" to be made—these kids have needs, too, and deserve an education tailored to meet them—at the policy level the likelier-to-succeed case is linked to economic competitiveness, technical and scientific leadership, and America's future standing on the planet. Sometimes this case can be made locally—as when northern Virginia business leaders prevailed upon county and state officials to establish the acclaimed Thomas Jefferson High School of Math and Science to grow scientists for the region's burgeoning high-tech sector (and to give present-day scientists a school where they'd happily send their own kids). State or regional competitiveness may also succeed on occasion.[1] Mostly, though, this case needs to be made for the country as a whole—an obvious problem in the United States and other countries where school policy making and funding are decentralized.

The challenge is somewhat less daunting in nations that have placed "human capital development" high on their priority list, particularly places with few other resources, such as Singapore, Switzerland, Hungary, and Korea. There we find wider public and political acceptance of cultivating talent. In the United States, however, and in many other Western nations, investing in high-ability youngsters is often viewed not simply as a diversion of resources from more urgent needs but also as outright discrimination, related to the fact that the student profile in such programs and schools frequently ends up skewed toward middle-class, white, and Asian kids. Never mind that this argument grows circular when one realizes that it's our *neglect* of high-ability kids from disadvantaged backgrounds that accounts in considerable part for the demographic discrepancies that trigger the policy animus.

DEFINITIONAL DISPUTES

Who is gifted and how does one determine this? As outlined in the introduction, such questions launch a journey into confusion and controversy, beginning with the possibility that the term "gifted" itself may be counterproductive. It implies that one was endowed at birth with some quality denied to others, a quality that—with no exertion or ambition on one's own part—entitles one to special handling in the education space. Yet we've all known individuals who entered the world with pronounced intellectual (or other) potential yet lack the drive or discipline to accomplish much. What makes them deserving of anything special?[2] On the flip side, we've observed people whose innate abilities may not be outstanding but whose pluck and drive lead them to scale impressive heights. Talent is properly viewed as something dynamic and able to be cultivated, developed, and enhanced, not a static "at-birth" quality. Yes, starting "smart" is a distinct advantage: given the chance, faster learners generally learn more. But personal qualities related to temperament and character also matter in terms of eventual accomplishment. So does how much one has already accomplished. That's why—as we discuss further in chapter 18—such respected education commentators and scholars as Paul Tough, William Damon, Carol Dweck, and Angela Duckworth declare effort, attitude, and aspiration to be at least as important as ability.[3] And that's why, in the messy business of defining "giftedness," we have come to favor theorists such as Joseph Renzulli, Françoys Gagné, Robert Sternberg, Rena Subotnik, Paula Olszewski-Kubilius, and Frank C. Worrell, whose multidimensional models take account of the intersection of several such qualities, not just one's at-birth "gifts."[4]

The deeper we dive into this bog, the more we're also drawn to phrases like "high ability" or "high achieving." In a number of countries, the preferred term is "talent"—and the relevant policy domain is called "talent development" rather than "gifted education."

Yet the phrase most often used in contemporary American discourse on this topic, "gifted and talented," carries baggage of its own. Although old-style conceptions of "giftedness" had significant problems, especially their reliance on IQ testing to demarcate those who possess this quality from those who don't, at least they had a clear focus—high intellectual ability—as well as a reasonably precise definition and a specific if controversial metric. As the field evolved toward "gifted and talented," however, the definition widened and the focus blurred. Such blurring made it ever more difficult to frame the issue, depict the challenge, document the problem, and measure its extent. That's why, even today, almost all the data that one encounters regarding "excellence gaps" relies on conventional measures of achievement in core academic subjects.

One may fairly ask whether adding "talented" to "gifted" has made matters better or worse.[5]

Whatever the name, there's also confusion and conflict over how many forms of gifts or talents matter for purposes of education policy, school structure, curriculum, and instruction. Almost everyone acknowledges that exceptional intellectual prowess and accomplishment in the traditional curricular core qualifies as a legitimate form of giftedness—and that is the form we focus on in these pages. But even within that core, does a talented poet warrant as much investment of policy energy, teacher time, and tax dollars as an exceptional physicist? Do historians and psychologists count as much as mathematicians and microbiologists? And when we move away from the core, how important is giftedness in the arts, which may be of greater value to a society's culture than to its economy? How about athletics? And what to do—if anything—with unusual potential or achievement in leadership, interpersonal relations, and other realms that today are sometimes termed "twenty-first-century skills"?

The sole federal program aimed at promoting education for gifted children, dating to 1988, employs this expansive definition: "Students, children, or youth who give evidence of high achievement capability in areas such as intellectual, creative, artistic, or leadership capacity, or in specific academic fields, and who need services and activities not ordinarily provided by the school in order to fully develop those capabilities."[6]

(Before moving on, observe the emphasis on these children's "need" for extra "services and activities.")

Ohio's statutory definition is almost as sweeping, though it doesn't mention "leadership" (or "services"): "Students are identified as gifted in any of four major categories: superior cognitive ability; specific academic ability; creative thinking ability; and visual or performing arts ability. Specific academic ability spans four fields: mathematics; science; social studies; and reading or writing, or a combination of these two skills."[7]

But no two states use quite the same definition and some are notably narrower, others vaguer. Indiana, for instance, puts no limit on the realms where a student may display "high abilities." Its definition could, in theory, encompass tightrope walking, marijuana growing, and omelet making.

Kansas, by contrast, confines itself to "academic fields" and "intellectual ability," while Kentucky adds such hard-to-detect strengths as "divergent thinking" and "psychosocial" prowess. Louisiana distinguishes between "giftedness" in academic domains and "clear evidence of unique talent" in visual or performing arts. Meanwhile, Massachusetts, New Hampshire, and South Dakota have no definitions at all.[8]

Just as varied are the definitions of giftedness that local school districts deploy. Here's Fairfax County again: "Children who have been identified as gifted and talented (GT) have the potential to achieve high levels of accomplishment that need to be recognized and addressed. These students exhibit unusual performance capability in intellectual endeavors in one or more academic areas: mathematics, science, social studies, and/or language arts."[9] Fairfax thus limits itself to traditional academics, really to the four subjects at the core of nearly every school curriculum. Downstate in Virginia Beach, however, the gifted and talented program is open to students who possess "advanced aptitudes demonstrated by skills and creative expression in general intellectual ability" without reference to particular subjects, as well as "specific aptitudes in selected visual or performing arts."[10]

Bottom line: giftedness, a bit like Justice Potter Stewart's famous definition of obscenity, seems to be in the eye of the beholder. The problem is that, while we recognize the virtues of diversity and local control in K–12 education, it's hard to rally people around a cause whose putative beneficiaries seem to differ so fundamentally from place to place.

IDENTIFICATION CHALLENGES

As confused as the definition of giftedness is the identification of individuals who possess it and who may (or may not) therefore qualify for special handling in the education realm. This challenge is deepened by two related considerations.

First, almost nowhere does the supply of that "something special" equal the demand for it. Plenty of families seek the benefits of gifted and talented education for their children, almost always more than can be accommodated. As with any system for rationing a scarce good, particularly in the public sector, and doubly so in our litigious era, the criteria used for deciding who is in and who is out need to "hold up in court." Accordingly, they should be transparent, preferably objective, and reasonably immune to politics, favoritism, and special pleading.

Second, because the very idea of something special for gifted kids is often seen as gilding the education lily, it's doubly important that the identification and selection system give a fair shot—even a boost—to youngsters from disadvantaged circumstances. But what if few of them apply? What if their parents don't know or perhaps don't care about the extra attention for which their daughters and sons might qualify? What if their third-grade teachers are consumed by the difficulties of other youngsters and fail to refer the high-ability pupils who are in their classrooms, quietly behaving and handing in their homework, even if, perhaps, a bit bored? What if tests (or other measures) that are used for purposes of selection seem to favor—or do in fact favor—kids with educated parents, rich kids, and white or Asian kids?

Face it. Gifted education, whatever its form (and there are many, as we discuss in the next chapter), is nearly always a rationed good that cannot be supplied to all who crave it—and from which some cravers may not even derive great benefit, indeed might even retard the progress of those who stand to gain the most. At the same time, fairness demands that any public education system bend over backwards not to deny this opportunity to youngsters who might benefit from it even if their parents and teachers fail to point them toward it.

Such dilemmas mean that a workable identification system must simultaneously deal with the challenges of recruitment, evaluation, and rationing. Here, as in every realm that seeks to select on the basis of merit or need rather than randomly or first-come-first-served, the system must consist either of objective, quantifiable measures or of subjective, holistic judgments about individuals. Or some combination of the two. Plus outreach strategies so that qualified individuals at least get the chance to be considered even if they do not beat a path to the door.

It's a problem either way. In the field of education, objective measures tend to be test scores of some sort, while holistic judgments typically involve written applications, interviews, and teacher recommendations.[11]

The test-score approach is relatively efficient—fast and cheap, compared to almost everything else—and enjoys the appearance of objectivity: those with a score over 130, say, get into the program while those with lower scores do not. A score of 131 means you're in; 129 means you're out. That's pretty much how New York City's most famous public high schools, such as Stuyvesant and Bronx Science, handle admissions (although they use a specialized assessment of verbal skill and math prowess, not an IQ test).[12] This straightforward, score-based decision process eases the job of program administrators and school heads who are phoned by upset parents, influential politicians, and rich benefactors and asked to justify their admission decisions. Yet kids who do well on tests may lack other qualities—ambition, stick-to-it-iveness, purpose, prior accomplishment—that also matter in this realm. Test-score results alone are also apt to yield a winner's list that's poorly aligned with community demographics—another source of discontent and pushback over special handling for some youngsters but not others. And because some high scorers are bound to be upper-middle-class youngsters whose parents paid for "cram" courses or tutoring to prep them for the tests, economic stratification is also likely to set in.

Holistic judgments, on the other hand, which elite private schools and colleges generally employ, involve close inspection of many attributes of prospective participants, often including school grades, recommendations by teachers and others, interviews, essays or personal statements, and perhaps evidence of prior accomplishment in various domains. This process makes it easier for a school or program to end up with "diverse" participants and to take account of other factors that a gifted education program may legitimately seek to cultivate, such as critical thinking and independent inquiry. But it calls for bulky files and time-consuming procedures, thus proving relatively costly for those involved with the process; it's vulnerable to lobbying by well-connected parents and other influentials; it smacks of subjectivity, which is always risky in public institutions; and it's far from transparent, hence viewed with suspicion by some and prone to being dubbed unfair, maybe even discriminatory in its own way. (So, of course, is extensive outreach to disadvantaged populations and other forms of "affirmative action" that some will see as "reverse discrimination.")

Scanning the selection criteria and procedures of school systems across the country, we are struck by how dissimilar they are. Here, for example, is Sarasota, Florida:

> Any Sarasota County student may be referred for a gifted screening to determine the need for further evaluation. Students who meet the minimum score (130) on the intelligence screening instrument may be referred for a full evaluation.[13]

Contrast that with the four-step "identification" process employed by Los Angeles:

1. *Search and referral:* The school develops an initial list of potential candidates through the process of search and referral. A referral for identification can be made by a teacher, administrator, parent, or student.
2. *Screening:* The school administrator or designee screens students by collecting data from existing sources, such as, the cumulative record and progress report card. School personnel may use the Student Information System's (SIS) potential list.
3. *Committee review:* When a candidate is deemed eligible for consideration, a member of the Local School Screening Committee

obtains parent consent and completes the referral. When appropriate, an intellectual assessment or an evaluation of academic abilities, or audition in the performing arts, or a demonstration in the visual arts may be required.

4. *District verification:* A designated District staff member reviews all screening and assessment materials and determines the eligibility of students.[14]

In essence, Sarasota emphasizes IQ tests and minimum cutoff scores that it makes public, while Los Angeles is vague, maybe intentionally so, about what exactly it's looking for—creating at least the potential for holistic evaluations—and vague again on who will make decisions based on what evidence, though it's clear that central office staff make the final call. (That may also be true in Sarasota, though the district website doesn't spell it out.)

Bottom line: as with discrepant definitions of giftedness, the variegated criteria and procedures by which districts determine which kids qualify, although consistent with America's devotion to local control, mean that whether your child is in or out probably hinges more on where you live than on what she's capable of—or has already achieved.

4

How the System
Slows Us Down

IN THE PREVIOUS CHAPTER, we considered three up-front obstacles to the education of high-ability children: philosophical disputes over whether they even deserve attention, confusion over who qualifies, and divergent practices in identifying them.

Now we turn to four more weaknesses in the current arrangements by which the U.S. public school system deals with such students: the extreme variability of program offerings, the lack of reliable data, the uncertain efficacy of gifted education as currently practiced, and the feebleness of its political support.

PROGRAM VARIABILITY

What exactly are children being identified for and selected into? The variety is mind-boggling. In chapter 5, we take up "differentiated instruction" within regular classrooms and schools. Here, we flag five prominent (and semi-overlapping) forms of separate or distinctive treatment for high-ability learners.[1]

- *Acceleration.* A student might skip an entire grade, proceeding from, say, third directly into fifth grade. Another option is to accelerate in one or two subjects, such as allowing a fifth grader to study science with seventh graders. In high school, that student might dual-enroll in a local college or take Advanced Placement classes that yield university credit. But that's just the beginning; the acceleration quiver holds many arrows.[2]

- **Supplementation.** After school, on the weekend, or during vacation time, a student might engage in independent study, work with a mentor in his lab, take part in a robotics workshop, enter the Intel science fair, or join a summer program on a university campus. Such programs abound, often run by organizations other than school systems.

- **Part-time "pull-out" classes.** A high-ability youngster might spend part of her day or week in a separate room with other advanced pupils. She might attend a full-fledged math or language class—perhaps Advanced Placement—or have an "enrichment" period during which she and her peers pursue individual research projects. The possibilities are many. What's usually distinctive about such classes is that their purpose is not quicker progress through the conventional curriculum (acceleration or "curricular compression," it's often termed), but going deeper, exploring alternative methods or explanations, conducting experiments, engaging in independent exploration of the subject—or deviating from the curriculum to examine other fields or topics of interest.

- **Full-time "pull-out" classes.** Besides wholly separate schools and "schools within schools" (see below), some programs (akin to the latter) cluster gifted students for the entire academic curriculum while generally commingling all pupils for homeroom, phys ed, and perhaps art and music. Examples include Seattle's Thurgood Marshall Elementary School and San Diego's Innovation Middle School. At the high school level, there may be an "honors track."

- **Complete separation.** Gifted students may enter a separate or semi-separate institution with a complete alternative curriculum such as the International Baccalaureate, a school-within-a-school such as California's North Hollywood High School or the Cincinnati Gifted Academy, or a stand-alone school such as Boston Latin or Austin's Kealing Middle School.

Wholly separate schools for high-ability pupils are scarce in American public education. When the senior author and a colleague searched recently for public high schools that are academically focused and entirely selective, we found just 165 of them in a country with some twenty thousand high schools.[3] But the U.S. education system contains many other forms of gifted education. Once again, it's largely up to individual districts and, as with the definitional and identification challenges noted earlier, one can search far and wide without finding agreement on which approaches are best. Some places do nothing. Others offer multiple options. From state to state and district to district—even within the same district—this isn't just apples and oranges. It's an entire fruit basket.

DUBIOUS DATA

Considering the lack of consensus on what giftedness means, what forms it comes in, how to identify it, and what to do (if anything) for those who display it, we shouldn't be surprised that few data are available to quantify and illumine the situation—and there's reason to be skeptical of the numbers that exist. Indeed, the main U.S. source of education data, the National Center for Education Statistics (NCES), relies for its tally on a shaky sampling process conducted by the Education Department's Office for Civil Rights (OCR). And the situation is even worse when we seek data on disadvantaged kids who are also gifted; according to a March 2015 report from the Jack Kent Cooke Foundation, "No state has a comprehensive system for tracking high-performing, low-income students."[4]

How many gifted youngsters are there in America? Don't look to federal sources for a clear answer, or to any other source we're aware of, save for a few states with nose counts based on their own idiosyncratic definitions and gauges. NCES reported that 3.2 million such children were enrolled in U.S. public schools in 2006, about 7 percent of the total pupil population.[5] Track this number, however, and it comes from an OCR estimate drawn from a sample survey of districts that included this two-part query:[6]

1. Does this school have students enrolled in gifted/talented programs? (Yes/No)
2. (only for schools with gifted/talented programs): Enter enrollment in gifted/talented programs.

So the federal estimate is not the number of gifted children in the nation but, rather, the number currently found in district-operated gifted education programs, a very different thing, and obviously dependent on what (if anything) a district does by way of supplying such programs. (In 2011, San Jose, California, reported *no* schools with gifted programs, while San Francisco reported ninety-three.)

Ohio's own data—districts must apply the state's multipart definition of giftedness to their students and report the number who meet one or more of those criteria—lead to an estimate of about 15 percent of Buckeye children who qualify. Yet OCR's number for Ohio works out to 4.6 percent. We know from Ohio sources that most of those "identified" as gifted are not served by gifted education programs so OCR may, in fact, be correct or nearly so with its estimate of how many youngsters are *enrolled* in such programs. But being enrolled is not the same as being gifted.

For its part, the National Association for Gifted Children (NAGC) estimates that the United States contains three million gifted youngsters. That's not very different from the OCR-NCES national estimate, but the latter is based on children enrolled in programs, whereas NAGC's is extrapolated from Commissioner Marland's 1972 report to Congress, which declared (based on what?) that 5 to 7 percent of all students are gifted. Yet if one were to extrapolate from Ohio's data, the national total would be closer to seven or eight million children.

And that's just the puzzle of how many kids *might* be identified for gifted education programs versus actual participation. Considering how many different forms such programs take, how loose are the definitions, how problematic the screening processes, and how iffy the policy mandates to "serve" those who make it through the screening, it's practically impossible to say how many kids really take part—and how many more may be "qualified" but don't participate, whether because they never knew about it, never wanted it, were rationed out of it—or because their locality simply doesn't offer it. Yet if we don't know how many are potentially eligible and how many actually participate, it's impossible to know how much more of it there should be.

Ohio data indicate that Buckeye school systems actually provide some sort of gifted education—by that name—to just one in five of the youngsters they have identified as gifted. OCR data for Ohio suggest that it's more like one in three. Either way, state law requires only that they be counted, not that they be served. And some undoubtedly take part in programs offered by universities and other entities and therefore might not appear in district-reported data on children served. (Let's not even get into the swamp of charter, private, virtual, and home schools.)

But pause for a moment on the one gifted child in five that Ohio districts say they currently "serve" (without considering whether that means a full-time classroom or half an hour a week of supplementation). And imagine the uproar if we woke up to read that only one-fifth of children with disabilities were being furnished with "special education" by their school systems. All hell would break loose. Yet in the world of gifted education, the only pushback comes from a few parents and a couple of small advocacy organizations. There's no powerful organized constituency, and no legal basis by which parents can push on behalf of their child.[7]

Before moving on, observe also that the data on eligibility and program participation, shaky as they are, further illustrate the education system's failure to spread these opportunities equally across the population. In Ohio's numbers, we see that while almost half the state's public school pupils qualify as "economically disadvantaged," among those identified as gifted the corresponding figure is 21 percent. And while 18 percent of white students and 28 percent of Asian students meet the definition of gifted, only 5 percent of black students and 6 percent of Hispanic students are so identified.[8]

The OCR numbers on gifted education participation across the country also engender no satisfaction on this front. They, too, show white and Asian students to be "over-represented," comprising 65 and 10 percent of program enrollees compared with 55 and 5 percent of the total public school population (in 2009). By contrast, Hispanic and black students comprise 15 and 10 percent of gifted-program participants, though they make up 22 and 17 percent of total enrollments. Oversimplifying, one might say that an Asian American pupil is about three times likelier to be enrolled in a gifted education program than is a student of either Hispanic or African American origin.

UNCERTAIN EFFICACY

None of this much matters if we can't be reasonably confident that special handling of high-ability youngsters truly benefits them. Research in this realm is skimpy and inconclusive, partly because, as we noted earlier, it's off the radar of most education scholars, and partly because the effectiveness of gifted education is truly hard to study. The programs are so different—in mission, philosophy, scope, content, intensity, admission criteria, duration—that gauging their impact on participants (much less their cost-benefit ratios, their consequences for other kids and the larger education system, etc.) is a nebulous and daunting assignment that is rarely tackled. Moreover, evaluation efforts in this domain face major methodological challenges, including selection effects, difficulty distinguishing between peer and teacher influences, the short time horizon of most evaluations, the problem of standardized test scores "topping out," and the limits of skill-centric tests as metrics for programs whose goal isn't necessarily to go farther or faster but, often, to dig deeper.

The respectable research that has been done yields mixed but intriguing results. In a 2013 paper, Sa Bui, Steven Craig, and Scott Imberman looked at the academic achievement of children who barely "cleared the bar" for admission into middle-school gifted education in a large U.S. city, and of other students who won the lottery for admission into the district's gifted magnet middle schools. They found, over the first year and a half, "that marginal students neither improve nor worsen in terms of achievement from GT services."[9] Not exactly heartening. A year later, however, David Card and Laura Giuliano looked at the impact of another district's gifted education programs on several different groups of students.[10] Their findings and policy implications are tantalizing enough to justify an extended excerpt from the summary supplied by the National Bureau of Economic Research:

> [F]ull-time classes set up for gifted students don't raise the achievement of gifted students, but have large positive effects on non-gifted high achievers in those classes—especially on the reading and math scores of low-income high achievers. The authors conclude that establishing "a separate classroom in every school for the top-performing students could significantly

boost the performance of [these] students in even the poorest neighborhoods," without harming other students or increasing school budgets.

Using detailed administrative data from one of the largest school districts in the United States, the authors tracked the progress of three distinct groups of students who were eligible for placement in classes for the gifted from 2004 through 2011. District policy required each elementary school to set up a separate gifted class for all students in the fourth or fifth grade who met one of two criteria. So-called "Plan A" gifted students scored at least 130 points on an IQ test. The policy also allows a lower threshold (116 points) for the "Plan B" gifted students—i.e., English-language learners and participants in the free and reduced-price lunch program. Finally, since many schools have relatively few gifted students in a grade, the remaining seats are offered to non-gifted students who scored the highest on the previous year's state-wide achievement tests (known as "high achievers"). Classes for the gifted are the same size as other classes in the district, and students follow the same curriculum and write the same standardized achievement test each spring.

The positive and relatively large effects on the math and reading achievement of the non-gifted high achievers was [sic] concentrated among free and reduced-price lunch students and black and Hispanic students. There was also a small positive effect on the writing scores of Plan B gifted students—especially boys and students at schools with high fractions of students who were eligible for free and reduced-price lunches . . .

[T]he authors speculate that many Plan B students may have lacked non-cognitive traits, such as attention-to-task and a willingness to meet social expectations. Such traits may have helped high achievers perform well on standardized tests of routine knowledge despite their lower IQ scores. Differences in these traits may explain why high achievers benefitted more from gifted classes than the Plan B students, and may also explain why Plan B students reported lower satisfaction with the gifted classroom environment than either the Plan A students or the high achievers.[11]

In essence, these findings suggest that moving children into gifted education classes on the basis of IQ scores does not boost their achievement, although this conclusion is limited by the fact that conventional state measures of achievement may "top out" (i.e., not do well at measuring gains for students already at the upper end of their scales) and do not even try to gauge other possible benefits of gifted classes, such as original thinking and independent research. But the Card-Giuliano findings show clearly that selecting children into such classes on the basis of strong prior achievement does benefit them academically (in ways that state assessments capture) and that the greatest benefit accrues to high-achieving disadvantaged youngsters. Moreover, that achievement boost seems to last.

One other body of research in this realm deserves attention, as it speaks to an old-fashioned version of gifted education that appears to have positive effects on the academic performance of those who benefit from it: acceleration by speeding up or compressing the regular curriculum, perhaps skipping classes or entire grades, and gaining earlier access to more advanced and challenging material.[12]

Although legitimate questions can be raised regarding the social and psychological effects of accelerating a given child (and many parents who have this option agonize over whether the potential academic boost offsets the possible loss of classmates and age-mates), considerable evidence suggests that these side effects are *not* harmful to most children who do accelerate and that the ensuing academic gains are notable, particularly for exceptionally high-ability, high-achieving students. We must add, however, that accelerating through the conventional curriculum will not necessarily yield other opportunities and benefits that many experts in the field view as important, such as independent research, critical analysis, original thinking, and access to mentors, labs, and other nonschool experiences.

It's a cliché in education (and other fields) to declare that "more research is needed," but in this case it's absolutely on point. Not nearly enough is known about what strategies, policies, and programs are most beneficial for which kinds of high-ability and/or high-achieving learners, selected through what means and at what stages of their lives. What are the long-term effects—and not just the academic effects—of such opportunities and interventions? What are the costs, as well as the benefits, of tailoring their educational experience in ways that differ from the experiences of other students?

Education policy choices and budget priorities in twenty-first-century America are increasingly driven by evidence regarding actual effectiveness, not just hopes, preferences, and pressures. Today, however, the gifted education field cannot supply enough evidence to answer such questions definitively. Few analysts and scholars are interested. And private and public agencies that commission and pay for research have neglected these issues. Combine such neglect with the squishy, uncertain data mentioned above, and we face a worrying paucity of reliable information for the decisions that lie ahead.

POLITICAL WILL

Partly because there's little reliable data and solid research by which the potential of gifted youngsters can be gauged and their performance tracked, there's not much political horsepower behind efforts to do more in this realm. The organizations are tiny. The middle-class parents most likely to fuss on behalf of their own kids often have options beyond what's offered by the school system. And one cannot engage in effective advocacy if one cannot explain to a school board member, legislator, or pundit how many gifted kids are not being served, much less the gnarly business of whether they're adequately and successfully served.

Combine those impediments with ideological challenges, heavy lobbying on behalf of sundry at-risk populations, the many other reform struggles under way in today's K–12 universe, and the tough resource trade-offs that state and local officials confront, and perhaps we shouldn't be surprised that gifted ed doesn't have a lot of champions in the domains of policy and politics or that, as the Jack Kent Cooke Foundation recently reported, "In most states, attention to advanced learning is incomplete and haphazard."[13]

Nor should we minimize Americans' ambivalence regarding the legitimacy of gifted education, and our horror of being called elitists. In September 2014, the *New Yorker* featured a cartoon showing two moms meeting on the sidewalk outside a school, each with a backpack-burdened child at her side. In the caption, one says to the other, "Zach is in the gifted-and-talented-and-you're-not class."

Amusing, sure, but it points to something deeper, something also voiced to the senior author during a recent flight. As he was explaining the present study to his seatmate, a woman in the row just ahead, obviously overhearing, turned to remark that "I went through gifted education when I was in school and I won't let my daughter do it, even though her school has it and she's eligible. It makes your head swell as if you're something special, it makes the other kids feel bad, and it doesn't cause them to like you, either."

5

Will Differentiation Move Us Forward?

THE POLICIES AND PROGRAMS we sketched in the last chapter, varied as they are, all entail doing something outside the regular classroom to advance the education of high-ability students. Yet many educators and policy makers favor keeping such pupils in standard classrooms and declare that their education needs can be satisfactorily met in "inclusive" settings. This approach is generally termed "differentiated" or "individualized" instruction. Tracey Huebner, senior research scientist at the Center for Applied Special Technology, defines it as "a process to approach teaching and learning for students of differing abilities in the same class. The intent is to maximize each student's growth and individual success by meeting each student where he or she is . . . rather than expecting students to modify themselves for the curriculum."[1] Professor Carol Tomlinson of the University of Virginia, who is perhaps the foremost theorist and advocate for this approach, adds, "The idea of differentiating instruction . . . is an approach to teaching that advocates active planning for student differences in classrooms."[2]

Differentiation takes many forms and teachers use sundry methods, from "tiering" their lessons to organizing small groups of students for projects (with each group generally containing at least one member who the teacher believes has mastered the topic) to teaming up with other teachers so their combined classes can be temporarily ability-grouped.

Despite, or perhaps because of, its many varied applications, as well as its obvious allure on grounds of both fairness and individualization, differentiated instruction is one of the hottest reforms in education today, not only in the United States but across much of the planet, and it's one with big-time implications for high-ability children. Almost everywhere we've been, at home and abroad, we've encountered some version of this assertion: "We don't really need to provide special programs, classrooms, or schools for gifted children because we expect every school and teacher to adapt their instruction to meet the unique educational needs of all children, including the very able, and to do so within a heterogeneous classroom."

A splendid goal for sure, but how realistic? How well is it being done by how many teachers in how many schools? And does it really meet these children's needs, or is it a politically defensible excuse for not doing anything special for them? Nobody really knows much about its actual efficacy, especially for educating high-ability youngsters. On balance, the evidence that proponents of differentiated instruction offer looks as mixed and inconclusive as what's presented in support of separate programming for such students.

The appeal of differentiated instruction has multiple origins:

1. "Brain research" that has (not always with the finest of scientific rigor) claimed to identify diverse "learning styles" and multiple forms of intelligence, thereby challenging teachers to customize their classroom practice to accommodate such student variability. (As Tracey Huebner put it, don't expect students to "modify themselves for the curriculum.")

2. Many in the special education world—parents and experts alike— favor "mainstreaming" disabled children in regular classrooms, thereby challenging teachers to adapt their instruction to accommodate these youngsters, too. Although high-ability learners in the United States are not generally treated as part of special ed, the "mainstreaming" impulse applies here, too.[3]

3. Mainstreaming—and then differentiating—is also a way to avoid, at least in concept, the practice of "tracking," which many view as tainted because of its historical association with invidious separation of children and deterministic thinking about their futures. (Differentiation does, however, commonly include versions of "ability grouping," which avoids most of the infamy of tracking but does separate children, at least temporarily.)

4. Ideological (and budgetary) considerations don't just lead to rejection of tracking. They often extend to unease over "pull-out" programs and other forms of educational separation, including acceleration and grade repetition, on grounds that such practices are morally wrong, socially and educationally undesirable, politically imprudent, psychologically damaging, possibly discriminatory, and just plain unaffordable.

5. Some educators and policy makers assert that the push for rigorous uniform statewide (and now multistate) academic standards will cause every child to become "proficient" (in NCLB lingo) or "college and career ready" (in today's preferred terminology). Hence all children can be taught together and any differences in prior achievement can be accommodated—and ultimately wiped away—within standard classrooms and schools.

6. Growing use of "blended learning" and other classroom applications of technology can indeed help teachers customize learning by enabling some students to move at their own pace with the aid of online resources while flesh-and-blood instructors focus on other kids one by one or in small, more homogeneous groups.

For these reasons and in response to all the zeal associated with differentiation, teachers are tasked with tailoring their instruction so that administrators and lawmakers can declare with straight faces—and perhaps authentic conviction—that their classrooms are diverse and inclusive *and* that every child's singular education needs are being satisfactorily met.

To equip teachers with the requisite pedagogical prowess, all sorts of courses, books, in-service programs, itinerant experts, and summer workshops are available. (Google "differentiated instruction" and "professional development" together and you get a half-million hits.) Organizations such as the Association for Supervision and Curriculum Development devote much energy to promoting this approach.

In other words, it's quite a big deal. But how well does it work?

As with "gifted education," the evidence is mixed, and the research is both tantalizing and frustrating. It's pretty clear that differentiation *can* work for many children, but also that it must be done with finesse and be accompanied by much planning, the versatile use of diverse instructional materials, better-prepared teachers, sophisticated and frequent review of students' performance, and the teacher's ability (and freedom) to group and regroup pupils in the course of a lesson, a day, or a unit.[4] At least in the usual low-tech classroom setting, differentiated instruction does not really mean individualizing the learning experience of every single pupil. It's more akin to adroit grouping of students. That's not the same as traditional tracking— it's more flexible and adaptive—but still may not do right by children at either end of the ability or achievement spectrum. Which is precisely why a way-behind child may find his education supplemented— beyond what the regular teacher is doing—by tutoring, help from a reading or math specialist (perhaps in a different room), extra time, special technology, or assistance from an aide (especially when the youngster also has a disability).

What about a way-ahead student? That's stickier because, as noted earlier, schools and teachers feel little pressure today (save perhaps from parents) and encounter few policy incentives to pay much attention to such pupils; because kids like that are generally thought to be doing fine; and because there's only so much any given teacher can be expected to manage, especially if she has a large class with pupils at many levels of attainment or instructs a group of students for less than an hour a day. As a result, many a way-ahead child gets little more than everybody else, perhaps some additional reading, maybe more challenging worksheets, possibly time to pursue a topic in depth on her own or encouragement to dig deeper outside school.[5] But she may also end up daydreaming while waiting for the rest of the class to catch up.

Effective differentiation is tough to pull off in a truly heterogeneous class that contains girls and boys with diverse needs and varied learning speeds. It's akin to presenting a physician with two dozen patients who manifest different symptoms, differing degrees of illness, and, upon examination, many different ailments. It's unlikely that any one doctor can do a great job with all of them, especially when strapped for time and resources. He's apt to engage in a form of triage, focusing mainly on those he can readily help and giving less attention to the mildly ill. The sickest may be sent to the hospital and others referred to appropriate specialists.

Teachers, however, are expected to be all things to (almost) all youngsters. Few, at least in the United States, have had much training in effective strategies for meeting this challenge. And most of those with whom we have spoken admit that, while technology and small classes surely help, they don't often feel that they're meeting it well.

Some manage better than others, of course, and some "inclusive" classrooms aren't all that diverse. It's obvious that the larger the class and wider the range of ability, achievement, or specialized needs within it, the greater the teacher's challenge. That's why, for example, severely disabled students are often still educated in "resource rooms," even in entirely separate schools. Such practices are far more widespread, however, in the realm of special ed than in gifted education.

Many teachers accept the premise of differentiation but then—triage style—pitch much of their instruction to kids in the middle of the achievement/ability/motivation distribution, doing less for pupils who are either lagging far behind or capable of surging ahead. But when policy or the principal intervenes to reshape such a teacher's priorities, it is invariably on behalf of the laggards, for they are the beneficiaries of major government efforts—such as NCLB and IDEA (Individuals with Disabilities Education Act)—to advance the education of youngsters who face difficulties and to reward schools and teachers that accomplish this.

By contrast, pretty much the only pressure on teachers to attend to their quicker, higher-achieving pupils comes from parents.

Plenty of teachers strive to do right by all their students and, with the help of sophisticated technology and quality online offerings, it will eventually be possible for more to succeed. Meanwhile, however, we've watched as "smart" kids doodle (or act out) in boredom and frustration while the instructor toils to get basic concepts into the heads of pupils who, for whatever reason, find them harder to learn.[6] And when speaking to audiences of teachers, we've observed that any suggestion that differentiated instruction works better in theory than reality elicits knowing chuckles—and frequently applause.

Some leading gifted education experts reach conclusions such as this: "Many gifted children's needs can be met in the regular classroom, if grouped with academic peers for part of the day and if under the reign of a very gifted teacher. The likelihood of getting a very gifted teacher is, however, too small." And "Differentiation doesn't typically address the needs of very highly able children." Differentiation specialist Holly Hertberg-Davis wrote in 2009: "It does not seem that we are yet at a place where differentiation within the regular classroom is a particularly effective method of challenging our most able learners."[7] More recently, gifted education specialist James R. Delisle wrote in *Education Week* that "although fine in theory, differentiation in practice is harder to implement in a heterogeneous classroom than it is to juggle with one arm tied behind your back. . . . Differentiation," he declares, "is a cheap way for school districts to pay lip service to those who demand that each child be educated to his or her fullest potential."[8]

This situation will likely improve in the United States, and educators in several countries that we visited are convinced that in their schools it already has. Technology will help. Smarter public policies would, too, as would better teacher preparation and greater experience. We applaud teachers who do their utmost to make differentiation work. Yet when a colleague of ours visited a Maryland school that places careful differentiation high among its priorities, he reported back that these arrangements look awfully "rickety, held together with lots of duct tape and chewing gum, and subject to collapse without just the right staff and parent support."[9]

Can reliance on individual teachers to meet all pupils' education needs possibly be robust enough to bear the enormous policy and professorial weight that's being placed on it today, particularly for high-ability pupils? Does anybody really know? Based on the evidence to date, it's impossible to be sure.[10]

PART II

Beyond Our Borders

6

How Do Other Countries Educate Smart Kids?

RECAPPING WHAT we've examined so far yields an unsettling scene:

- U.S. achievement at the high end is nowhere near where it should be—and far weaker than the levels reached by a number of other countries. Nor are our trend lines as promising as we see elsewhere, particularly in the upper grades.

- The lag is even starker when we examine high-end achievement by young Americans from disadvantaged backgrounds and compare it with their overseas counterparts. Though the data show some welcome upward ticks, considering our multidecade push to boost the learning of poor and minority kids, we're still doing a woeful job of boosting the ablest among them as far as they could go and thereby narrowing the "excellence gap."

- Maximizing the achievement of high-ability children is not a priority for American K–12 education, and hasn't been for many years. Evidence of that neglect abounds, from incomplete data to limited access into a hodgepodge of programs and policies, and

69

from disagreement over which kids (if any) need "something different" to what forms (if any) that something should take.

■ So far as we can tell from the scanty research, sketchy data, and skimpy evidence available, with the exception of acceleration much of what passes for "gifted education" in the United States today is not reliably effective at boosting the achievement of high-ability youngsters, although it appears more valuable for those selected on the basis of prior achievement rather than IQ.[1] But the variability of such programs raises doubts as to whether the "intervention" being studied is sufficiently coherent to lend itself to rigorous evaluation at this time—and whether findings from one city's program can legitimately be generalized. Parallel doubts must also be raised, however, about the practicality and adequacy of educating high-ability pupils by differentiating instruction within heterogeneous classrooms.

All of which is ample reason to explore other countries, seeking to understand the policies and practices of places that mostly do better at producing high achievers, often including children from tough circumstances. How are they tackling the problems we've outlined? How are they responding to the challenges? Has anyone really figured out—and put into practice—a better way of educating high-potential youngsters?

WHERE TO LOOK?

Over the years, Americans peering into the cloudy globe of other countries' education practices—and that's not a lot of people, considering the insularity of most U.S. education debates—have often slipped into two simplistic traps:

■ *Mimicry:* Why can't we be more like (fill in the blank: Finland, Singapore, Japan, etc.)? Couldn't we just copy what they do?
■ *Exceptionalism:* The United States is so different from everyplace else in size, diversity, and decentralization that there's little to be gained by examining how they do it elsewhere.

We sought, in the present study, to shun such stereotypical thinking. But where should we look? This was no topic for a random sampling of countries as there would be no point in looking closely at places that do poorly in producing high achievers. And ten or a dozen sites were all that time and resources (and, perhaps, readers' patience) could handle. We chose them by applying four criteria:

- Places where sizable fractions of students score at the high end on international assessments such as PISA and TIMSS.
- Reasonable diversity of continents and regions, plus some countries with federal structures akin to ours.
- Nations prominent enough on the world scene that American readers might take them seriously.
- Places where we could identify willing, knowledgeable, English-fluent informants.

We contacted potential respondents in more countries than we could afford to visit and received useful feedback from several in places (e.g., Hong Kong, New Zealand) that did not make the final cut because we judged that their approaches to gifted education resemble other countries already on our list. Some places that seemed potentially interesting (e.g., Israel) did not yield a respondent willing to help us in a constructive way. Others were too bureaucratic (e.g., New South Wales in Australia). We wanted to examine Alberta in Canada, but floods there consumed the attention of the people who were initially willing to cooperate. China would, of course, be fascinating—Shanghai's scores on PISA, although suspect, have certainly captured the world's attention—but of the many potential respondents we contacted there, none would even return an e-mail. Ditto Russia. India is riveting in many ways, but far too complex for an abbreviated study. And although the energetic young educators running high schools for gifted students in Kazakhstan volunteered to participate, we were not confident that many American readers would understand why they should pay close attention to that country at this time. The same goes for several lands around the Persian Gulf. What they're doing is interesting, but not likely to move the U.S. policy needle.

Sadly but unsurprisingly, few developing countries have yet tackled gifted education in an organized way, save for private schools that typically serve prosperous elites. They're mostly consumed by the challenges of basic literacy, opening schools, getting kids (and teachers) to attend, and other fundamentals. We could not find places in Africa, much of Asia, or the smaller lands of the Pacific that seemed ripe for further exploration at this time. Perhaps we should have dug deeper in Latin America, but the PISA and TIMSS scores we found there were not inspiring.

Where we settled on a "federal" country—Canada, Germany, Australia—it made sense to focus on a particular state or province because these are analogous to U.S. states, where most of the education action (and inaction) is located.[2] Why we wound up examining two of Germany's sixteen *Bundesländer* is a long story. Suffice it to say, we were persuaded by people who know the Federal Republic better than we do that both differences and similarities would prove interesting. They weren't wrong. In this connection, it's also important to note that several countries we entered thinking they had tightly unified national education systems (e.g., Korea, Japan, Taiwan, Switzerland) turned out to be far more decentralized in their school practices than we expected.

In the end, we chose a dozen sites in eleven countries, which we divided into three clusters: Asia, Europe, and the Anglophone world. The first includes Japan, Singapore, Korea, and Taiwan. The European cluster consists of Finland, Germany (Bavaria and Berlin), Hungary, and Switzerland. With apologies to Singapore, where English is the language of instruction in schools and universities, we have designated England, Ontario, and Western Australia our Anglophone lands.

In each location, we carried out three stages of research: advance reading and reconnaissance, multiple communications with our "informants," then site visits organized with their help. We sought to determine why and how each locale deals with the education of high-ability students and how this fits within its broader education strategies and structures. How important is equalizing opportunity—for both smart kids and poor kids? What about human-capital development and international competitiveness? What's working and what's not?

In this section of the book, we first report some of what we learned from querying our informants and advance reading. Then we look closely at each locale.

BEFORE VISITING

We questioned at least one willing respondent in each locale, using online survey forms and much e-mailing. The survey population was so small, however, and the informants' roles in their respective countries so varied (academics and government officials, on-the-ground educators and wise observers, critics and advocates), that we decided we would better serve readers by outlining what we learned from these helpful people (plus our reading and surfing) rather than by presenting systematic data.

Student identification and participation

When and how are gifted youngsters identified? Across the twelve locales, we found some identification going on at every stage of education, but it's most common during the middle grades and somewhat less so in the upper secondary years, at least in part because many able students at that stage attend selective-admission high schools rather than take part in separate "gifted ed" programs.

The factors most often considered during the identification process are achievement test results, school grades, and IQ scores, all depicted by most of our respondents as having great influence. Teacher recommendations and parent preferences are given fairly substantial weight, too, followed by recommendations from school principals.

Most of the locales we selected enroll some children in gifted education programs by age eight. By age eleven, all but one have students in gifted programs of various kinds. The student numbers are generally small, however, only once exceeding 10 percent of the pupil population and most often in the 3 to 5 percent range.

Many respondents indicated that participation is limited (by policy, capacity, or resources) to a fixed number or percentage of qualified and interested children. The reasons are most often budgetary but sometimes philosophical, based on beliefs about how many children qualify as gifted.

A majority of informants said their locales collect data regarding participation by children from different population groups and regions, including minority and disadvantaged populations, yet few were aware of purposeful efforts to enhance such participation. Only a couple of locales offer programs in alternative languages. Fewer than half identify high-ability children from disadvantaged families at a young age and direct them to opportunities crafted to optimize their abilities, and not many reported that such youngsters receive information and encouragement from nonschool sources such as churches or social organizations.

Program content and benefits

The content of gifted-student programs varies not only among countries, but frequently also among regions within them, even localities. Yet we found some commonalities.

Most students in gifted programs devote additional time to them outside the regular school day. As one might expect, the curriculum in such programs also differs from that in regular classrooms, with the extent of difference varying by subject. Math is most changed, followed by science, then by languages (primary and secondary) and history.

All our informants indicated that at least a few teachers of gifted students in their locales receive supplementary professional development and most reported that this is the case for "many" such teachers. Compensation follows a somewhat similar pattern, with at least a few gifted education teachers getting extra pay for this work; in some locales, many receive this benefit.

Workloads and budgets vary, too, with roughly half our informants suggesting that gifted ed classes in their countries are generally smaller than regular classes, and about half also indicating that extra money is spent on the education of these children. Few said that families are expected to contribute, but in one-third of these locales some nongovernmental resources help to support such programs.[3]

What advantages, if any, accrue to participating students, beyond the enhanced education that the programs themselves try to supply? We asked about distinctive diplomas, certificates, or other documentation of completion, and responses were again split, with students in just half our sites receiving something extra or different. Participation in gifted education often brings other benefits, however: access to special activities or opportunities (such as travel or research projects) as well as mentorships and internships. In nearly half of these locales, such students may accelerate to the next grade level, graduation, or university entry, perhaps even receive priority admission to desirable schools or universities.

Yet despite expending extra resources and conferring extra benefits on students who take part in gifted education programs, few countries track what later becomes of them, and few evaluate their programs. Just a couple of respondents said that monitoring the longer-term paths of participants is customary, and formal appraisals of the programs themselves are rare, save for those sporadically undertaken by doctoral students or individual schools.

There were few clear patterns across countries. What was clear, however, from our advance study and queries to knowledgeable individuals was how seriously most of the places in our sample take the education of high-ability students. Although the number of children participating in gifted education programs is generally small, sometimes tiny, we definitely saw things worth examining more closely. So we bought some plane tickets and Chester Finn flew off to all twelve sites, while Brandon Wright remained in the control tower.

7

Japan: Early Neglect, Later Intensity

JAPAN FACES CHALLENGES aplenty as it strives to modernize its education system for the twenty-first century, including uncertainty and unfairness in what passes for gifted education. Let us begin, however, by acknowledging the accolades that the overall quality and performance of that system have drawn for decades. It's free, compulsory (through ninth grade, although nearly everyone stays through twelfth), carefully planned, rigorously monitored, and generally successful on such measures as completion rates and international assessments. Literacy is universal, teachers are respected, students work hard, and the culture is bullish on educational achievement, which most families understand is an important prerequisite to a good job and a prosperous life.

Along with strong—and improving—average performances on PISA and TIMSS, Japanese students have done well at making their way into the loftier ranks of test scorers—further evidence that societies with high overall achievement also generally notch solid results at the upper end of the distribution. (See table 7.1.) On the PISA math assessment in 2012, 24 percent of Japanese test takers reached the two top categories, compared with an OECD average of 13 percent (and U.S. performance at 9 percent).[1] Japan also does exceptionally well in

TABLE 7.1   Japan average scale scores and percentages of high scorers on
international assessments over time, with trend lines

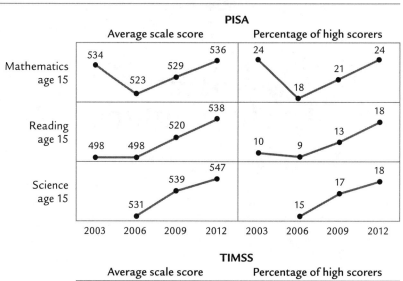

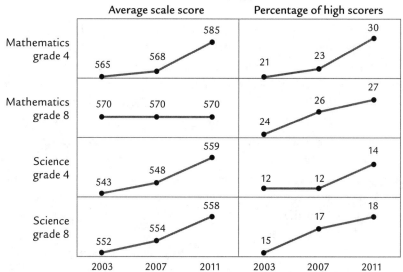

math on TIMSS and is strong in science on both assessments, as well
as on PISA reading.

Not everything, however, is cherry blossoms under the rising
sun. Japanese education leaders—like those in other Asian countries

with impressive test scores—have agonized at least since the 1980s over what they regard as systemic weakness in fostering curiosity and creativity.[2] The competitive pressures for high school and university admissions are intense. And the system as a whole has been inward-looking, weak at imparting fluency in other languages, and sluggish at sending young people to study overseas—a problem that worsens as the world economy interconnects while Japan's domestic economy, immense as it is, continues to stagnate, a problem since the boom years of the 1980s.

Demographics also exert a powerful effect on Japanese education. The population has been aging rapidly, fertility and birth rates are down, and school enrollments have plummeted—from 5.6 million high school pupils in 1990 to 3.4 million in 2010.

Though it cannot reverse population trends, the multitasking Ministry of Education, Culture, Sports, Science and Technology (MEXT) has been tackling other challenges—boosting STEM education, mandating the study of English beginning in fifth grade, subsidizing private schools and universities, and taking steps to diversify the system and revamp the curriculum. (A new "competence-based" course of study is due in 2016.)

MEXT has limited sway over the schools themselves, however. Although Japan is widely viewed as having a centralized education system, the country's forty-seven prefectures operate nearly all of its public schools and, like American states, they vary in size, politics, traditions, philosophies, and more.

But the prefectures don't control everything, either. In sprawling Tokyo, twenty-three municipal subdivisions known as "wards" manage most of the schools. A handful of selective-admission secondary schools are run by national universities. Other schools are designated by the central government as "super" (with an extra focus on science, English, or "globalism"), and a huge number of private schools operate alongside them, enrolling almost one in three high school students. (In Tokyo, it's more than half.)

The umbrellas over all this are a historically bossy if constrained education ministry, a national curriculum, and national approval of teacher-preparation programs, combined with complicated subsidies for schools and students. Yet much autonomy is also evident, at least in the high schools. There, it was explained to us, the national curriculum is more a list of courses than actual delineation of content. And school heads have considerable say over who teaches in their buildings, partly because so many people covet those jobs—especially in high-status schools—and so few leave them.

GIFTED EDUCATION FUNDAMENTALS

Alongside institutional autonomy and geographic diversity, at least since World War II Japan has placed heavy emphasis on equality, community, and uniformity. In the primary and lower secondary grades, this reveals itself in inclusive classrooms and scant special provision for high-ability youngsters. Here, as in many countries, the regular teacher is expected to provide for students of differing ability levels—a challenge that is stiffened by large classes but eased by the small number of pupils needing remediation and the fact that many children with disabilities are educated in other classrooms or schools.[3]

Prewar Japan had an official version of "gifted education" consisting mainly of acceleration: grade skipping and early admission into elite universities. After 1945, however, as Nobutaka Matsumura (perhaps the country's leading scholar on these issues) has stated, "Extreme egalitarianism by teachers and parents led to uniformity in education, and also to a high quality of education."[4] But it also exacted costs on the "excellence" front. Matsumura explains that:

> Respecting effort rather than ability raised average academic achievements efficiently without discriminating against low-achieving students; however, this post-war attitude did not properly address individual giftedness. Talking about gifted education became taboo. . . . At the turn of the millennium and even today, 2010, there is no agreed-upon, official definition of giftedness and gifted education. Today, gifted education does not exist officially.[5]

Still, it hasn't vanished entirely—and there are signs that some versions of it are returning (though not acceleration). In Matsumura's words, elements of gifted education exist "'virtually' inside and outside of school. Academic abilities and achievements are respected, and there are competitions for examinations. . . . Learning beyond the regular curriculum, developing special talents, is allowed." Special provisions for high-ability youngsters are creeping into the regular curriculum. And high school is another story altogether.

PRIMARY AND MIDDLE GRADES

Nationally, a handful of free but selective primary schools affiliated with teacher-training institutions function as a limited "gifted and talented" bolt-hole for those who can gain entry. Each prefecture has at least one—and Tokyo has ten. Private schools are another option for families that can afford them, though they play a small role at the primary level.[6] Both kinds of schools have traditionally functioned as sources of enriched or accelerated education, especially for children from affluent families.

Regular primary schools may seek government approval to group students by ability in math and science, and may receive extra staff to assist with this. In Tokyo, individual wards may also provide after-school and summer supplements for high-ability youngsters. Wards and schools must initiate such practices, however, and resource constraints impose limits. Hence the supply of such special arrangements does not match the demand. We sensed that, as we found in many other places, these options are more available in communities with impatient, education-minded parents. High-ability students from disadvantaged circumstances are less well served by this uneven approach.

HIGH SCHOOL

The picture alters considerably in secondary education, where nationwide practices, pressures, and offerings cause much greater differentiation in students' educational experiences and where more options exist. For the most part, these differences tend to benefit high-ability (or at least high-scoring) youngsters.

In Tokyo, for example, an old senior high school was rebooted in 2006 as a six-year secondary school, now one of ten such in the prefecture. Koishikawa High School's students enjoy an integrated curriculum that focuses on "determination, exploration and creation" built around "broad culture," science, math, and "global understanding" (including English-language instruction). Some one thousand youngsters apply annually to enter the school's 160 seventh-grade places, with selection based on a three-part aptitude test plus recommendations from the primary-school principal.

This illustrates the big difference between the "inclusiveness" that prevails in primary schooling and the competitive procedures that govern which students end up where in secondary schools and universities.

Indeed, to understand how the high school system functions for high-ability students (and others), one must begin with the university challenge. Although Japan contains some 740 degree-granting institutions, a person's social status and career prospects are both closely linked to attending one of the country's eighty-six "national" universities and, even more so, to graduating from one of seven former "imperial" universities, including Tokyo University (Todai) and Kyoto University.[7]

Admission to these prestigious institutions is intensely competitive and procedurally complex.[8] It has long been based on exam scores, so prospective attendees are well served by enrolling in secondary schools with strong records of producing graduates who do well on the entrance tests that follow. Besides the common test (given just once a year!), every Japanese university designs and administers its own exam, so strategic students (or, more likely, their parents) consider which high school has fared best in producing solid scores for applicants to particular universities.

High schools, in turn, as part of establishing their own status and attracting able students—particularly as the youth population shrinks—advertise how many of their graduates get into which universities. At a respected "national" high school that we visited in Tokyo, for example, they are hugely proud of the fact that some one hundred graduates a year—from a class of just 160—end up at Todai.[9]

The high schools that do well at university admissions, not surprisingly, appeal to more students than they can accommodate. So they, too, practice selective admissions, sometimes based on holistic evaluations of prospective students and recommendations from middle school principals, but more often relying on scores on their own entrance examinations.[10]

It's at this point in Japanese K–12 education that separation actually occurs between high-ability (or high-scoring) youngsters and others. This de facto tracking system partly contradicts the earlier grades' emphasis on uniformity and community.[11] Those who ace the admissions process end up in high schools with others like themselves, schools featuring teachers, courses, activities, and peer groups that, taken together, have proven effective in university admissions. It isn't called "gifted education," but it amounts to high-powered—and separate—education for those who can get in.

Which is its own story, because doing well on the admission tests set by competitive secondary schools—and one can apply only to a single school in any admission cycle, so the pressure is intense—is understood to hinge on intensive study not just in regular schools but also, for many pupils, in supplementary cram schools known as *juku*.[12]

Juku attendance can start as early as first grade and roughly a quarter of primary students enroll, including those seeking to enter schools like Koishikawa, where admission decisions are made during sixth grade. By middle school, about 60 percent of pupils attend juku, and by the end of high school, the practice is nearly universal.[13]

The supply of selective schools varies greatly from place to place. In small and rural communities, there may be only a single public high school with little extra to offer its swifter learners. Even in major metropolitan areas, government policies differ widely, as does the supply of—and rules for getting into—the strongest schools. Policies have also been known to change in the aftermath of elections and in response to various reform initiatives.

In Tokyo, for instance, a socialist metropolitan government abolished high school entrance exams during the 1970s on grounds that they were elitist and unfair. Students were instead assigned to high schools based on their residence, much like the primary schools. In 2002, however, a more conservative regime restored entrance exams. It also offered citywide choices to students—with admission based on exam scores—and inaugurated a program of partial differentiation and diversity among upper secondary schools. It now operates three tiers of academically distinctive high schools. Seven (of about two hundred) have been designated for high-ability students.

Most sizable prefectures have their own assortments of competitive-entry schools, a mix of municipal, national, and private. As in Tokyo, these vary in reputation, success in university placements, and competitiveness. It follows that, in most places, there's an unofficial but widely understood hierarchy of desirability among these schools.

That's not quite the whole story, however. Since 2002, the national government has also designated "super science" schools—by 2007 there were a hundred of these—and gives them extra resources to strengthen their offerings in STEM fields.[14] "Super global" high schools are on their way, emphasizing English fluency and understanding of the world. At least in principle, such schools are also intended to cultivate individuality and enable students to go deeper into subjects that interest them as well as engage in more independent research and less formulaic ways of demonstrating what they've learned.

Most "super" high schools are operated by prefectures, but some are university affiliated—descendants of earlier "lab schools"—and operate outside the prefectural system.

DIVERSITY AND DISADVANTAGE

Selective high schools often engage in outreach activities to make their offerings known to more families and thereby diversify their applicant pools. They hold open houses, send literature to primary and middle schools, and participate in informational meetings that are sometimes sponsored by the juku themselves. But knowing about a high-performing school is not the same as having the means to prepare one's child to gain entry.

Japanese parents, even those who patronize public schools, are accustomed to out-of-pocket education costs. At a time when U.S. families with school-age kids were estimated to spend about 3 percent of their income on education, parents in Japan were investing five times that share.[15] But many families are far from wealthy, and Japan's wealth gap is widening even as its economy is stumbling.[16]

Juku are not cheap—and most of their costs are borne privately, meaning participation is slanted toward more prosperous families.

Nor are all juku equal. They, too, have a hierarchy of status, quality, and price. Those deemed best naturally charge more. No official data exist, but Tokyo officials say juku costs nearing $10,000 per year (per student) are not unusual, and these often continue for years.[17]

Considering the country's sizable juku industry and large private school sector, we see how Japan's cultural commitment to equality and universality is not fully honored. This may be gradually changing, however. Prominent juku chains have been closing some centers—a reflection of Japan's shrinking population but also, perhaps, of the improving odds of entering well-regarded high schools and universities without the juku boost.

Whether or not their families can afford such supplements, youngsters from less advantaged circumstances in Japan have done better than in most countries at racking up high scorers on international assessments. On the 2012 PISA math test, almost 12 percent of Japanese participants from the lowest SES quartile reached levels 5 and 6, versus 38 percent from the top quartile, a ratio of nearly 1:3. That's not as good as the best, but better than the OECD average and far better than the U.S. ratio of 1:8. In reading, Japan had the most equitable ratio of the countries in our sample. And in science it placed second, with a 1:3 ratio, notably better than the OECD average of 1:6. (See appendix table A.3.)

Looking at how students do in relation to their parents' education, Japan also fares quite well. In math, equating PISA scores to NAEP's Advanced level in math, 10 percent of Japanese students whose parents' education was low attained that level, compared with 29 percent with better-educated parents. In PISA science and reading, again looking at equity in the percentages of each group reaching levels 5 and 6, Japan placed second and fourth among the dozen countries (including the United States) in this study. (See appendix table A.4.)

DILEMMAS AND CHALLENGES

Even in elite schools, most Japanese classes are enormous—forty students is not uncommon—which inevitably impedes a pupil's ability to get extra instruction and inhibits a teacher's capacity to do more than lecture. We spotted few signs of "discovery learning," individual attention, or lively, student-initiated discussion. The dominant ethos seems to be, "The teacher will impart what he knows to his students, who will record it." Nor did we see much use of technology—surprising for such a high-tech country—to supplement or extend the teacher's reach or to individualize instruction.

Yet we did see widening recognition that kids differ and that it's important to nurture individual "excellence" as well as "equality." Government policy is moving in that direction, and not just for public schools. Japan readily makes use of private schooling, too. As one of our Japanese advisors explains:

> The rapid massification of high school and university education in the post–World War period was made possible by the expansion of private schools and universities. The government has relied on, partnered with, and publicly supported private schools in this sense. Once the schools have saturated society, private schools have strategically positioned themselves as providing alternatives to public education, some with pedagogical character—pursuing elite/gifted education, or applying the philosophies of Dewey, Steiner, Montessori, etc., or providing extra support for deviant children, etc. Public policy generally respects the historical roles that private schools have played, and continues to support them financially.[18]

Another challenge for Japanese education is opening its windows to the wider world. Schools still judge themselves mainly by success in getting graduates into eminent domestic universities. We encountered little international benchmarking of standards, curriculum, or post–high school trajectories. Even the schools' much-loved "festivals" and popular competitions seem to confine their horizons to domestic rather than international "Olympiads" and contests. Nor do many graduates go abroad to study.[19]

The new government is striving to alter this mind-set. In addition to the "super global" high schools, MEXT has conferred that designation on several dozen universities, and granted extra funding for upgrades to help them compete in the world market. Initiatives such as this will ultimately reverberate in the primary-secondary sector, too, including its handling of high-ability students and their education. Moves are underway, for example, to incorporate "higher-order thinking" and "real-world applications of knowledge" into the university admissions process. This signals a widening interest in "competency" and the use of multiple indicators of success. Todai and Kyoto universities have indicated their intent to move in this direction and, if it gains real traction, it will inevitably cause the schools, too, to rethink how they prepare their pupils.[20]

TAKEAWAYS

In the late 1980s, while working at the U.S. Department of Education, the senior author led the American side of concurrent evaluations by Japan and the United States of each other's K–12 systems. In an admiring epilogue, Education Secretary William J. Bennett wrote:

> Japanese education works. It is not perfect, but it has been demonstrably successful in providing modern Japan with a powerfully competitive economy, a broadly literate population, a stable democratic government, a civilization in which there is relatively little crime or violence, and a functional society wherein the basic technological infrastructure is sound and reliable . . . We Americans, being a pragmatic people, would therefore be well-advised to learn what we can from Japanese education if only because of its manifest success. But there is a more abstract reason, too: It is the American belief in the value of universal education that the Japanese have so successfully put into practice, and the American quandary over "equality" and "excellence" that the Japanese seem rather satisfactorily to have resolved.[21]

Three decades later, that quandary is again visible in Japan and it feels like time for this country to update its approach to both equality and excellence and to find better ways of balancing them. Americans, meanwhile, would do well to keep trying to emulate Japan's success at bringing almost everyone up to a solid standard of basic achievement. On the gifted education front, however, until their latest moves in this realm bear fruit, perhaps the most useful lesson we can borrow is the practice of establishing high schools explicitly aimed at high achievers. We would do well, though, to resist Japan's use of parent-pay juku to prepare children to enter such schools.

8

Singapore: Enough of a Good Thing?

SINGAPORE'S EDUCATION and policy leaders radiate awareness that the main resource of this miniature Asian tiger is its human capital—and the capacity of its people not just to be smart in traditional ways but also to innovate, discover, create, and make things more efficient. They're paying the requisite attention to STEM issues but are also now putting more of a premium on other skills, attitudes, and behaviors—and they view the schools' job as developing qualities in their pupils that go beyond the purely cognitive. We encountered unabashed honoring of academic ability and achievement—but also widening recognition of other forms of excellence.

Save for Shanghai (whose exam results are suspect), Singapore has long earned top marks on international assessments. As we see in table 8.1, on the 2012 PISA math assessment, a stunning 40 percent of Singapore test takers scored in the top two tiers, compared with an OECD average of 13 percent (and a U.S. score of 9 percent). In reading, too, Singapore trailed only Shanghai, with 21 percent of its fifteen-year-olds in the top two tiers, versus the OECD average and the U.S. score (both near 8 percent).[1] Its science results are also strong by any reckoning—on TIMSS even more than PISA.

TABLE 8.1   Singapore average scale scores and percentages of high scorers
on international assessments over time, with trend lines

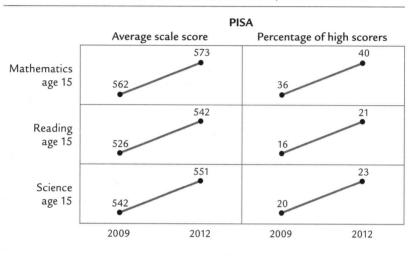

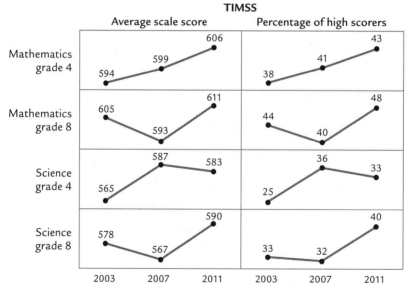

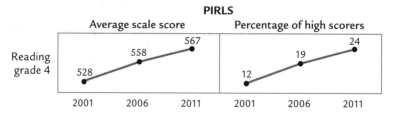

Singapore is more city-state than nation-state, with a total population smaller than that of New York or London. It's compact, stable, law-abiding, and prosperous, with policies that strive to balance equity and excellence. It also helps enormously that the culture and population value education, that the benchmarks they respect are international, and that instruction takes place primarily in English. General acceptance of tracking is a further advantage when—as here—it's accompanied by opportunities to change tracks and an education system that makes valiant attempts to equalize such opportunities.

That system also features intensive, top-down policy making, combined with efforts to build autonomy at the school level. This, in turn, all happens within a complex sociopolitical framework that labors to preserve harmony and national unity in a multiethnic society.

Schooling is universal and compulsory (through sixth grade), but it's not quite free. Parents are expected to pay something, arising from the government's conviction that everyone should have some "skin in the game." Fees are very low in the primary grades, however, and in government secondary schools. It's costlier to attend independent schools, but most are government subsidized and also offer financial aid to those who need it.

Here, as in other realms, Singapore takes the wider world seriously. Where a Tokyo school might focus inwardly on its own "festival," a comparable Singapore school is apt to compete in an "Olympiad" involving multiple countries. Many officials, educators, and students themselves travel overseas and take part in foreign exchange programs. A nontrivial number, particularly those emerging from top schools, go abroad for university. (Once again, English fluency is an asset.) Singapore views this as an important investment—provided these students either return to their homeland or otherwise benefit it.

GIFTED EDUCATION FUNDAMENTALS

A highly structured and buttoned-down country that is hypersensitive to issues of fairness across its three major ethnic groups, Singapore has an education system that features systematic gifted education beginning in fourth grade, carried out in carefully chosen schools with selective admission based on children's test scores. A universal testing regimen is intended to create equitable access to this opportunity. Participation in the core gifted education program at the primary level is limited, however, to 1 percent of the pupil population, although individual schools may provide supplemental education to other strong pupils. There are also outstanding selective-entry high schools and an efficient, broadly knowledgeable administration that can respond to changing needs and opportunities.[2]

The website for the Ministry of Education (MOE) declares that the agency "has a commitment to recognize, nurture and develop the potential of each pupil. This means that it must provide an education of quality and relevance which stimulates individual growth and helps pupils realise their full potential."[3]

Such statements are common in many education systems but their realization is not, especially at the upper end of the ability/achievement distribution. In other countries, such young people may end up "realizing their full potential" only when they or their families cause this to happen.

Singapore seeks to differ. It wants educational success to be based on ability, ambition, and hard work. And for three decades, it has made special provision for gifted youngsters, fine-tuning and adding to its programs over time as experience has accumulated and societal needs have changed.[4]

Although Singapore's government and society are obsessively committed to equal opportunity for everyone, they also recognize that individuals are not identical, that goals and talents differ, and that the country's human capital requirements are multiple. (The MOE also pays close attention to vocational and technical education.[5])

Hence everyone's interests can best be served—it is believed and enshrined in policy—if the education system engages in various kinds of tracking and ability grouping, so long as everybody has a fair shot. Often, however, such fairness is operationalized via sorting based on test scores, with all the positives and negatives associated therewith.

PRIMARY AND MIDDLE GRADES

The Gifted Education Program (GEP) spans the second half of Singapore's six-year primary school sequence, with student selection based on tests administered three-quarters of the way through third grade. This timing results from the MOE's desire to equalize children's opportunities, mindful that they come from differing home circumstances but, by then, will all have benefited from almost three years of formal schooling. This equalizing may be especially important for English proficiency, one of three subjects (along with math and "general ability") that are tested for entry into the GEP, as many children speak other languages at home. Though there are certainly drawbacks to the exclusive use of test scores for selection, the universality of the screening system is one way to ensure that all kids at least have the chance to be considered—and it seems very Singaporean to settle on a method that is so sterile, quantitative, efficient, and seemingly objective.

The first round of testing is given to all third graders—unless children opt out. (About 70 percent end up participating.[6]) Among these, the 8 percent with highest scores (averaging 4,000 youngsters) take a second round of tests two months later. Of this group, about 550 are offered places in the GEP, and roughly 450 typically accept. That's approximately 1 percent of the age cohort which, indeed, is the policy target.[7] (Resources permitting, this may rise as a consequence of the policy review that was under way in 2014.)

Once accepted, children are assigned (based on myriad factors, including residence) to one of nine centers inside schools strategically scattered around the country. (Singapore operates about 135 primary schools.) These function as "schools within schools," averaging 150 pupils each, with their own teachers (selected, trained, and then mentored by MOE staffers), smaller classes (20 to 25 pupils versus about 38), and other extra resources. Most of the students' academic instruction takes place within the GEP classrooms, though they mix with other children for noncore subjects and activities.

Although GEP classes must cover the basic Ministry-prescribed course of study, they go deeper, they are more interactive, they pay greater heed to humanities and social studies, and their pupils engage in independent research.[8]

The GEP is not the only form of gifted education. In addition to widespread tracking and ability grouping within classrooms, primary schools are encouraged to supplement the education of the next

4 percent of pupils (dubbed "high ability learners" or HALs, again determined via testing) and may also use other means to identify and add more children to that population.[9] The content of such supplementation is pretty much up to individual schools, though the Ministry offers some standard options in English, math, and science as well as teacher training.[10] Because schools rarely have more than a handful of "official" HALs, they may team up with nearby schools to offer specialized classes. (And by adding more youngsters, they may beef up their own programming options.)

This "bottom-up" approach to serving high-ability children beyond the GEP—that's how MOE officials explain it—was intentional when launched in 2007 and it definitely allows for school-level initiative and customization. The predictable result, however, is unevenness. Some schools have created what amounts to their own home-grown gifted programs, even separate classrooms; others do little. Hence another likely outcome of the present policy review will be greater structure and standardization, perhaps also expansion beyond the 5 percent target.[11]

HIGH SCHOOL

Singapore's gifted education arrangements at the secondary level are more complex and diversified. It's helpful, first, to understand the regular structure.

All students take the Primary School Leaving Exam (PSLE) at the end of grade 6, which appraises their performance in English, math, science, and their "mother tongue." For most families, the PSLE generates much angst because that score determines which secondary school they will attend. These schools fit into three tracks, currently dubbed "express," "normal (academic)" and "normal (technical)." As in other countries with similar fate-shaping exams, there's a thriving industry of tutoring centers, cram schools, home tutors, and online programs designed to boost children's scores (provided that their families can afford such things).

Most secondary schools end with grade 10, when students sit for the GCE O-level exams, administered jointly with a Cambridge-based examination board.[12] Results on this traditional academic evaluation lead to further tracking. Those seeking to attend university (and doing well enough on the exams) enter pre-university programs in "junior colleges"—grades 11 and 12—which culminate in British-style A-level exams, then (for those who succeed) university entry. Singapore has four national universities as well as several private institutions and branches of international universities. The current MOE goal is for 30 percent of the age cohort to receive university education, though they haven't reached that target yet.

Other students—termed "post-secondary"—go into "polytechnics," career-oriented tertiary institutions, of which Singapore has five, or into other technical-vocational programs. About half the age cohort exits formal education after tenth grade.

The progression from primary into secondary school works somewhat differently for GEP children. During sixth grade, the Ministry evaluates their academic performance and ratings by teachers (particularly in regard to attitude!), as well as their PSLE score, then decides whether to "promote" them to the secondary level. If they qualify—most do—their school fees are paid by the MOE. (Such subsidy makes a difference for those who enroll in privately operated secondary schools such as the high-status Raffles Institution, which charges several hundred dollars per month.[13])

At one time, Singapore also had a centrally run, secondary-level gifted education program in a handful of centers that roughly paralleled the primary GEP program. Policy changes over the past decade have altered this pattern. The centralized program is gone but individual schools have ramped up their offerings for high-ability students and much of that ramping has taken place in the traditionally elite schools that had housed the old program.

The ramp-up includes curricular changes meant to focus less on test prep and more on learning. At sixteen schools, O-level testing has been scrapped for some students. Instead, they operate continuous (university-oriented) programs in grades 7–12, thus freeing their pupils from the rigors of exam-cramming and affording them greater flexibility in curriculum and instruction. These are known as Integrated Program (IP) schools and most also house "school-based gifted education" programs.

A number of high schools now also accept some students directly, without reference to PSLE scores. This system, limited to a small percentage of seventh-grade places, is meant to help schools build diverse student bodies and offer a more "rounded" educational experience.

Direct admission is also meant to reduce exam fever and cramming. Instead of using PSLE scores alone, participating secondary schools engage in more holistic admission decisions, also weighing teacher recommendations, interviews, school grades, and their own customized exams. Children admitted this way still take the PSLE but it doesn't count as long as they meet a low threshold that serves to confirm their direct-admission place. It does, however, serve a sort of backup function: if they don't get in via direct admission, they can still be "placed"—often in the same high school—by the Ministry based on their PSLE score.

In practice, some 90 percent of GEP graduates now enter secondary school via "direct admission" and, in some top IP schools, direct admission now accounts for many of their students. This essentially allows them to pick and choose their pupils (although the MOE still manages the process). This, in turn, fosters choice among students and energetic recruitment on the part of the schools.

Yet overreliance on direct admission via "holistic" decisions that are not based solely on test scores invites allegations of favoritism. As a result, some schools opt not to fill their allotted openings via this method. It was explained to us that "when students are offered a place via [direct admission], people don't know why some are offered places while others are not. However, when placement is based on the score on the national exam, it is transparent. . . . Everyone has an equal chance of getting into the school of choice."

Collectively, the sixteen IP high schools are meant to accommodate the top 6 to 10 percent of Singapore students and prepare them well for university and beyond.

Within the schools we visited, the dominant mode of instruction in regular classes was lecture-style, but in the gifted classes, we saw lively, interactive, even Socratic engagement intended to draw kids out, make them think, and engage in complex reasoning.

We also observed a great deal of independent (and team) research, outside mentoring, and individual projects, as well as participation in community service programs and international exchanges.

As for technology, the schools we saw have impressive on-site resources, although we observed scant use of this capacity. We were told that this is intentional because the kids are awash in technology outside and are therefore supposed to use their brains and voices while in school—a sort of sanctuary from nonstop electronic bombardment.[14]

DIVERSITY AND DISADVANTAGE

Singapore has succeeded better than almost everyplace else at advancing lower-SES children into the ranks of high scorers on international assessments and—unlike most countries—girls are almost as likely as boys to be found there on the PISA math test (and well ahead of boys on the reading test). The government has striven to equalize opportunities for poor but able youngsters from all backgrounds to participate in the country's gifted education offerings (although our eyes told us that Chinese youngsters are most likely to end up there).[15]

As shown in appendix table A.3, a very impressive 21 percent of Singaporeans from the bottom SES quartile (as gauged by OECD) scored in the two highest tiers on the 2012 PISA math test—more than reached that level from the *top* quartile in the United States! Among students from the top SES quartile, an astonishing 61 percent attained the two highest PISA tiers, creating a ratio of 1:3 between the two quartiles, markedly better than the OECD average (1:5) and one of the lowest to be found anywhere. Singapore's ratio falls to the middle of our twelve-nation pack on (PISA) reading and science, but always beats the United States and OECD averages—and always posts impressive percentages of low-SES top scorers.

When we turn to parents' education, Singapore's equity performance is particularly impressive in reading. A full 9 percent of its students with poorly educated parents reach PISA's top ranks, compared to 29 percent with highly educated moms and dads—a ratio of 1:3. No other country beats any of those numbers—especially the United States. (Our figures are roughly 2 percent and 12 percent, a ratio of approximately 1:6. See appendix table A.4.)

We need to remind ourselves, however, that perfect equality would be a ratio of 1:1. Even in Singapore, more than three times as many students with well-educated parents shine in reading than do children with poorly educated parents. This is due, at least in part, to the fact that children from wealthy, education-minded families enjoy clear advantages in Singapore, as they do everywhere else. Income inequality is wide here and Singapore is home to many private tutors and juku-style "cram schools" to prep kids at every level, beginning with the GEP test in third grade. This continues during the primary grades, even for many children who take part in the GEP, both to augment the standard curriculum and to boost their scores on the PSLE.[16] Cram schools also help other children get ready for that momentous sixth-grade test. And this happens all over again as students prepare for the O-level exams that determine where—and whether—they will finish their secondary schooling and prepare for university.[17]

Although the MOE seeks to discourage such tutoring, and insists that it doesn't help with entry into the GEP or selective high schools, the practice remains widespread, meaning that it's more accessible to wealthy families and likelier to be used by achievement-driven parents.

DILEMMAS, CHALLENGES, AND TAKEAWAYS

For high-ability students, Singapore offers a set of carefully considered opportunities, and tries conscientiously to make these accessible to children from different backgrounds. And its outcomes, by pretty much every measure we have seen, are remarkably strong.

Yet Singapore, like other countries, must navigate cross-currents that resemble those roiling U.S. education waters. What, exactly, is "fairness" when it comes to educating high-ability children? Should admission into gifted programs and schools continue to be based so heavily on test scores, or should it rely on more holistic judgments about children's performance and potential? What about kids whose families opt them out of the third-grade qualifying tests? What happens when the system winds up admitting more boys than girls or more Chinese than Malay and Indian youngsters? Should across-the-board meritocracy be modified to produce a more balanced outcome? Is there a trade-off between pure intellect and, say, morality and creativity—and not only in science and math? How best to ration scarce resources in a democratic society?

Such dilemmas are never permanently resolved and there's no reason to expect this small nation to settle them. But so far Singapore has done a pretty good job of holding them at bay, and there's every reason to expect that it will continue doing at least as well at this as anywhere else on the planet. Singaporeans understand how directly their future depends on it.

American educators have long taken Singapore seriously, from its acclaimed math curriculum to its high-quality technical schools, from its efficient education ministry to its well-prepared teachers. In the gifted education realm, perhaps the most notable takeaways are universal screening of children at the end of third grade—admittedly easier to do in a "city-state" than in a sprawling school system—and its commitment to full-time classrooms in the middle grades for those who make it through the screening process, classrooms that manage to be both different and comfortably housed within regular elementary schools. Less appealing to our eyes is Singapore's heavy reliance on test scores at several stages to determine which children end up where.

9

Korea:
Too Much
Pressure?

KOREA (AKA "REPUBLIC OF KOREA" AND "SOUTH KOREA") is known for its impressive student achievement, education-obsessed parents, and hypercompetitive pupils. This turns out to have as much to do with culture, tradition, social structure, and longstanding employment practices as with public policy. But there is no denying that the Korean economic miracle of the past sixty years—the country faced poverty and devastation at war's end in 1953—owes much to its ardent attention at every level to educating its populace.

Comparative data also attest to this accomplishment. Any number of international measures make plain that Korea has been exceptionally successful at propelling large numbers of students into the world's highest ranks in math and science. As we see in table 9.1, 31 percent of Korean test takers reached the two top categories on PISA's 2012 math assessment, compared with an OECD average of 13 percent (and U.S. performance at 9 percent).[1] TIMSS results also show Korean students to be very strong in math and robust in science. PISA science and reading scores are less impressive but still far ahead of most other countries in our sample. (See also table 2.3.)

At the secondary level, Korea has a number of schools—extremely hard to get into—that seek to supercharge their pupils, mainly in

TABLE 9.1   Korea average scale scores and percentages of high scorers on international assessments over time, with trend lines

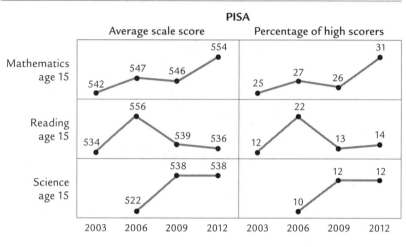

PISA

Average scale score — Percentage of high scorers

Mathematics age 15: 542, 547, 546, 554 | 25, 27, 26, 31

Reading age 15: 534, 556, 539, 536 | 12, 22, 13, 14

Science age 15: 522, 538, 538 | 10, 12, 12

2003 2006 2009 2012 | 2003 2006 2009 2012

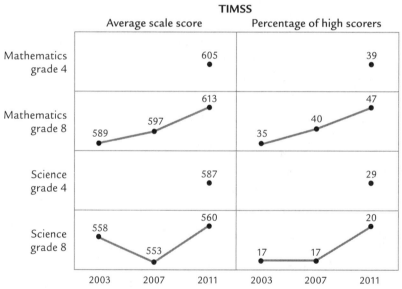

TIMSS

Average scale score — Percentage of high scorers

Mathematics grade 4: 605 | 39

Mathematics grade 8: 589, 597, 613 | 35, 40, 47

Science grade 4: 587 | 29

Science grade 8: 558, 553, 560 | 17, 17, 20

2003 2007 2011 | 2003 2007 2011

STEM subjects. It takes seriously the challenge of cultivating, even force-feeding, top performers in fields that make a difference to the national economy, which also turn out to be the fields in which Korean parents are generally keenest to have their children excel—because, of course, that's where they see the brightest career opportunities.

Yet the education system that served Korea well for half a century is now stressed by several forces. Economic shifts are escalating attention to information technology, communications, and the challenge of "creativity" in these and other realms, as Korea moves toward the postindustrial era. Anxiety is also mounting that education-related competitiveness—the "pressure cooker," Amanda Ripley terms it—is not only harming kids; it's also costing parents so much that it discourages them from having more children.[2]

Like Japan and Taiwan, the crush to gain entry to a limited supply of top schools and universities, combined with the need to excel on exams that dominate the admissions process, has led to heavy emphasis on private "cram schools" (known here as *hagwon*) that attempt to boost students' grades and prep them for the crucial tests. Factor in a shortage (albeit a slowly growing number) of systematic "gifted and talented" options in the primary and middle grades and it's not surprising that the kids most apt to make their way into competitive institutions come from families with the motivation and means to purchase extra instruction and keep their kids up late cramming it in.

Policy makers understand that this push for admission isn't healthy for kids—Korea really does have a worrisome suicide rate among young people—and does little to foster imagination or critical thinking. Hence government policy in recent years has sought to reduce the roles of testing and test prep. Indeed, the national government that came into office in 2013 has introduced the unfamiliar notion of "education for happiness."[3] Yet the culture continues to emphasize competition and the economy still rewards accomplishment in STEM fields.

So Korea invests sizable sums not only in schools that cultivate excellence in these subjects but also in labs, technology parks, and centers of advanced study. For instance, the Korea Advanced Institute of Science and Technology (KAIST) is surrounded by an array of high-tech firms and other institutions, akin to what one sees near Stanford or MIT. Included therein is a lavishly resourced high school for students who excel in the STEM disciplines.[4]

Although the country has few truly private schools, the for-profit hagwon have grown into a large vested interest. As of 2011, reported the *Wall Street Journal*, Korea contained some 95,000 of them plus another 80,000 or so individual tutors, not counting those that fly under the radar to avoid paying taxes.[5]

Their influence is real, too. The "private sector has swallowed the public education system," complained one observer. "The Education Ministry has set academic standards and exam cutoffs so high that conventional teachers and schools cannot meet them, thus necessitating hagwon." So while government is trying to discourage cramming, those who operate the hagwon are fanning flames from the opposite direction—and, knowingly or not, the same government may be collaborating.

Competitive parents also press hard for their children to get into better colleges, working all angles and seeking every advantage—and this, we were assured, would persist whether government-set education standards were high or low.

Cramming can get very expensive and may indeed be one cause of the current demographic crash. (The fertility rate has fallen well below replacement levels.)[6] The *Wall Street Journal* estimates that Korean "parents routinely spend $1,000 a month" for hagwon services for each child, with this outlay repeated month after month, year after year.[7] Add the major lifestyle adjustments and parental supports needed to get those youngsters through the long evening and off to school the next day, and it's not surprising that many families stop with just one child.

Meanwhile, on college admissions testing day, Korea comes to a semihalt. Air traffic is suspended (so as not to make distracting noise, especially during the English "listening test"), commuters come to work later (so as not to cause traffic jams), and some middle and elementary schools are off for the day so high school seniors can use their facilities as testing sites. Parents pray in temples, buy lucky amulets, even invest in oxygen tanks to pep up their test-taking kids.[8]

GIFTED EDUCATION FUNDAMENTALS

Specialized attention to gifted and talented education is a relatively recent development in Korea. Though some science-centered high schools have operated since the 1980s, the main gifted education law was passed (after a decade of effort by advocates) in 1999 and its "enforcement decree" came in 2002.[9] Included therein was establishment within Korea's principal education-research agency of the National Research Center for Gifted and Talented Education, which monitors, evaluates, and encourages this part of the K–12 system, as does the Global Institute for Talented Education based at KAIST.

The enabling statute defines a gifted child as one "who possesses extraordinary innate abilities or visible talents requiring special education to nurture them." Five domains of giftedness are itemized plus a catchall category termed "other special talents."[10] Authors of the policy were clear that such children "should be identified early and provided with appropriate and differentiated education programs" and that these should include "special schools for gifted high school students."[11]

Such offerings are supposed to emphasize students' curiosity, independence, and adventure, "not just [be] limited to the intellectual components" of the subjects that form their core. Though such emphases will not strike many U.S. educators as unusual, they're scarcer in Korea, where teachers typically view themselves as sources of knowledge to be poured into the unquestioning heads of eager yet docile pupils—what's known in American education as "sage on the stage" pedagogy.

Options for high-ability learners have gradually expanded, spurred by gifted-student advocacy groups and a bit of competition among ministries. The government's third "comprehensive" plan for gifted education is now under way.

Yet schooling in Korea is more decentralized than we knew. Other than a handful of "national" high schools, public education is actually delivered by sixteen separate cities and counties, each with its own elected superintendent. In realms such as gifted education, they set their own priorities and budgets. That includes determining whether to underwrite gifted programs at all or make parents pay for children to participate. (The exception is disadvantaged kids, up to 10 percent of total gifted-program enrollments, for whom the national government provides a subsidy.) The results vary widely, according to local politics and preferences. In some places, parents pay. In others, the program is free.

The extent of such offerings varies, too. Particularly in metropolitan Seoul and Kyonggi, although there are plenty of educated and demanding parents, the public schooling system actually provides less by way of opportunity for high-ability learners, partly because of local officials' political orientation but partly out of concern that parents' education fever will rise to unmanageable levels. In such circumstances, families that can afford it are even more apt to turn to hagwon to provide their children with supplemental education and superior preparation for high school and university admission. In poorer and more remote areas, where the entire community is likely to welcome gifted education—and where hagwon options are fewer or less affordable—local officials are apt to provide more gifted opportunities within the public system.

PRIMARY AND MIDDLE GRADES

Korean schools do not practice ability grouping or separate classes for high-ability students during the regular day, even though that would make pedagogical sense, especially considering that regular classes are the largest among OECD countries.[12] It was explained to us that, again due to parents' competitive impulses, education officials view it as unworkable to separate kids on the basis of ability during normal school hours. (There might be a riot!)

So while the entire national curriculum was meant by its creators to be "flexible" and "level-differentiated," with children moving at their own speeds, explicit "gifted and talented education" (GATE) in the elementary and middle years is limited to enrichment programs, beginning in fourth grade. School systems may offer these after school, on weekends, and during vacations, and so may universities, county education authorities, research institutes, and other organizations.

Participants are selected—and must be rescreened annually—based on evidence of their giftedness. That process has been changing to discourage parents from sending young children to cram schools. Instead of basing it on test scores, screening now begins with an individual "nominator" (ordinarily the classroom teacher), followed by a school-level selection committee (presumably to counter any favoritism by teachers), then another review by the gifted center to which a student is applying.

Even after all that, the supplemental programs may be thin—typically a few hours on Saturday morning—although they may also include multiday "camps" during vacations. But because kids are ambitious (and vulnerable to premature specialization), parents are intense, and the hagwon habit runs deep, even a meager GATE program may be further supplemented (for those who can afford it) by private options. We visited a program for gifted dancers that operated just once or twice a week but, we were told, these kids—girls around nine years old—all took part in afterschool dance classes of some kind at least five days a week. That's because they were all bent on becoming ballerinas!

Dance, art, and humanities are not, however, the core of Korea's offerings for gifted students. Math and science comprise 90 percent of the supplements.

None of this guarantees that even a qualified child will find a GATE opportunity in something that interests him, has space for him, and is within striking distance of his home. (Transportation is a family responsibility.) This is a real problem in rural areas, although they're beginning to make some use of online programming.

Limited public funding further constrains access. Even in education-minded Daejeon City, where the superintendent believes gifted education is important and there's ample public demand, the amount spent on "supplemental" programs worked out to about $280 per participant per year.

Still, such programs have been growing, from 58,000 children nationally in 2008 to 118,000 in 2012. More than half are elementary pupils and most of the rest are in middle school. Just 13,000 are high-schoolers. That tapering off, we were told, is because the parents of older children are focused on college admission and so tend to concentrate their kids' efforts on school grades and hagwon offerings. One observer added that when the Education Ministry—again struggling to dampen competitiveness—decreed that participation in supplemental gifted programs would no longer be part of children's school records, interest in such programs fell off.

Despite Korea's shrinking pupil population, government policy makers intend (in the "third comprehensive plan") to continue growing gifted education, although they do not appear to be adding to its budget. The present goal is to cover 3 percent of all students by 2017—not, by our lights, a very large number, though it would represent a considerable advance from today's 1.9 percent.

HIGH SCHOOL

Korea's approach to gifted education changes dramatically at the upper secondary level. Here, supplementation continues (with scant participation) but is joined—perhaps superseded—by full-time high schools for high achievers, all of them specialized, mainly in science and math.[13] These institutions practice selective admission and the competition to get in is keen.

Eight such schools will soon operate at the national level—there were six when we visited—open to qualified students from the whole country, with most kids boarding during the week in school dorms. These schools are exceptionally difficult to get into because they're small, accepting in the aggregate fewer than 1,000 students per year—this in a nation with some 700,000 tenth graders. The one we visited had 2,250 applicants for 93 openings.[14]

Admission here is multitiered. At the school we visited, they first use paper applications, an essay, teacher recommendations, and school marks to winnow half the applicants. Those who remain in contention take a special test in "creative problem solving" and the three hundred who do well on it then come in for an interview and observation during "science camp," which functions as a kind of performance assessment.

The resource level in these schools can be remarkable, with student-teacher ratios of 4:1, classes of twenty or so (versus thirty-five or forty in regular Korean public schools), and exceptional facilities.

Teachers earn the regular salary but teach fewer than ten hours a week in order to keep time free to work with students on independent study and research.

When we asked if the extra resourcing causes resentment, the responses were that most people don't really know about it and that, among those who do, there may be some resentment but Koreans also understand that gifted kids are a national resource. Particularly in science, the public believes that exceptional talent will eventually work for a brighter future for the country and thus for themselves.

Because the demand for such souped-up education vastly exceeds the supply of national schools, districts also operate their own special high schools.[15] Each district runs at least one selective science-oriented school and others may specialize in languages, arts, technical training, career training, even sports. In Daejeon City, for example, some 19 of 60 high schools are specialized. Countrywide, there are now some 140 such public schools, as well as a handful of private options for those who can afford them.[16]

Thus fallbacks exist for kids who don't get into the most exclusive schools, although the public views these as less desirable. That's not altogether wrong: as the uber-selective high schools increase, their graduates fill more places in elite universities, meaning that students in lesser schools fare worse in this key competition.[17]

DIVERSITY AND DISADVANTAGE

Including more disadvantaged children (from poor families, immigrants, North Korean refugees, etc.) within the "gifted" population is a challenge. The government target is to boost them to 10 percent of the gifted enrollment but, as of 2013, it had not quite hit 4 percent.[18] In principle, 10 percent of the slots in every program are now "reserved" (and subsidized) for such youngsters, but to qualify individually they—like others—must be identified and referred by teachers. The suspicion is that many teachers—because it's easier and more defensible if challenged—simply refer those with the best grades, which likely does not include a full measure of the disadvantaged-yet-able.

At the super-science high school we visited, they hoped to enroll ten disadvantaged children in the following year's entering class but said they were able to find just three they were confident could succeed in doing the work.[19]

A further challenge is gender diversity. Boys now make up 58 percent of the enrollment in supplemental gifted programs, and in the special science high schools it rises to 80 percent. This may help explain why, on the 2012 PISA math test, Korea found 35 percent of its boys scoring in the two top tiers, versus 26 percent of its girls.[20] (The latter, however, is still quite impressive.)

Raising the numbers of girls and disadvantaged children won't be easy. Nobody seems disposed toward the kind of "affirmative action" that might countenance a lower entry standard for some youngsters than others. The playing field apparently remains level. But so long as qualifying for such programs and schools hinges to some extent on attendance at costly hagwon and/or referrals by teachers who may be consumed by problems characteristic of disadvantaged children, it's going to be a continuing tribulation, particularly for children whose families have limited awareness or motivation to push them forward.

Still, as we see in appendix table A.3, Korea does better than most countries in our sample at propelling youngsters from relatively disadvantaged circumstances into the ranks of high scorers. On the 2012 PISA math test, 16 percent of students from the lowest SES quartile scored in the top two tiers, creating a 1:3 ratio with those in the highest quartile. In both reading and science, the ratios were 1:4, which beat the OECD averages (1:6 for both).

Fifteen percent of Korean youngsters whose parents are not well educated made it into the upper math ranks, as did 38 percent of those with well-educated parents, producing the most equitable ratio among our twelve countries. In the other two subjects, Korea was middling—but always better than the U.S. ratios. (See appendix table A.4.)

DILEMMAS AND CHALLENGES

The education of high-ability students in Korea faces multiple trials, from scarce resources and fierce competition to overlapping authority, weak coordination, and rivalry across ministries, research centers, and such.

The budget challenge is real, too. We were told by advocates that the national government has been devoting more resources to welfare-type programs, leaving less for education in general and gifted education in particular.

Underlying such complications is a more fundamental dilemma: what exactly is the role of formal "gifted education" in a society full of education-obsessed parents and sleepless, pressured-to-succeed children, a society where much of the learning that affects a person's future seems to occur outside the formal education system—and beyond the direct reach of public policy? What, one might ask, is even the justification for gifted education when international data make clear that plenty of Korean students are making their way into the top tiers with or without it? And when a keen observer such as Amanda Ripley sees the present system as a "hamster wheel" in which "joyless learning" leads "mostly to good test scores, not to a resilient population" as well as to students whose "famous drive dropped off dramatically once they got to college"?[21]

Is it more important to beef up the opportunities for high-ability youngsters or to ease the pressure? How to inculcate ethics and morality in schools where the students are accustomed to cutthroat competition? How to foster flexibility and resourcefulness in a regimented system where exam scores still matter greatly? How to balance the obvious economic and popular priority for STEM education with the desire to develop creativity and imagination?[22] How to become more egalitarian without lowering standards?

TAKEAWAYS

In little more than a decade, Korea has mounted an impressive if limited array of options for high-ability youngsters. Place that accomplishment atop an education system that emphasizes—perhaps to a fault—achievement for all its pupils, and a culture that—perhaps to a fault—pushes children in the same direction, and we ought not be surprised that Korea's educational results at the "high end" are as strong as they are. The million-*won* question is whether it can maintain that level of performance while addressing today's challenges.

American states and districts might usefully borrow from Korea's recent practice of having teachers nominate kids for supplemental gifted programs rather than relying on test scores. But perhaps the most valuable examples we could draw are at the secondary level, where the national "super" schools resemble our handful of statewide (and usually STEM-centric) residential high schools such as the Illinois Math and Science Academy.[23] The United States would benefit from more such institutions, which are especially valuable for able students from troubled neighborhoods, small towns, and rural communities. We would also benefit from more nonresidential but selective-admission academic high schools serving high-ability pupils in large districts and metro areas. These are widespread in Korea but far scarcer today in the United States.

10

Taiwan:
Do as We Say,
Not as We Do

FOR A COUNTRY beset by as many political and economic challenges as Taiwan has faced since 1949, it's been a remarkable success, including strong performance on a host of education indicators. But the country's economy, though still robust, is less vibrant than it once was, with jobs harder to come by and salaries generally stagnant. The demographic picture is also worrying, as one of the world's lowest fertility rates portends a rapidly aging population.[1] School enrollments are therefore down and teacher career prospects dimmed. There's mounting concern about a brain drain—and a domestic work force that may be keener on comfort and security than innovation and leadership.[2] Overshadowing all else, Taiwan's political status has long been ambiguous, and its stressful relations with the People's Republic across the Formosa Strait remain complicated.[3]

When it comes to education, Taiwan's overall performance is still solid, but attitudes are a bit schizophrenic, with parents extremely competitive on behalf of their own children while also embracing a cultural value of uniformity and inclusion. They want their daughters and sons to attend the best schools, yet they don't really want those schools to discipline their precious progeny.

The education of high-ability children also suggests ambivalence. Despite forceful wording in national policy, prior to the high school level it's up to local governments to decide what, if anything, will be done in this realm. National funding for gifted education is about 5 percent of the special education budget and no more than 3 percent of children are supposed to be labeled gifted. In most of the country, parents themselves must initiate—and pay for—intelligence testing to gauge whether their daughter or son even qualifies.

Yet Taiwan's high-end results are especially impressive in math. (See tables 10.1 and 2.3.) On the 2012 PISA test, "Chinese Taipei" (as the OECD calls it, perhaps to appease Beijing) found 37 percent of its fifteen-year-olds scoring in the top two tiers, thrice the OECD average and bested only by Singapore and (if one believes the numbers) Shanghai.[4] Taiwan's results in reading have been improving, although those scores stay below math. Science appears to be weakening, though the country fares better on TIMSS than PISA in this subject.

Is Taiwan settling for an exceptional showing in math? Resting on those laurels? We detected little popular concern about human-capital development on behalf of the country's economic future, at least not the kind that percolates into primary and middle schooling. But the government's most recent "white paper" (see below) signals that this issue is ascending on the policy horizon.

GIFTED EDUCATION FUNDAMENTALS

Gifted education in Taiwan occupies a complicated place at the table today, a sort of impoverished member of the special education family.

National policy asserts that all children with "special needs" must be suitably served by the education system and defines giftedness as a qualifying category. In other words, gifted education is officially *part* of special education—and has been for three decades. Here is how the Ministry of Education describes its intentions:

> An educational program for the gifted is implemented to encourage a variety of plans that nurture students' different abilities and skills based on their intellect and aptitude, artistic and creative qualities, leadership and other special attributes. By combining

TABLE 10.1   Taiwan average scale scores and percentages of high scorers on international assessments over time, with trend lines

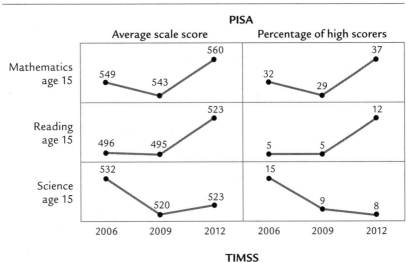

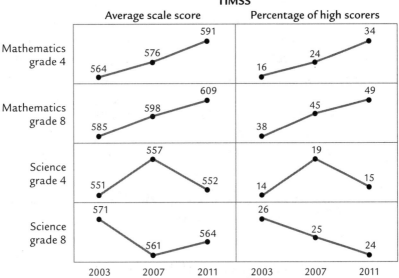

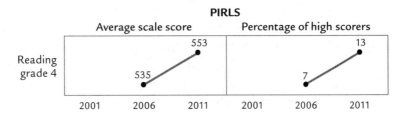

resources inside and outside of schools, we hope to admit gifted students to schools early and shorten their length of study.[5]

Government policy recognizes six forms of giftedness (although formal criteria exist only for the first three): "general intelligence aptitude" (aka "intellectually gifted," to be determined by IQ testing), specific academic aptitude (i.e., really good at some subjects), visual and performing arts, creative and productive thinking, leadership ability, and "other aptitudes."

The Ministry's 2008 "White Book of Gifted Education" admirably set forth this rationale for such attention:

> The gifted brain is the country's most precious resource and core power of social progress. It is also of great importance in the pursuit of excellence and innovation. Gifted education is crucial to the development of the country because of: 1. the need of human resource development (High quality human resource comes from high quality education); 2. the need of individual development (The basic idea of special education lies in the development based on the aptitude of each individual and the chance for students with special needs to explore their potentials); 3. the need for educational reform (Gifted education emphasizes creative, critical, and practical thinking, which can improve the quality of education and holistic reformation is expected under all pervasion [sic]). It is, therefore, a major mission of all educational professionals.[6]

We couldn't have said it better ourselves. But there have been many slips between assertion and reality.

PRIMARY AND MIDDLE GRADES

In the early and middle grades, schools in Taiwan seldom practice ability-grouping or tracking—and citizens are said to view accelerated classes suspiciously, as shortcuts that give a few lucky kids advantages in the race to enter the next level of education. Couple this with the widespread convictions that schools should treat everyone alike and that "smart kids can pretty much look after themselves," and we can understand why any heavy emphasis on gifted education would breed resentment. So does the fact that gifted classes qualify for additional resources.[7]

To minimize resistance and curb misuse of gifted opportunities, particularly their use as an end run around other policies that mandate inclusive ("mixed ability") classrooms, many local governments pay scant attention to high-ability pupils, and the national government has cut back, tightened entry into these programs, and limited their visibility. Indeed, at least through 2011 the number of children identified as gifted in Taiwan schools was declining, and only about 15 percent of the country's primary and middle schools provided any sort of gifted program (versus 50 percent with programs for disabled youngsters, whose numbers—of course—have no limit placed on them).

At the primary level, gifted education programs exist only for "intellectually gifted" students, with admission based entirely on IQ test scores above 130. Most such programs consist of part-time pull-out classes, up to ten hours a week. A recent policy change says any primary school with more than fifteen gifted students ought to have a full-time resource room for them, but such rooms are so far scarce. Across Taichung's 275 elementary schools, for example, there are just four.

On the positive side, once a child is identified as gifted, she has the right to transfer to another school with an appealing program—provided one exists within reach—if her original school offers nothing suitable. (Schools generally discourage such movement, however, not wanting to reduce enrollment or lose their ablest pupils.) Schools that can afford it are also free to supplement their regular offerings with extra learning opportunities for able youngsters who may not meet official standards of giftedness.[8] Another option is acceleration, whereby pupils skip subjects or grades and move faster through the regular curriculum. Such speeding up does not, however, lead to the deeper learning and independent thinking that most gifted education specialists believe is valuable for high-ability youngsters.

A further challenge is weak coordination between the gifted education offerings of primary and junior high schools, even within the same city.[9] The latter programs come in three forms: intellectually gifted, subject-specific, and arts-focused. Admission to the first category is again based on IQ tests. For entry into subject-specific programs, a student must have top school marks, score more than two standard deviations above the mean on an aptitude test, and pass a subject exam. One can also get in via exceptional success in a local or national competition.

Such competitions take place all over Taiwan, even at the elementary level, including Olympiads and science fairs, and spanning many different specialties. Some are local, some national, some international, and much is made of the trophies and prizes that a school or its pupils win. This is consistent with a culture that is competitive in many spheres, and preparation for these contests may in some ways compensate for the scarcity, thinness, and unevenness of formal classes and programs for high-ability students.

HIGH SCHOOL

The high school picture is somewhat different, and visibly in flux.[10] Senior secondary schools in Taiwan have historically been optional. Although nearly everyone went, which school you attended was based on exam results—and was not free. Government schools charged about $200 per semester while private high schools (serving nearly half the upper secondary pupils) charged about four times as much.

This is shifting, as of 2014, with mandatory attendance extended through twelfth grade, entrance exams mostly phasing out, free tuition becoming the norm in government schools, and subsidies supplied to most students in private schools.[11]

These changes are intended to equalize opportunity, sustain enrollments, diminish the pressure to cram for ninth-grade exams, spread resources more equitably around the country, and tame the "star system" by which people have traditionally ranked the country's high schools and competed for places in the most prestigious. But these changes also show the fingerprints of the country's politically influential teacher union, which claims to deplore the pressure that exams place on students but which also—like its counterparts in most countries—opposes anything that smacks of elitism, selectivity, or status hierarchies.[12]

From the perspective of able students and the high schools they have historically scrambled to enter, such changes are a mixed blessing. Although special classes for gifted pupils will evidently continue (more on this in the next paragraph), in practice the country's high-status schools have been able to use exam-based admissions to ensure that essentially all their pupils are strong scorers, thus enabling the schools to develop curricula and build instructional teams that are well suited to educating such students across the whole institution rather than in enclaves. Losing that selectivity, their leaders fear, will not just darken the schools' lustrous reputations but also make it harder to assemble and retain teaching teams and other benefits that result from enrolling a critical mass of ambitious, high-scoring, and high-achieving students.

Taiwan has almost five hundred high schools, two-thirds of them academically oriented. Although these include some that have long drawn top students, the country lacks high schools devoted exclusively to gifted pupils (save for one that focuses on the arts). Instead, it has a half-dozen schools that contain special programs for students judged to be "highly gifted" in science and a larger number with separate classes for young people who are merely "gifted" in science, math, language, humanities, or other subjects, as well as the arts.[13] In Taipei City in 2012, for example, there were thirteen such high schools in the academic sphere, accommodating some 54 classes and 1,450 pupils. Taipei also operates seven high schools with 21 classes serving about 675 gifted students in music, fine arts, or dance.[14] Taichung's fifty senior high schools include five with programs for gifted students in academic subjects and three with programs in the arts.

Across the country, such high schools enroll approximately 10,500 youngsters in their gifted classes. That's 2.7 percent of the total enrollment in academically oriented high schools (though barely half that when vocational students are included in the denominator). Among these "talented" pupils, about 54 percent are academically oriented, the rest art-centric.

In contrast with the earlier grades, where school-sponsored gifted education is usually part time, being in a gifted high school class means you stick with your classmates through the entire curriculum, even music and physical education, and throughout your years in that high school. This is why a "class" of gifted students is the unit that matters to schools, policy makers, and budgets.

Admission to such classes at the high school level is based on scoring more than two standard deviations above the mean on an aptitude test, followed by a paper-and-pencil test in the subject one seeks to specialize in, and sometimes a performance assessment as well. So far as we can tell, this selection process will continue for gifted education classes even as test-based entry into regular high schools fades away.

DIVERSITY AND DISADVANTAGE

Like the other three Asian countries in our sample, Taiwan does considerably better than the OECD average—and far better than the United States—at propelling disadvantaged children into the ranks of high scorers in math. As shown in appendix table A.3, Taiwan's ratio of lowest-quartile to highest-quartile SES students who scored in the top two tiers on the 2012 PISA math test was 1:3, about the same as Japan, Korea, and Singapore. (The OECD ratio was 1:5 and the U.S. ratio was 1:8.)

Unlike the other three Asian countries, however, Taiwan's good record on the equity front in math doesn't extend to other subjects. In science, for example, only 2 percent of lowest-quartile Taiwanese test takers reached levels 5 or 6, yielding a 1:10 ratio of lowest to highest quartile, worse than the OECD average (1:6)—and a bit worse than the United States (1:9).

Math is clearly Taiwan's strength. And, as in most places, boys surpassed girls in that subject—40 percent in the top-scoring tiers versus 34 percent—while girls bested boys in reading (15 versus 9 percent).[15]

Taiwan fares somewhat better on the equity front when disadvantage is gauged by parents' educational attainment, but even on that metric it remains in the bottom half of our countries in both reading and science. (See appendix table A.4.)

More disadvantaged children would likely make it into the ranks of high scorers if access to first-rate gifted education opportunities in the early and middle years were more equitably distributed, but

TAIWAN'S CRAM SCHOOLS

Competitive, exam-based admission to "name" high schools has fostered in Taiwan, as in other Asian nations, both heavy pressure on kids (especially in the middle grades) and a thriving cram-school industry (known here as *buxiban*).[16] As elsewhere, these profit-seeking schools, run by private firms, are believed by parents to boost grades and raise test scores, and to access these benefits families that can afford it must pay fees that are reported to average about $3,300 per year, a sizable fraction of many Taiwanese salaries, more than many low-income families can swing—and more than many other families could swing if they had multiple children.[17] As with the hagwon in Korea and perhaps the juku in Japan, one must seriously consider the possibility that the buxiban habit is contributing to Taiwan's fertility decline.

The end of most exam-based admission to high schools will likely shrink the buxiban market somewhat, but plenty of customers will remain. Surveys suggest that as many as 80 percent of students in high school patronize these afterschool tutoring services to help them prepare for university entrance, and considerable fuss has been made recently about parents enrolling very young children—under age six!—to boost their English and math prowess.[18] It must be noted, however, that Taiwanese families also patronize such centers to obtain child care and supplement their children's education with subjects that the regular schools do not provide enough of—or maybe none at all.

such access has long been limited by multiple factors, beginning with policy caps and meager funding at the national level and unequal resources and uneven demand at the local level. Even in major urban centers that take this seriously, education officials acknowledge that they don't succeed very well at identifying and cultivating disadvantaged children with high ability. Families living in poor or rural communities find fewer opportunities to enroll their children in suitable and accessible programs. Even where such programs exist, most offered at the primary and lower secondary levels are so skimpy as to be unreliable sources of propulsion toward desirable high schools and universities. Lack of coordination from primary to middle to high school also means that children without savvy parents may easily be lost in the shuffle.

Family economics play a role, too. In most of the country (although not Taipei City), parents wanting their children to be evaluated for giftedness must pay about $100 out of pocket just to get them tested so they can be considered for admission. High schools have, until now, charged tuition. And cram schools are pricey.

DILEMMAS, CHALLENGES, AND TAKEAWAYS

At the level of national policy, the education of high-ability children in Taiwan may be starting to turn a corner. The latest government white paper on "talent training and development," released in December 2013, devotes much attention to this issue. Declaring that "Talent is our most important resource, and is the key to the development of our country," education minister Wei-ling Chiang introduced a long series of themes and strategies intended to equip Taiwanese people with "key traits such as global mobility, employability, innovation, cross-domain skill sets, information technology, [and] civil awareness," all of them intended "to increase our overall competitive edge on a global scale."[19]

In the realm of gifted education, the paper spotlights a number of shortcomings in the present system, especially the missing synchrony from one level of schooling to the next and the failure of colleges to pay special attention to those who were deemed "talented" just a year or two earlier.

It then lists a number of policy changes, some vague, others quite concrete (such as allowing for dual enrollment of high school students in college courses). The overall thrust is toward stronger coordination, more flexible methods of identifying talent (presumably going beyond IQ testing), greater attention to students' psychological and "coaching" needs as well as their cognition, more frequent use of acceleration, and wider application of performance measures to gauge student progress rather than relying on one's age and the number of years spent in school.

Undergirding many proposed changes is continuing, even intensifying, emphasis on STEM education, ranging from professional development for teachers to better evaluation and quality control in their classrooms, and from strengthened "science competitions" (and preparation for them) to a wider "range of science education," including newer fields such as information science alongside the traditional disciplines.

Skeptics note that past government pronouncements in this realm have not reliably been matched by action, resources, or conscientious enforcement. This could happen again. Gifted education experts also legitimately note that the white paper pays scant attention to curriculum, independent study, internships, and other important elements of the enterprise. (A student might move faster through the standard curriculum but will he also go deeper? Engage in original research? Have his thinking challenged—and enjoy the freedom to challenge that of others?)

Nor does the white paper address other dilemmas that are evident in Taiwan's present approach to gifted and talented education: its awkward fit under special education and its "poor-relation" treatment there; its uneven provision around the country; the limits of "inclusive" classrooms for high-achieving youngsters; staffing rigidities that cause inefficient deployment of teachers; the drawbacks of part-time pull-out programs and paucity of full-time resource rooms; discrepancies between those from fortunate and disadvantaged households; the inherent contradiction between gifted education and other prominent policies (such as maintaining heterogeneous classrooms in the early grades and ending test-based high school admission); the ways in which "cram schools" intersect with gifted ed; and, perhaps above all, the ambivalence with which the Taiwanese people—and their government and education system—seem to view giftedness in the first place.

Still and all, whether it's something in the water or the culture, despite the relative scarcity of explicit gifted education in Taiwan and the contradictions and unevenness that seem to beset it, the country's overall achievement in primary and secondary education deserves praise, as does its success in producing high achievers, particularly in math. Taiwan may well demonstrate as well as any place that programs and classrooms labeled "gifted" are not the only path to developing such achievers. One wonders how much better the country would do if that path were wider, straighter, and more welcoming.

From the U.S. perspective, we might do well to pay greater attention to the competitions and Olympiads that loom large in Taiwanese schools (although this would prove distasteful to American educators who reject competition in general). And the most recent government white paper includes several points worth taking seriously at home: openness to student acceleration, the suggestion that "mastery" rather than years-in-harness should determine a pupil's progress through school, and the emphasis on better synchronization of gifted education programs and criteria from one level of the education system to the next. This echoes the problem cited by Caroline Hoxby—strong achievers in high school not even applying to top colleges—and would also help high-ability disadvantaged children in our communities to get spotted early and put on a path toward success in high school and beyond. Retooling incentive structures so that schools pay more attention to the educational progress of all their pupils, not just low achievers, is a much-needed reform in both countries.

11

Finland: Not Quite as Advertised

FINLAND HAS BEEN widely hailed as an education success story, deserving of study and emulation, since it came in first on PISA in 2000 and maintained strong results on that measure through 2003 (reading) and 2006 (math). Educators from around the world hastened to Helsinki to sample the secret sauce, hoping they might recreate it back home. And most of them loved the taste, for the recipe that Finland had formulated over several decades contained many ingredients that educators generally like and shunned those they typically find repugnant.

Here is the simple version of that recipe, courtesy of the OECD:

> Finnish schools seem to serve all students well, regardless of family background, socio-economic status or ability. . . . The possible factors behind this success . . . include political consensus to educate all children together in a common school system; an expectation that all children can achieve at high levels, regardless of family background or regional circumstance; single-minded pursuit of teaching excellence; collective school responsibility for learners who are struggling; modest financial resources that are tightly focused on the classroom and a climate of trust between educators and the community.[1]

Finland's reputation also benefited from a masterly advocate in Pasi Sahlberg, a charismatic, articulate (in English as well as Finnish) educator and scholar who served as spokesman, interpreter, and publicist, tirelessly circling the globe, writing prolifically, and welcoming visitors to his homeland. His 2011 book, *Finnish Lessons: What Can the World Learn from Educational Change in Finland?*, sold well, won prizes, and (as we write) will soon be reissued.

Even as Sahlberg's evangelistic tome was winning prestigious awards, however, clouds were forming over the education cloudberries. Although still solid, Finland's PISA scores and rankings were slipping (in 2009 and again in 2012). And 2013 brought a scathing report from the University of Helsinki that Sahlberg himself interpreted in these words:

> The change between the year 2001 and year 2012 is significant. The level of students' attainment has declined considerably. The difference can be compared to a decline of Finnish students' attainment in PISA reading literacy from the 539 points of PISA 2009 to 490 points, to below the OECD average. . . . Home background was not related to the change in students' attainment, however. A decline could be discerned both among the best and the weakest students. . . . It is time to concede that the signals of change have been discernible already for a while and to open up a national discussion regarding the state and future of the Finnish comprehensive school that rose to international acclaim due to our students' success in the PISA studies.[2]

Alarmist, perhaps. But there had been earlier signals that not all was working as intended. There were significant gender differences. And while Finland doesn't make data available on academic achievement by ethnic groups, observers had long detected weakness among the country's immigrant and minority populations. (The latter are small but the immigrant influx is growing and in some parts of the country is highly visible.)

Not everyone was troubled. Many looked at the PISA dips, saw scores that were still robust, and, recalling how many "education tourists" they had hosted, concluded that nations now surpassing

Finland were doing so because they were putting into practice the lessons they had learned there.

Nor did it go unnoticed that Amanda Ripley's much-praised book, *The Smartest Kids in the World*, also appearing in 2013, termed Finland an education "utopia."

The education minister at the time was among the untroubled. During a visit to the United States in early 2014, she noted that the OECD's own assessment of adult literacy showed that Finland's education reforms were working well because people who went to school after the changes were made did better than those educated earlier. "Our educational system," she declared to a journalist accompanying her, "is creating people who have extremely good skills and strong know-how."[3]

Sahlberg, too, seemed to recover from his own anxiety attack when he wrote in the *Washington Post* in December 2013 that it was Finland's very success in propagating effective strategies and envy around the world that had caused more countries to surpass it. "As a norm-referenced test," he wrote, "PISA is graded on a curve. What other nations have learned from Finland and put into practice has necessarily brought down Finland's results." He went on to caution his own country—and, implicitly, the world—against embracing "market-based reforms" and "tougher test-based accountability." He argued, instead, for Finland continuing to be Finland, "let[ting] national education and youth policies—not PISA scores—drive what is happening in schools."[4]

It seemed odd to watch the foremost spokesperson for an education system that owes its celebrity to impressive PISA results now suggest that Finland should not let newer, lower PISA results cause it to change. Although the 2015 election results may lead to policy shifts (and curriculum revisions were already under way), as of this writing the government was steering a steady course.[5]

GIFTED EDUCATION FUNDAMENTALS

A key ingredient in Finland's "secret sauce" is its belief in inclusive, child-centered instruction delivered in similar schools by exceptionally well-prepared teachers whose skills include the capacity to differentiate their instruction according to the needs, capacities, and prior achievement of their pupils. This would seem to point away from separate educational arrangements for high-ability children, and indeed there are few such arrangements in the primary and middle grades, at least not overt ones. As we shall see, however, alternatives are available in parts of the country for families that seek them, and some of those alternatives could reasonably be said to resemble gifted education.

With or without gifted education, Finland continues to propel a goodly fraction of its fifteen-year-olds into PISA's top ranks: 17 percent in science in 2012, 15 percent in math, and 13 percent in reading. (See table 11.1.) This doesn't match the Asian tigers but, by Western norms, it's fairly impressive. Finland looks good on PIRLS, too, though its students' high-end performance on TIMSS worsens between fourth and eighth grade in both math and science.

This relatively strong showing at the top may be attributable to Finland's solid overall performance. (Education systems that do well in general also tend to produce high scorers.) Possibly it can be ascribed to the de facto gifted education arrangements that we sketch below. Or it may arise from the motivation of people living in a nation—akin to Singapore in this way—whose main asset is its human capital and whose employers have made clear that they need skilled people to hire.

Three fundamental values undergird Finnish education, nearly all of which is state run or state controlled. The first salutes inclusion, uniformity, and group consciousness, particularly in the early and middle years of schooling. It's unseemly to "stand out" except in music and sports. This one-size-gets-stretched-to-fit-all comprehensiveness is a legacy of the education reforms of the 1970s.[6] "Elite" is a pejorative term here—as in many lands—but disdain for it appears to shape education policy more definitively in Finland than in a lot of places.

The second fundamental value is trusting teachers to do right by students. They are respected professionals, concerned with the "whole child"—and every child—and expected to adapt their methods

TABLE 11.1   Finland average scale scores and percentages of high scorers on international assessments over time, with trend lines

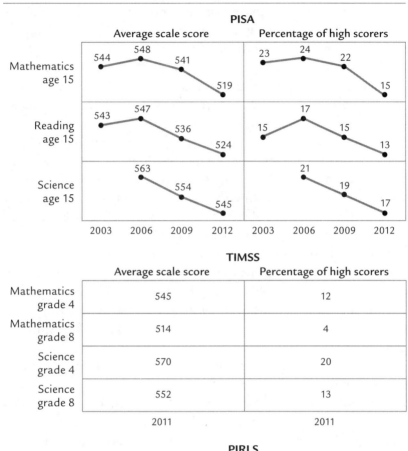

PISA

	Average scale score	Percentage of high scorers
Mathematics age 15	544 · 548 · 541 · 519	23 · 24 · 22 · 15
Reading age 15	543 · 547 · 536 · 524	15 · 17 · 15 · 13
Science age 15	563 · 554 · 545	21 · 19 · 17
	2003 2006 2009 2012	2003 2006 2009 2012

TIMSS

	Average scale score	Percentage of high scorers
Mathematics grade 4	545	12
Mathematics grade 8	514	4
Science grade 4	570	20
Science grade 8	552	13
	2011	2011

PIRLS

	Average scale score	Percentage of high scorers
Reading grade 4	568	18
	2011	2011

to meet the needs of dissimilar children. Don't shackle them with needless mandates or spurious accountability schemes. That's part of what educators elsewhere love about Finland. Equally appealing is the system's success in attracting smart, well-prepared, and highly

credentialed (with master's degrees, even in the primary grades) people to work in its classrooms: only about 7 percent of would-be teachers even get admitted to the preparation programs. There's essentially
no external accountability for schools or teachers (all of whom are
unionized); no inspection teams; no national assessment system,
indeed no national testing at the building (much less the classroom)
level; no value-added calculations, and so on. "We don't need an ethos
of excellence," we were advised, and "we don't collect data that we
don't need."

A third value, almost as fundamental, and familiar to policy makers in many other countries, including the United States, is to give priority (time, money, etc.) to uplifting the downtrodden, helping those
with problems, and boosting the achievement of those who haven't
done well. We often heard that "the smart kids will do okay regardless. So let's work on those who might not."

Backstopping these values is politics, not just strong unions but
also a national government that was dominated for many years by
Social Democrats. Its policy and budgetary priorities have long tilted
toward the neediest (although Finland's recent national election,
combined with sagging economic indicators, augur likely shifts in
some priorities).

Given all that, "gifted" education isn't something that Finland
has been well disposed toward. Government policy and curriculum
documents feature nothing that bears that label, although there is
talk about it, there are experts on it, and teachers are—briefly—admonished not to ignore their smart students. But there's no systematic
identification of them. The regnant ideology in the primary and lower
secondary grades says every school ought to offer great teaching to all
its pupils.

Finnish education experts insist that, while such terms as
"gifted" are taboo, attention to high-ability children is already sig-
naled under such phrases as "different learners," "diverse learning
styles," and "learning models."[7] These are meant to encourage teachers to determine which pupils need what sort of instruction at what
level. There's also widespread interest among Finnish educators in the
"growth mindset" articulated by Carol Dweck. Properly interpreted,

that means encouraging students, whatever level they're at today, to strive ever forward, not settle for past achievement or present status.

PRIMARY AND MIDDLE GRADES

In accord with these values, teachers in Finland are expected to pay suitable attention to moving their ablest students ahead at a rapid pace. Yet veteran observers acknowledge that teacher preparation, while carefully addressing students with disabilities, all but ignores high-ability youngsters. Future teachers hear, at most, a single lecture on their characteristics and needs.[8]

The upshot is that whether such students in fact have their educational needs met in Finnish primary and lower secondary schools depends entirely on individual teachers and principals. Hence it works well in some places but not others. Even where educators have the inclination, they may lack the requisite know-how in this specialized domain.

Nor does Finland offer much by way of supplementation for gifted students. There are all manner of afterschool clubs and "hobbies." But they're open to everyone and likelier to focus on music and sports than academics.

Still, the emphases on flexibility, individual needs, and school-level decision making mean that some pathways are available for youngsters of exceptional ability to obtain an education that works for them, even in the primary and middle grades. Some of these paths lead to an invisible or underground system of gifted education, although it's never talked about that way—and isn't always fair in terms of who benefits.

Within regular schools, teachers may engage in "ability grouping" for math and other subjects, so long as such divisions are temporary. Another option is acceleration, whereby children begin school at age six instead of Finland's unusually late school-entry norm of seven. This needs to be initiated by families, however, and isn't always granted by the system. Nor is it something that many parents push for in a society as concerned about children's play and socialization as about maximizing academic achievement.

Options can also be seized via school choice. Despite the tradition of attending one's nearest school, Finnish law permits enrollment elsewhere if space is available.[9] How that works is determined by the local education authority; some communities promote choice while others discourage it.[10]

Choice, however, works only when there's more than one school within range and when the schools differ. In many parts of Finland they do, particularly in metropolitan Helsinki, where one-fifth of the population lives. And some of these differences amount to schools for high-ability students, often with selective admission. The Helsinki Education Department website lists thirteen of them, and education-minded parents also learn about such options via informal channels.[11]

Some specialize in art, music, or sports—more culturally acceptable than academics—but some concentrate on languages or other subjects.

In a Helsinki school that we visited, for example, a combination lower and upper secondary school that enjoys a strong reputation, the lower school has a special Latin class that admits students on the basis of a language exam. They can apply from anywhere for this school and about one-quarter of each entering class arrives this way; for the other three-quarters, it's the "neighborhood school." But because it's customary for the entire "class" to stick together for all subjects, the selective-admission Latin students generally also remain together for science, Finnish, English, history, math, and so on. While they aren't necessarily "gifted," they and their parents are motivated to seek this kind of schooling and they're able enough to do better than others on a competitive entry test.[12]

Nearly everyone we met cited similar examples in the metro region: the person who sent all three children to a competitive-entry "art" school that in fact is full of high-ability youngsters who go on to university. The person whose friend moved into the zone of a school that offers German as well as Finnish. The person whose own education from third grade onward took place in a "music school." These are often limited-admission situations that are bound to favor children with educated, motivated parents.

Special classes (such as the Latin class noted above) can also be requested by parents and, if enough ask for it to reach a minimum enrollment threshold, the school is obligated to provide it. This is, apparently, a frequent ploy for creating selective options within comprehensive schools.[13]

Special-emphasis classes of this kind may occupy as little as an hour or two per week, yet acceptance into them may determine one's classmates across the curriculum. Hence such access is also a way for parents who want such exclusiveness to enroll their children with other "kids like them." One controversial result, again mostly in greater Helsinki, is that schools may be effectively segregated by ethnic background, language, wealth, or social class.

Finnish schools, like those everywhere, also differ in performance. The government won't report school-level academic achievement (at the primary and middle-school levels) in ways that can be compared. Yet enterprising parents have ways to determine which schools are better. For example, low-performing schools and those with lots of poor or immigrant families get extra resources—and lists of such schools are public.

Those who can afford it may even change homes in pursuit of a neighborhood school that appeals for various reasons, which might be demographic, religious, or linguistic, or simply because it is known as a "better school."[14] Such real-estate-based school shopping is controversial and un-Finnish because it, too, leads to more segregated neighborhoods, yet the practice is spreading.

Thus, education-minded families can find alternatives, including some that work well for high-ability children. But nobody examining Finnish education in 2014 would say that policy makers have intentionally advanced the education of such children. It's happening in spite of them.

HIGH SCHOOL

Finland's "invisible" system of gifted education is most visible at the upper secondary level, which is not compulsory but highly meritocratic, both for those headed toward university (about half the cohort emerging from "basic" education) and those headed into vocations (most of the other half).[15]

Although total enrollments are declining, admission to the most respected high schools remains extremely competitive (some two thousand applicants for ninety places in one that we visited) and is based primarily on school grades. In fact, nobody with a GPA lower than 9.1 (out of 10) was admitted to that particular school, which ruled out two-thirds of the graduates of the lower secondary school that shares its building and many teachers. This competition and placement system is run nationally—one can apply to any senior high school in the country, indeed to several in order of preference; then a computer-matching system managed by the National Board of Education works out most placements.[16]

But it's not that simple, for Finland's 418 upper secondary schools (in 2012) include 56 "special" schools that, according to Helsinki University professor Kirsi Tirri, "can just as well be called schools for the gifted and talented as it is very difficult to be accepted into them."[17] By her count, half of these specialize in "creative talent in art or sports" while others focus on science, languages, or the International Baccalaureate. And she observes that, in addition to applicants' GPA, these schools "may also have an admission examination." Some may require interviews, auditions, or additional evidence of readiness.

The city of Espoo alone—Finland's second-largest municipality—has a dozen upper secondary schools with specialties that range from football and golf to information technology and theater.[18] One is a Swedish-language school. Two offer the International Baccalaureate—and handle their own admissions.[19]

Thus Finnish education at the upper secondary level also contains institutions full of high achievers. And it's easier at this level for families to determine which schools are "best" because school-level results on the university matriculation exam are public. Whether the big differences visible there are caused by what happens within those schools or a consequence of who is admitted in the first place, it's no surprise that parents and students with their eye on the university prize will gravitate to places with the strongest results.

Academic competition and supplementation are also more common at the upper secondary level. Finnish schools and students take part in all manner of Olympiads, both domestic and international. There are summer science and math camps run by universities and a museum, even a "Millennium Youth Camp" that draws STEM-minded kids from around the world (although evidently not many from Finland itself).[20]

At the end of high school, those headed to university take the national matriculation exam, akin to England's A-levels. Universities typically add exams of their own. Admission is again extremely competitive, with just a third of those who sit for the matriculation exam actually gaining entry to universities.[21] Yet we saw little evidence of "cram schools" to prep students for the admissions gauntlet, and the climate within high schools is more collegial than dog-eat-dog. Much of what Amanda Ripley prized about the experience of an American girl who spent a year in a Finnish high school was how different it was from South Korea's "hamster wheels" and "pressure cookers."[22]

DIVERSITY AND DISADVANTAGE

Compared with the rest of the world, and despite its lack of explicit "gifted education," Finland does a pretty good job of moving less privileged children into the ranks of high performers. Using the OECD's version of socioeconomic status, for every lowest-quartile fifteen-year-old in Finland who makes it into the top tiers in math, science, or reading, three students from the highest quartile get there. It's not equality, but it's closer than the OECD average ratios of 1:5 or 1:6. It's perhaps the best track record in Europe, which is Finland's usual frame of reference. And it's far better than U.S. ratios of 1:8, 1:9, and 1:11. (See appendix table A.3.)

Finland also does decently compared with most countries when student performance is examined according to parents' education levels. Using NAEP's Advanced level in math as the benchmark, 5 percent of Finnish youngsters with less educated parents get there, versus 17 percent with highly educated parents. That ratio of almost 1:4 is about the same as the U.K. and Australia, far better than France, but a bit worse than Germany, Canada, Japan, and Korea. Finland's performance in reading and science is similar.[23] (See appendix table A.4.)

The reading results show a different discrepancy, however, that is out of harmony with Finland's sense of equality: whether one looks at PISA reading or PIRLS literacy, girls in Finland do *far* better than boys, a gap that's among the widest on the planet, leading one education expert to remark that young women in her country are encountering difficulty finding mates who are as well educated as they are.[24]

CHALLENGES, DILEMMAS, AND TAKEAWAYS

We were told repeatedly that Finland is a classic "Nordic welfare state"—with commensurate taxes—and that people assume the state will look after their interests. There's an ethos of collective responsibility and common provision rather than individualism and competition, and there's been widespread trust in government, hence little call for formal accountability systems.

Yet almost nobody we met thinks Finland is doing a good job of educating its high-ability children, and there's fairly wide recognition that the "invisible" system that serves some of them well favors those with resourceful, energized parents—and those with the means to, for example, start their kids early on private music lessons so as to boost their admission prospects at a special music school.

Although Finland has many high achievers, its de facto gifted education options are not equally accessible to able children from all sorts of families or all parts of the country. Yet problems like this seem unlikely to be solved so long as both the government and the political culture deny that such children need attention and fail to ensure that the country's decentralized, school-and-teacher-centric education system does right by all of them.

One feature of Finnish education that is most admired by American educators—its success in staffing classrooms with teachers who are generally smart, well educated, highly regarded, and carefully trained—is surely good for many of the country's high-ability students, as it would be in the United States, and it surely improves the odds that differentiated instruction will work better for them than in places with weakly educated teachers. Yet think how much better it might work if those teachers were explicitly prepared to deal with fast learners and if the system were more accepting of acceleration and other strategies for adding to the education of such children without depending on parents to maneuver through it. Though high achievement is more equitably distributed across Finland's population than in most other (non-Asian) nations in our sample, certainly more equitably than in our own country, it's still a long way from full equity and seems to be an almost inadvertent byproduct of policies and practices designed for other ends.

12

Germany: Differentiating Without Differences

THE FEDERAL REPUBLIC of Germany is so large and educationally decentralized—with sixteen *länder* that resemble American states in the ways they shape and pay for their school systems—that we wound up with two sites there: Bavaria and Berlin.

Germany's tens of thousands of schools come in at least thirteen varieties, further complicated by differences in länder education structures, making it a challenge to describe the system simply.[1] Typically, however, primary schooling consists of four grades, followed by a middle level that generally goes through tenth grade but takes place in three different kinds of schools. By and large, the "gymnasium" (which sometimes starts in fifth grade, thus subsuming the middle level) continues through twelfth grade and is the main path to university matriculation.[2] The *realschule* and *mittelschule* are more oriented toward vocational and technical education.

This system was fairly static—and complacent—through the latter part of the twentieth century. The economy was strong, east-west reunification was succeeding, employers and unions made decisions together, and the integration of vocational schooling with apprentice-style training produced a well-functioning workforce.

Then came the "PISA shock" of 2001.[3] Much like the U.S. reaction to *A Nation at Risk* in 1983, Germans were stunned to learn from the first PISA data that their children were scoring well below the OECD average in reading, results that had been foreshadowed, although less noticed, by disappointing math and science scores on TIMSS a half-decade earlier. The PISA data also showed that achievement and career opportunities were far from equal, especially for poor and immigrant youngsters and those not fluent in German. Academic standards within the country varied greatly, and few fifteen-year-olds reached the ranks of top scorers. Much debate followed and then, slowly, a series of reforms commenced, many of which are still under way.[4]

The national government brokered a move toward common curriculum standards (as well as more preschool), but in most realms the länder did their own thing.[5] Many extended Germany's notoriously short school day and strove to boost teacher quality. Schools were given greater autonomy in return for more accountability. And rigid tracking was eased so that the post–primary education paths incorporated ways to shift among them if one's interests or career plans changed.[6]

It worked, too—at least gains began to appear on PISA in 2009, primarily in math but also visible in reading and science, with fewer weak achievers and improvements among disadvantaged youngsters and immigrants. The correlation between low scores and low socioeconomic status has definitely weakened.

At the high end, however, Germany cannot boast much improvement, although it does respectably in math, with 17 percent of fifteen-year-olds scoring 5 or 6 in 2012, versus OECD and U.S. percentages of 13 and 9, respectively.[7] (See tables 12.1 and 2.3.) PISA reading is less impressive, however, with just 9 percent of Germans in the top two tiers, only a point ahead of the United States and the OECD.[8] TIMSS results (available only for fourth graders) show Germany with a low—and declining—percentage of high scorers in both science and math. And on the PIRLS reading test in 2011 (also just grade 4), the United States had almost twice as many high achievers (for the country's size) as Germany.

TABLE 12.1   Germany average scale scores and percentages of high scorers on international assessments over time, with trend lines

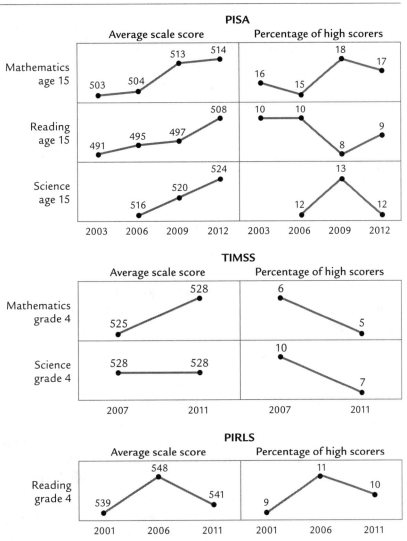

This being Western Europe, a strong social norm favors equality, and people are uneasy about singling anyone out as better than anyone else. This being Germany, with its troubled history, it's even less acceptable to suggest that a person is in any way superior. And nobody

in the education sector here wants to be seen as elitist (although business leaders are less skittish). Yet because Germany also has a long tradition of grouping children homogeneously and tracking their education into different kinds of schools, the equality-uniformity ethos coexists with the realization that not everyone is headed to the same place, that capacities and ambitions differ, and that the education system needs to accommodate such diversity.

Attitudes and practices toward gifted education vary from state to state and there's no national strategy in this realm, although a number of private organizations have imparted a modicum of coordination and information-sharing. There are also some nationwide competitions, summer programs, and such.

BAVARIA

Bavaria is the largest of the länder by area and second largest by population, with 12.5 million residents, similar to Pennsylvania. This prosperous region is traditionally conservative—and proud of its educational and research institutions, as well as its thousand-year history. Its 5,500 schools range from tiny rural primary schools to large high schools in bustling Munich.

Primary Grades

Through grade 4, Bavaria offers little systematic help to high-ability students, although several hundred schools permit acceleration—essentially speeding through a four-grade curriculum in three years. (A new curriculum in the works, expected to be more competency based, may bring added opportunities for subject-specific acceleration keyed to accomplishment, rather than full-grade skipping.)

Some schools also offer afterschool supplementation and child care—primary schools here traditionally end their day at lunchtime—but these are not generally designed for gifted pupils. Both acceleration and supplementation call for extra staffing, and thus are hard for many schools to afford.

Inclusion is the watchword, even for many children with disabilities, and the education system seeks to treat everyone similarly while relying on teachers to address individual needs. Some "coaching" programs try to help them get better at spotting and supporting gifted pupils, but participation in these is spotty. Ordinary teacher preparation, although extensive in other ways—particularly subject mastery—pays no attention to giftedness.[9]

Bavaria employs school psychologists for testing and counseling, but there are no gifted education specialists in the primary schools, nor have their principals had special training of this kind. Individual schools are free to engage in such heterodox practices as team teaching and ability grouping, but all such choices are up to them.

As with NCLB in this country, Bavarian educators feel pressure to get all their pupils to a threshold passing score, in this case the GPA needed for admission into gymnasia. So there's much emphasis on boosting the performance of kids below that threshold and a risk of slighting those above it. Unlike the United States, however, where the pressure tends to come from school accountability systems, in Bavaria the pressure comes mostly from parents concerned about their own progeny.

Middle Grades and High School

At the gymnasium level, programs for the "highly gifted" (HG) operate in eight schools distributed such that every major region of the state has at least one. (Greater Munich has two.) Bavaria funds these programs on top of regular school budgets, but admission is limited to twenty students per entering (fifth-grade) class, meaning that, in an age cohort close to 120,000, only about 160 are admitted into HG classes.

The HG program runs through tenth grade. During the last two years of gymnasium, its students join the school's regular pupils. This is done for both economy and egalitarianism—lest HG pupils emerge from school feeling superior—but it doesn't mean they're slowed, as the overall curriculum for everyone at this stage focuses on preparing for the statewide university-entrance exam (*Abitur*).

A gymnasium with an HG program may specialize in science, languages, or both. Students choose a major subject, but can shift later. The school we visited offers both specialties, partly to attract both boys and girls (which it has done).

Students must apply to the HG program, presenting primary school marks that qualify them for gymnasium, plus IQ test results from a psychologist, plus teacher recommendations. (Forty to fifty youngsters typically apply for twenty seats in the school we visited near Munich.) There follows a three-day screening period of additional testing and observation, hypothetical lessons, group activities, and so forth. School staff then determine who is admitted.

IQ test scores loom large because Germans, we were told, tend to regard giftedness more as "potential" than "achievement." Individual schools, however, may consider additional student attributes, and educators themselves tend to view giftedness Renzulli-style as "potential in combination with achievement." (See chapter 3 for an explanation.)

HG students take their main academic courses together in grades 5 through 10, from instructors who also teach regular gymnasium classes. Teachers must volunteer to tackle the HG program. In the view of the principal with whom we spoke, perhaps 70 percent of her teachers are "up to the challenge." It's her job to work out who does what in the HG classrooms.[10]

The statewide curriculum is ambitious but not detailed, so teachers can move at different speeds and customize lessons for able students. For example, the ninth-grade English-language curriculum fills just a few pages. It's the teacher's responsibility to develop the actual lessons.

Because external exams are few, most student assessment (prior to the Abitur) is internal to the school. Teachers develop tests, which are reviewed—along with students' work and the marks given—by department heads. The principal said she wants to know when more than half the pupils in a class get low marks because then she tends to suspect a problem with the instruction.

At the end of high school, all students, including those from the HG program, sit for the Abitur, scores on which count for 28 percent of their record (along with grades and other elements) in determining university entry.[11]

The HG program is clearly Bavaria's showpiece when it comes to gifted education at the secondary level, but it's not the only offering. Each region has a coordinator of gifted-student programs, and supplementation is available after school. Some universities run programs—and provide scholarship opportunities—for highly qualified students. Also available are residential summer programs akin to the "talented youth" programs on some U.S. college campuses.

In addition to its HG classes, the gymnasium that we visited operates a program for eleventh and twelfth graders, developed jointly with Munich Technical University. Admission is based on grades and interviews by school and university staff. Participants spend a day a week on campus, sampling the university experience and engaging in independent STEM projects—and most go on to study science later. It's small, however, enrolling just fifteen students per year—due, we were told, to budget limits as well as operational complexities that had to be worked out between school and university.

Several more gymnasia and universities have recently entered into similar arrangements, and some universities engage in other kinds of outreach to secondary schools and high-ability students. An education ministry staffer estimated that perhaps three hundred students across Bavaria benefit. Again, not a large number for a big state.

BERLIN

School enrollments are shrinking in the "federal state," especially among German families, and the proportion of immigrant students keeps growing. About three hundred thousand students attend government schools—Berlin's population is only a quarter of Bavaria's—and another thirty thousand study in private schools.[12]

The state government is strapped for funds. People spoke of it as "bankrupt" and recent economy moves have caused pain in the education sector. Teachers, in particular, are disgruntled because they were relatively poorly paid (by German standards) to begin with; then the system was changed such that new teachers no longer receive the raises and benefits of regular government employees. As a result, more than a few are job hunting in nearby states.

At the secondary level, Berlin has amalgamated the traditional *realschule* and *hauptschule* into a "comprehensive" alternative to the university-oriented gymnasium. Today it operates about 120 comprehensives and 100 gymnasia.

Berlin's distinctive history complicates the education picture. In most of Germany, reunification meant bringing the states under a single federal structure. In Berlin, it meant actually integrating two very different systems.

During the Cold War, West Berlin had little by way of gifted education, other than accelerating some children so they might enter and leave the gymnasium at a younger age. East Berlin, however, had some special schools, especially in math, serving a mixture of high-ability and politically well-connected students.

After reunification, there was a desire in the public sector to build "lighthouses of learning" that could compete with private schools, as well as ways of providing more equal opportunities for smart kids who weren't necessarily well connected.

So beginning in 1993, Berlin commenced a three-school pilot program for gifted students, starting in grade 5. It was English-based and accelerated by a year, essentially skipping eighth grade and pushing students through grades 5–10 in five years. That meant the standard curriculum was compressed but not otherwise altered. It wasn't an effort to go deeper or study additional subjects.

Thus began Berlin's "highly gifted" (also known as "fast learner") program at the gymnasium level, with all three of the original schools in the west and three more added in 1996, two of these in the east.

Primary and Middle Grades

A 2004 law says Berlin's schools must provide for giftedness—these children, too, have the right to have "their needs met"—but it's up to individual schools how seriously to take this requirement and how to carry it out. As elsewhere in Germany, the fundamental view here is that primary classes should be inclusive. Most schools rely on teachers to differentiate the education of their high-ability pupils as they see fit. (Elementary teachers in Berlin generally have the same students for two or three years.) But instructors in thirteen primary schools were offered advanced training in "giftedness," which gave those schools added cachet for families with high-ability youngsters. Choice is permitted in Berlin if the "receiving" school has space, but today those thirteen schools cannot satisfy the demand. (Budgetary constraints, we were told, keep the program from expanding.[13])

In addition to these schools, supplemental and enrichment courses are offered at various locations in grades 3–10. These take place once a week after school and are limited to a dozen pupils each. Students join them upon the recommendation of teachers in their home schools and may continue if the enrichment-course instructor finds them suitably engaged. All told, the "learning by gifted students in the afternoon" program can accommodate about 840 kids at a time in some fifty-five classes, with topics picked by the teachers. There's demand for more but, again, the budget is limited.

High School

Berlin (like most German states) recently reduced from thirteen to twelve the years that a university-bound student spends in school. This vitiated the practice of accelerating gifted pupils by a full year (else they'd find themselves in university while still minors). So what now to do for such youngsters? The answer turned out to be "enrichment" during the regular school day.

In retrospect, this appears obvious, but it was hard to develop at the time. Five lesson periods per week are now carved out of the gymnasium schedule—meaning students still accelerate in a sense, covering the standard curriculum in fewer periods—and the time thus freed up is given over to enrichment courses for "fast learners." This yields the instructional equivalent of six weeks per year on top of the standard curriculum.

Also needed was a selection system that would both admit qualified students and be politically sustainable in a place allergic to elitism and haunted by its history of distinctions among people. The new arrangement needed to be affordable, too, so eligibility was limited to 5 percent of the pupil population.

Meanwhile, the number of gymnasia with gifted programs had grown to thirteen by 1999, and apparently they weren't all prepared for a successful shift to enrichment. So the number of "lighthouse" schools was cut to the present seven (plus other special schools discussed below.)

These aren't "whole schools" for gifted pupils. Rather, they are standard gymnasia that enroll most of their pupils in grade 7. But they also admit a class (or two) of thirty or so students into the gifted program starting at grade 5, much as in Bavaria. Applicants (aged nine or ten) may apply to three such schools, must take IQ tests, have their primary school records and teacher recommendations considered, and sit for an interview, generally with the headmaster, at each school to which they apply.[14] Those with IQ scores above 130 are admitted—the top 2 percent—and the headmaster has discretion to admit others with scores as "low" as 120, so long as there is room in the class. This enables him to "discover" able students who don't necessarily have a strong primary school record. It's also a way of giving consideration to more children from disadvantaged backgrounds.

As in Bavaria, pupils in the gifted program have separate classes for all their subjects through grade 10. Instructors follow the state curriculum but may go deeper into issues as well as speed up. Participating schools then use the enrichment-lesson time in different ways. Some offer students a broad menu of course options; others might double down on science or math. All, however, expect their HG pupils to take a third foreign language in grades 8–10.

Those who are university bound—essentially all the "fast learners"—remain in the gymnasium through grade 12 but, as in Bavaria, the courses offered during the final two years may be taken by both gifted and regular students. This, again, is intended to have an equalizing effect on the "fast learners" but also enables kids who didn't originally enter the gifted program to take the same advanced classes. A teacher observed that, in these final two years, he can't really tell the difference in terms of students' original mode of entry to the school.

Besides seven gymnasia with highly gifted programs, Berlin operates five that specialize in math and science.[15] The schools themselves are open to all who qualify for gymnasium but also offer special classes for gifted students in science and, particularly, in math. Here, too, those who qualify can begin in grade 5, with admission again based on test results (IQ, math, and science) as well as primary school marks, teacher recommendations, and interviews. Collectively, the math schools admit about three hundred new students each year, selected from two to three times that many applicants.

The five schools cover the regular curriculum but also the introductory university level in math, much like the U.S. Advanced Placement program, enabling graduates to move directly into advanced math at the university.

Another option available to high-ability youngsters in Berlin is dual enrollment at the Technical University whereby about sixty gymnasium students take courses on campus and receive university credit for doing so. (This serves as a recruitment strategy for the university, too.)

Also on offer here, as in Bavaria, are vacation-time "academies" and residential summer camps for gifted youngsters. These provide enrichment and networking opportunities for able students who may not have access to other options.

DIVERSITY AND DISADVANTAGE

Germany seems to be allergic to generating data by which the achievement of schools and länder can be compared, so we can report only at the national level. As we saw above, Germany does not do very well at producing high scorers on PISA, TIMSS, or PIRLS, but it's at roughly the OECD average in bringing lower-SES students into the top ranks. Looking at high scorers on PISA 2012, Germany's ratio of those who got there from the lowest SES quartile to their counterparts from the highest quartile was approximately 1:6 in all three subjects. (See table A.3 in the appendix for more detailed information.)

Viewed in terms of parents' education, Germany does better than most places in our sample, with 8 percent of students from families with poorly educated parents scoring at the PISA equivalent of NAEP's Advanced level in math, surpassed only by Japan and Korea. (The United States was at a sorry 2 percent.) Yet that "better" needs to be viewed alongside the 25 percent of German students with college-graduate parents who attain that level. Still, with a ratio of 1:3, only Korea did better (1:2.5). And this level of equity also holds for reading and science, in both of which Germany had the third-lowest ratios among all the nations in our sample. (See appendix table A.4.)

Because Germany is also allergic to demographic data, there's scant information on the ethnicity or language background of students who participate in gifted education programs and only hints regarding their economic status. Educators in both states that we visited acknowledged, however, that they've found it difficult to get disadvantaged youngsters even to apply to gymnasia, much less to gifted programs that may entail more commuting.

In sprawling, agrarian Bavaria, a couple of rural HG gymnasia have dorms where students can stay during the week. Even then, however, poor families—and those with settled, farm-based lifestyles—may be loath to send their sons (and especially their daughters) off to school by train, particularly if the parents aren't sure that this souped-up education is necessary. They may not have university aspirations for their children—and may want them not to forsake the family farm or business. Politicians in smaller communities, fighting to retain a secondary school for their town, may accept a "consolidated" school rather than maintain the traditional three-track secondary system. That brings some pluses but also means the community has no actual gymnasium option for its children.[16]

Three Bavarian gymnasia have special programs for disadvantaged students who are also gifted and motivated. These feature smaller classes, extra mentoring, and other supports. And while there's no general program to support such pupils, each year 1,500 youngsters with middling school grades are granted probationary entrance into gymnasia. (About half meet the schools' standards and remain there.)

In Berlin as in Bavaria, some high schools with gifted programs are undersubscribed, particularly those in disadvantaged neighborhoods. They may be able to fill only a single gifted class, instead of the two classes maintained by similar schools in more affluent areas. Indeed, the two Berlin HG schools in the poorest parts of town cannot always complete even a single class with qualified students. Simple efficiency would argue against retaining those schools, but equity and politics make it desirable to do so.

A major challenge faced by these schools is language, a nontrivial issue in immigrant-heavy Berlin. One gymnasium that we visited is located in a neighborhood inhabited by many newcomers. Indeed, some 80 percent of its students live in homes where other languages are spoken. (Statewide, the figure is a whopping 34 percent!) For the highly gifted program at this school, the language situation poses a real obstacle because the IQ testing that's a crucial element of the admissions process is administered only in German. In essence, this limits participation in the HG classes to youngsters fluent in German. Unfair, perhaps, although not altogether unjustifiable, considering that German is also the primary language of instruction within the schools.

Language isn't the only barrier, however. When this gymnasium strives to recruit high-ability students who would then exit their primary schools after fourth grade, it finds teachers and headmasters reluctant to lose their best pupils. Instead of encouraging able students—whose parents may not be aware of this option—to apply to the HG program at the gymnasium, they sit on their hands.

Gymnasia with gifted programs strive in various ways to spread the word in primary schools, sending out flyers and staff members, even using current students as "ambassadors." They have web pages and hold open houses for parents and primary teachers. School psychologists are also urged to make referrals.[17]

Still, everyone we spoke with in both states acknowledged that finding and attracting disadvantaged kids to programs like this is a challenge, and finding disadvantaged kids who can pass the threshold requirements (both grades and test scores) is even harder. One must wonder, however, whether this might get easier if the education system did more to develop high-ability youngsters in the primary grades.

DILEMMAS, CHALLENGES, AND TAKEAWAYS

As is true everywhere, politics and personalities strongly influence the nature and extent of gifted education in Germany, as do changes wrought by elections and personnel shifts. Because gifted education is a relatively small, even marginal, activity of state education departments, it may be even more vulnerable to such shifts.

In Berlin, for example, a previous secretary of education who was bullish on gifted education did much to develop the program. After the 2011 election, however, he was replaced by a former kindergarten teacher with no evident interest in the highly gifted. She leaves heavy policy lifting to a deputy who hails from the liberal wing of the majority party and believes everyone should be treated equally. So at the time of our visit, Berlin's "gifted education" community was nervous about the future of these programs in a place that's generally anti-elitist and left-leaning.

The effectiveness of German gifted education programs (as opposed to the overall effectiveness of the education system) is also hard to demonstrate. Evaluations are few and data scarce—and much of the data that exist are not made public. Analysts who evaluated HG programs in Bavaria and Baden-Württemberg, for example, were admonished not to publicize state-to-state comparisons.[18]

Germany's special efforts on behalf of high-ability children are obviously limited. What's not obvious is why demand for them does not hugely exceed supply, at least in Bavaria and Berlin. Perhaps many parents are not aware of their children's potential, don't know about the available education options, or don't want to take advantage of them.

Here, as elsewhere, family motivation matters enormously. German education officials emphasized the limited extent to which government can make decisions for kids that differ from what they and their parents want. As one remarked to us, "You can only change attitudes to some extent without behaving in a totalitarian way that no one wants."

Perhaps because Germany is still thriving in the world economy, we sensed little urgency about boosting the achievement of high-ability students or turning more young people—particularly from disadvantaged backgrounds—into high achievers. At the primary level, inclusion remains the watchword and, while teachers are urged to differentiate their instruction, little effort is made to prepare them to do this for high-ability students. Various supplemental programs are available for such children, yet this feels half-hearted. At the secondary level, a handful of gymnasia offer terrific "fast-track" options for gifted pupils, but their scale is small for so large a country and entry into them relies more on IQ-type testing than on children's past performance or other evidence of potential. On balance, it appears to us that, while the "PISA panic" has prompted some worthy changes at the low end of German education, it hasn't yet made much difference at the high end.

Seeking lessons that the United States might borrow from Germany—another large, prosperous land with state-run primary-secondary education—we find two, both at the high school (gymnasium) level. Although entry into the HG programs in Berlin (as in Bavaria) depends heavily on intelligence-test scores, school principals have some flexibility to add students who don't quite make the cut, enabling them to attract at least a few more disadvantaged children and diversify the participant population. And we're tantalized by the practice (in both Bavaria and Berlin) of reintegrating the HG students into the general gymnasium during the final two years. (By then they will ordinarily have had six years of separate instruction in HG classrooms.) We're mindful, though, that they're being incorporated back into a selective-admission, university-oriented school for all its pupils and that similar efforts at reintegration within typical American high schools could leave high-ability students hanging.

13

Hungary:
Much Talk,
Less Action

HUNGARY HAS A long tradition of nurturing "talent"—they don't much use the term "gifted"—and a reasonably ambitious national program for doing so, joined to a novel financing mechanism. It also boasts many civil-society organizations that are engaged in this effort. Yet the country's high-end results on international assessments are modest, some are slipping, and, despite sundry efforts to rectify the situation, the "excellence gap" between Hungary's more and less advantaged students remains wider than in most other nations—despite a relatively equal income distribution.[1] (See tables 13.1, 2.3, and A.2 and figure 2.5.)

Among the students reaching 5 or 6 on PISA in 2012, Hungary saw slight improvement from 2009 in science and reading, offset by slippage in math. Although math is where Hungary has the most high scorers, it ranks just thirty-fourth among participating countries (down from twenty-ninth in 2009).[2] On TIMSS, Hungary is up a bit in grade 4 math but down in grade 8, and its high-scoring ranks are thin.

Reading results are better on PIRLS. In 2011, 12 percent of young Hungarians were high scorers, better than the international average of 9 percent and reasonably similar for girls and boys. The PISA

TABLE 13.1   Hungary average scale scores and percentages of high scorers on international assessments over time, with trend lines

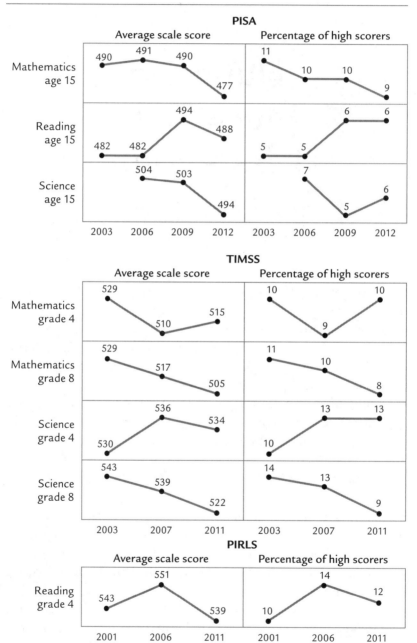

reading picture is less bright, however; only 6 percent of Hungarians scored 5 or 6—the OECD average was 8 percent—and girls did twice as well as boys.[3]

Hungary's population has been slowly shrinking for years. Not surprisingly, its public school enrollments are also declining, though private schooling surged after the Iron Curtain fell. (Preschooling has risen as well.)[4]

Hungary is also experiencing a brain drain.[5] Its economy is anemic.[6] And the current government appears less than riveted by education improvement. Indeed, it is described by some as broadly inattentive to the public interest and mainly attuned to the attitudes and interests of its own supporters. Recent moves in education have mostly to do with nationalism, religion, and centralization of control.[7] (The ruling party has, however, continued to make election gains, most recently in October 2014.)

Post-Soviet education in Hungary was quite decentralized until 2012, when the government installed a new constitution that shifts to a French-style model of control over schools, teachers, curriculum, financing, and more.[8]

Greater equality was part of the stated rationale, as Hungary has enormous school-to-school variability and a history of wide disparities in its education system. Some regions, primarily in the east, are markedly less advanced than others; some demographies (especially the "Roma," aka gypsies, comprising 3 to 5 percent of the population) are seriously disadvantaged; and some parents are ill-schooled themselves and not very knowledgeable about the education of their kids.[9] This is the case both in neighborhoods within major cities (including Budapest) and in small towns and rural areas.

The recent centralization includes a single, government-sponsored textbook publishing company, a curriculum prescribing 90 percent of what schools teach, and considerable loss of local and building-level control of instruction. The sweetener was a sizable boost in teacher pay, which had been punishingly low for many. Yet this raise wasn't a total plus for teachers, who simultaneously saw various supplemental payments abolished and their work week lengthened, leading them to complain that, while their take-home compensation may have risen, their *rate* of pay hasn't necessarily improved.[10]

Primary schooling in Hungary generally lasts eight grades, from age six to fourteen, followed by four years in a technical or vocational school for those headed into the workplace or in a gymnasium oriented to preparation for higher education.

The secondary school structure is complex, however, as some gymnasia, including certain of the oldest and most prestigious, start in fifth or seventh grade rather than ninth—and we visited one that contains all twelve grades. Selectivity is the norm at the secondary level, with elite gymnasia attracting many more applicants than they can accommodate; a combination of a national written exam and a school-specific oral exam determine which would-be attendees get how many points toward admission. Students designate their school preferences and a government-run system matches those preferences with students' point scores to determine which school one goes to. A student who applies to multiple schools must take all of their oral exams, and the points assigned to the applicant by one school will not be the same as the points assigned by another. Because schools have different emphases and degrees of selectivity, their oral exams vary, too. Moreover, one isn't just applying to a school; one may be applying to a specific "class" (e.g., humanities, science, or math) within that school, and each has its own exam. (One may also apply to multiple classes within the same school.)

About 80 percent of secondary students in Hungary end by taking the "matura," which is both a high school exit exam and a university entrance exam. It comes in two levels, with the more demanding of them attracting the more advantaged students.[11]

GIFTED EDUCATION FUNDAMENTALS

Hungary has long celebrated intellectual excellence, especially in fields like math and chess—such topics were politically acceptable even when Moscow ruled—and has long been home to competitions and Olympiads meant to encourage striving and reward excellence.[12] For more than a century, the student-oriented *Mathematical and Physical Journal for Secondary Schools* has sponsored "correspondence competitions" among able young people, and it inspired the 1989 launch of the U.S.A. Mathematical Talent Search, which continues today (under the aegis of the National Security Agency!).[13]

Hungarian students have fared well for decades in the International Math Olympiad and the best of them also do well in science competitions.[14] Much of the competitive energy and success, however, emanate from Hungary's higher-status gymnasia and universities, places not apt to include many poor or rural students.

Starting with the formation of the Hungarian Talent Support Society in 1989, when eighty-four influential individuals came together to coordinate this pursuit, the country has developed quite an array of initiatives and mechanisms. ("Bewilderingly complex" is how one outside observer describes it.[15]) The guiding force behind much of this is Peter Csermely, an energetic and well-regarded biochemist whose day job is professor at Budapest's Semmelweis University and whose enthusiasm for the support of talent reaches beyond Hungary's borders to include such ambitious (if slowly developing) multinational ventures as the European Council for High Ability and the European Talent Support Network.[16]

Hungary's talent program has both government and civil-society elements. On the former side, it involves parliament, the education ministry, and a body called the National Talent Forum. On the latter side, it engages associations of educators, academics, churches, and NGOs. Forty such groups plus government officials are joined in the National Talent Support Council. The melding of official and NGO support makes these ventures fairly broad based and multipartisan, if structurally elaborate.

The biggest governmental boost came in 2008 with a "parliamentary decree" setting forth a long-term (twenty-year) plan for talent support, as well as a two-year programming cycle and annual funding cycle.[17] But money for this enterprise comes from multiple sources, including NGOs, grants from the European Union, some private funds, and a novel arrangement whereby citizens can earmark 1 percent of their tax payments for the "national talent fund"—or for their church.

The National Talent Forum oversees distributions from the "1 percent fund," making some nine hundred grants annually. Those made to schools support teacher workshops, field trips, equipment and supplies, additional pay for teachers who do extra work, and stipends for local scientists and artists.

Talent-support advocates have also striven to insinuate it into the EU consciousness, both to obtain funding from Brussels for their work and to create external recognition and legitimacy that may help sustain the program amid Hungary's shifting political winds.

At present, the biggest EU-financed program is called "Talent Bridges." (It's the successor to the "Hungarian Genius Programme," also paid for by the EU from 2009 to 2013.[18]) Its fourteen activities include school-year enrichment, summer camps concentrating on disadvantaged areas, a national "talent day" (on the birthday of composer Bela Bartok), and public-affairs-style communication with the general public regarding the need to find and cultivate talent. (Such communication may also boost contributions to the "1 percent fund" and popular support for the overall talent initiative.).

Elitism per se does not appear to be much of an issue in Hungary, although equalizing opportunities for an elite education across various social strata and regions remains an enormous challenge. Such equalizing is, therefore, an important mission of the national talent program, both encouraging weak schools to do better by their talented pupils and giving such youngsters the option of going to better schools. The focus is on high-ability disadvantaged kids, defined by socioeconomic status, geographic region, and disability, as well as Roma youngsters and children "in care" (i.e., not looked after by their parents).

Talent is broadly defined and, while the main objective is to cultivate it in the young, much programmatic activity consists of training adults and enlisting local partner organizations to carry out the goals. In contrast to nations where most of the action is centered in schools, in Hungary schools are definitely not the only players.

PRIMARY AND MIDDLE GRADES

Prior to age fourteen, there's no nationwide gifted education program, although most parts of the country have offerings in music, math, sports, and more. Finding high-ability children and matching them with such activities depends on local schools, individual teachers, and NGOs. A thousand so-called "talent points" scattered around the country are part of this matching effort.

Primary schools themselves sometimes run pull-out programs for children identified as exceptionally able, particularly in math, science, and languages, but this is decided locally and is not widespread. Supplementation through afterschool programs and activities is more common but, once again, these are often organized and conducted by entities other than schools and frequently focus on music or sports rather than academics.

There's disagreement as to whether waiting until age fourteen for more systematic attention to high-ability youngsters forfeits a lot of talent, because by that point many disadvantaged kids may have been shunted into boring classrooms in weak schools with meager resources in communities that also lack alternative sources of education.

HIGH SCHOOL

As noted above, Hungarian high schools are selective, with each gymnasium setting its own curricular focus and entrance requirements, followed by a computerized matching system that's intended to connect students with schools they want to attend. (It was reported that, in 2011, three-quarters got their first choice.[19])

Included among the options are schools that specialize, typically in math, music, or the arts, but we were unable to obtain a list—or even a total number—of such institutions. These schools have exceptionally competitive admissions and thus tend to serve high-scoring students.

An admirable feature of Hungary's talent-support program is its emphasis on helping disadvantaged youngsters gain access to such schools, which give them a leg up on university entry and social mobility. Thus, when students are fourteen, the national (and government-funded) Arany Janos program kicks in, with three subprograms that actually move kids out of their homes and communities into dormitory-style arrangements that may be a distance away (though usually within their county of residence) and are attached, tightly or loosely, to upper secondary schools.[20] About forty institutions currently participate.

This is an intensive and costly effort, hence not large. The first subprogram is nationwide but focused on disadvantaged youngsters with uncommon ability, designed to beef up their secondary school opportunities and propel them into higher education. Schools, teachers, and NGOs that work with the disadvantaged are the main identifiers of these young people.

The selection process is multistage, entailing nomination by the primary school, endorsement by the mayor's office in the child's town, a two-hour "talent identification" test, reading comprehension and numeracy tests, and finally an interview by teachers in the secondary school that would enroll the student.

Once selected, participants—about six hundred per cohort—enter a "bridge year" meant to prep them for the transition to a more demanding school. That's the first stage in a five-year sequence that operates as a joint venture between the schools that educate them and the dormitories that house, tutor, and counsel them, while working on their "self-regard."[21]

Two smaller subprograms also operate under the Arany Janos umbrella, both focused on furnishing young people from disadvantaged regions with better secondary education options than they would otherwise have. One of these, also aimed at university entry, is organized through dormitories that work with several different schools. The other—said to be aimed at the "most seriously disadvantaged" youngsters—concentrates on vocational preparation.

Akin to the SEED schools in Washington and Baltimore, the residential feature has clear pluses, especially for kids from tough home situations (and those from rural areas without decent schools nearby). But it's limited both by resources and by families' willingness to part with their children (and the kids' ability to thrive in a dorm setting at age fourteen). The reason that subprogram 1 seems to work best is because participating gymnasia actually take responsibility for their students—and because the launch of that program was accompanied by what one of our Hungarian advisors terms "massive teacher training for the schools and dorms," which evidently did not happen under subprograms 2 and 3.[22]

Besides Arany Janos, the National Talent Support Forum makes grants to schools, universities, and other organizations to deliver teacher professional development, underwrite competitions and Olympiads in multiple fields, and subsidize some student field trips and international experiences.

Hungary's gymnasia themselves also strive in different ways to identify and nurture high-ability young people. Teachers spot strong performers and offer them extra instruction. They also help coach high-ability pupils for competitions and Olympiads—and those who win get extra points toward university entry. But the traditional base for these competitions has long been the high-performing gymnasia, which are difficult to get into, especially for disadvantaged youngsters who may have ample ability but didn't have much done to cultivate it in elementary school.

DIVERSITY AND DISADVANTAGE

Hungary's recent PISA (and TIMSS) results are underwhelming, both on average and in terms of high scorers. On gauges that compare the high-end attainments of less and more advantaged students, Hungary is the weakest country in our sample. Using the OECD's quartile-based version of socioeconomic status, for every lowest-quartile pupil in Hungary who reached the top PISA tiers in math in 2012, a stunning fifteen pupils from the highest quartile got there, far worse than the OECD average ratio of 1:5 (and the U.S. ratio of 1:8) and among the worst in Europe.[23] We see similar pictures in science and reading, in both of which Hungary had the smallest percentages of top scorers at both ends of the SES spectrum among the countries in our sample, as well as the least equitable ratios of lower SES to upper. (See appendix table A.3.)

Much the same pattern emerges when pupil performance is examined according to parents' education levels. Using NAEP's Advanced level (in math, once again) as the benchmark, less than 1 percent of Hungarian youngsters with weakly educated parents get there, versus more than 15 percent with highly educated parents. Only two countries for which this analysis has been done fared worse.[24] The story with reading is much the same: Hungary has a 1:18 ratio of students from poorly educated parents to those from highly educated ones. (The next worst country, the United Kingdom, had a ratio of 1:8.) (See appendix table A.4.)

Psychologist Eva Gyarmathy of the Hungarian Academy for Sciences is critical of what she views as wrong-headed ideas about giftedness in her country and selection methods that tend to favor the already-advantaged:

> The view of giftedness currently still prominent in Hungary is the ideal of the 20th century, that is, the school talent, who learns his or her lessons and tests well. A great part of the population who are identified as gifted comes from middle class students who perform well in competitions. Children from a favorable family background are at an advantage, as selection is, in most cases, not preceded by wide-scale gifted education, which would increase the manifestation chances of gifted children with no effective background for development. . . .
>
> The easiest way to select children for gifted programs is to select those who have already demonstrated ability, but this comes at the price of rejecting many children who have potential but have not yet demonstrated ability. Pursuing past achievements results in the loss of many real talents and makes the evolution of true gifted education difficult.[25]

For Gyarmathy's preferred approach to talent identification—observation of children's "interest and active engagement"—to work on a large scale, however, teachers would have to be trained as sophisticated observers of a great many pupils. That would be a heavy lift, for while many Hungarian teachers have had postgraduate university training—more than in a number of other European countries—only a small fraction (one knowledgeable observer estimates 10 percent) have had specialized preparation for identifying talented children through observation.

Because opportunities for high-ability students are scarce in primary schools, it appears that the principal mechanism for screening talent in Hungarian education, as Gyarmathy notes, remains the selection process by which students enter competitive gymnasia that boast strong track records on university admission. In many parts of the country, however, such schools are few or nonexistent. And because this sorting generally takes place at age fourteen, which is also when the most explicit (but rather small) outreach for talent among disadvantaged children commences, it is not surprising that Hungary has not yet registered much success in boosting the representation of poor and minority youngsters among its high scorers.

DILEMMAS, CHALLENGES, AND TAKEAWAYS

Hungary's minister of education in 2007—under the leftist government of the day—issued a comprehensive diagnosis of what ailed the country's education system. It was sweeping and urgent, akin to *A Nation at Risk*, linking the need for reform to Hungary's future economic vitality and much else, and charting a series of ambitious reforms.[26] As in most countries in our sample, and in line with the ideology of the government at that time, it focused primarily on lifting the floor, equalizing opportunity, and boosting the performance of historically disadvantaged populations. It did not single out the challenges of educating high-ability students or advancing gifted education—an interesting omission considering that this manifesto emerged the same year as the parliamentary decree encouraging "talent development."

In any case, 2010 brought into office a very different government with education-reform interests that so far appear focused more on control than either quality or equality.

Hungary's "talent support" efforts remain earnest and multidimensional—and semiremoved from primary-secondary education policies and ministers. Despite their organizational complexity and innovative funding arrangements, however, they're small and weakly resourced. (One outside observer estimates that Hungary's total expenditure on talent support between 2009 and 2014 was about $95 million, or roughly ten dollars per capita.)[27]

Long before its current political divisions and tensions arose, Hungary was a famously talkative, even argumentative place, where people love to voice opinions, disagree with others' views—and claim credit for many of humankind's historic accomplishments. Policy clarity and consistency are apt to suffer.

The smallish cadre of people committed to talent support in Hungary do argue among themselves from time to time, but they're not about to cease their efforts, nor is there any sign that talent support's several manifestations in the primary-secondary education system are going away. That's a very good thing—because this country still has a steep hill to climb.

From the American perspective, aside from interesting examples of competitions and Olympiads at the secondary level, perhaps the most useful lesson to extract from the Hungarian experience to date is the engagement of many nongovernmental organizations in "talent development" and the constructive interplay of these entities with public policies and budgets. Gifted education in the United States would benefit greatly from the mobilization of interest and support from more constituencies.

We're also intrigued by the provision in Hungary's tax system whereby individuals can direct 1 percent of their payment toward the talent program. Several U.S. states have tax-credit-supported scholarship programs; the long-standing charitable deduction is built into the Internal Revenue Code; and some taxes are "dedicated" to specific public purposes (e.g., federal gas tax revenues go into the Highway Trust Fund). So Americans are not unaccustomed to special financing arrangements of this sort. But to the authors' knowledge, nothing like Hungary's tax set-aside has yet been tried on behalf of talent development or gifted education at the local, state, or federal level.

14

Switzerland: Decentralized to Excess?

MINDFUL THAT, much like Singapore, skilled people are its main asset, Switzerland is exquisitely attentive to human capital development. As our principal Swiss advisor, Victor Mueller-Oppliger of the Northwestern Switzerland University of Education and Teacher Training, has written, his "is a nation whose economy relies on [the] knowledge, innovations, excellence and expertise of its population."[1]

This attention spans the spectrum of education and training, including quality options in the technical-vocational realm and sophisticated apprenticeships, as well as plentiful advanced learning opportunities for future scientists and technologists.[2]

Unlike Singapore, however, the Swiss education system is decentralized at the primary-secondary level, with most decisions made by the country's twenty-six cantons, loosely coordinated by regional and national networks of educators and programs and by a "conference" of cantonal education ministers. The central government in Bern has very little say.

In former times, primary schooling here lasted four, five, or six years, depending on the canton, and the gymnasium lasted another six. The new structure almost everywhere in the country consists of six years in primary school, then three years of "secondary" (of which there are several types), then four years of gymnasium (or another option, generally in the vocational realm). Because major shifts in one's trajectory occur at the end of grades 6 and 9, families must begin early to chart their children's courses.

Judging by its overall PISA results, the arrangement is working pretty well for Switzerland, whose fifteen-year-olds came in ninth in the world in math in 2012, bettered only by Asia's "tigers" and the tiny (adjoining) European principality of Liechtenstein. Switzerland, in other words, surpassed Finland, Germany, and others, including—by a considerable distance—the United States, which ranked thirty-second.[3]

Switzerland also does exceptionally well at the high end, with 21 percent of its students scoring 5 or 6 on PISA math, again lagging only the "tigers" (and Liechtenstein!).[4] (See table 14.1.)

Science and reading are solid but less impressive, with 9 percent of young Swiss coming in at levels 5 or 6 on both PISA assessments, compared with OECD averages of 8 percent in both and American proportions of 7 and 8 percent on science and reading, respectively.[5] (Switzerland has not participated in recent TIMSS or PIRLS assessments.)

TABLE 14.1   Switzerland average scale scores and percentages of high scorers on international assessments over time, with trend lines

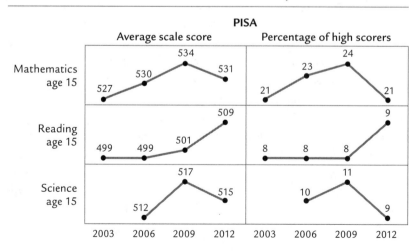

GIFTED EDUCATION FUNDAMENTALS

Gifted education experts in Switzerland describe the main program options for students under "four pillars": acceleration, enrichment, pull-outs (and ability grouping), and teacher preparation and support.

As we have observed in other countries (Finland, Germany, and Japan, for example), the Swiss are disinclined to talk about some kids being more able than others, and people manifest considerable angst about "elitism." On the other hand—as we have also observed in other countries that profess egalitarianism—there's a long tradition of selective-admission schools at the upper secondary level, the traditional route into university, and some of them are quite hard to get into. Only about 20 percent of young Swiss attend gymnasia—and their graduates do generally make it into universities. Historically, the Swiss have viewed such schools as the country's main gifted education program, and families compete vigorously to get their children admitted to the best of them, including tutoring and "cram schools" that constitute a sizable private industry, particularly in parts of the country such as Zurich where scores on entrance exams (rather than school marks and holistic evaluations) determine who gets into which gymnasium.[6] This naturally advantages kids from prosperous, motivated families.

The education of high-ability children in Switzerland takes many forms because cantons have different policies and practices, and how these get put into practice also varies by school. Moreover, it's up to the canton whether and how to fund and staff such programs and how (if at all) to handle enforcement. (All of this, we were told, tends to be more energetic in German-speaking cantons than in the French- and Italian-speaking regions.)

Historically, Switzerland, like most countries, associated giftedness with exceptional intellectual ability that could be identified early via intelligence testing. Over the past decade or so, however, Switzerland has broadened its definitions and (in most cantons) altered its approach. The "majority of educators, boards of education and cantons," writes Mueller-Oppliger, now recognize and promote "musical, artistic, sportive and social abilities . . . as well as academic abilities."[7]

In deciding which children qualify, many Swiss educators employ Joseph Renzulli's "three-ring" model of giftedness, which examines the intersection of a child's ability, creativity, and commitment.[8] Just two cantons still rely on IQ testing. Most draw instead on teacher recommendations and signs of student interest, although here, as elsewhere, parents often initiate the screening process, which opens this opportunity to the progeny of educated, motivated, prosperous families more often than to poor, immigrant, or otherwise disadvantaged families. Children of the latter depend more on the motivation and perspicacity of teachers, as well as the existence of suitable options in their community.

Most cantons expect each school to address giftedness in its multiyear education plan, and most cantons also evaluate their schools every few years to determine how well they're carrying out those plans. But what criteria to use? We found much disquiet about standardized testing in Switzerland, so such results are rarely made public and definitely not used to evaluate or compare schools or teachers. (One also detects teacher-union fingerprints.) This means, however, that evaluations of gifted programs tend to rely mostly on observation, satisfaction surveys, and trust (that a school is doing what it says it is to meet pupil needs).

PRIMARY AND MIDDLE GRADES

Especially in the primary grades, the principal mechanism for educating high-ability children is believed to start with regular teachers in inclusive classes. They're responsible for differentiating instruction to meet their pupils' varied needs. Everyone we spoke with agrees that such individualization is desirable in theory but most also acknowledged that it's difficult to execute—and grows harder as a child's abilities or needs become more esoteric.

Ability grouping and team teaching make differentiation more feasible, and schools are generally free to organize themselves that way if they so choose. They may also accelerate a child through the regular curricular sequence. Or they may mount pull-out programs (during or outside the school day). These include resource rooms, external competitions, even early access to university courses.

Some schools end up doing quite a lot in these areas, others very little. Whether a high-ability child finds herself with a suitable program of independent study, acceleration, and enrichment hinges on where she lives and what the staff in her school have chosen to do—and what sort of staff that school employs. Does it, for example, contain relevant specialists and support personnel? Does it allow for team teaching? All of this is spotty, as is the political and budgetary priority attached to gifted education.

In practice, then, gifted education at this level is a mix of "each teacher should do it herself" plus pull-out and supplemental programs in some schools plus (in some cantons) regional centers to which kids may come for programs unavailable at their own schools.[9] For example, thirty of Canton Argau's eighty-four schools have internal pull-out programs; in addition, five centers around the canton offer afterschool and weekend options in topics like robotics and writing. But Argau is regarded as uncommonly organized, ambitious, and attentive to the needs of high-ability youngsters.

Within-school pull-outs may consist of mentoring, group projects, individual research, enrichment, and more. They're often interdisciplinary. In one that we observed, each child (or team) was working on his own unique project, although all students had to go through a fairly elaborate process of refining their interests and justifying their projects to teachers (and sometimes classmates) before plunging ahead.

The demand for such programs exceeds the supply. Screening for them may include testing, or gifted education coordinators and teachers may do more holistic assessments. (Such coordinators are present in perhaps 30 percent of Swiss primary schools, maybe 50 percent in larger cantons such as Lucerne and Basel.)

Some schools in Basel actually screen all third graders for giftedness. In most cantons, however, students must apply for screening. Teachers may start the process, but parents more often initiate it. Parent initiative also makes a difference in whether the school has a gifted pull-out program of any kind or a gifted education coordinator on staff.[10]

Advocates have been pushing for specialized teacher training in gifted education, and two universities currently offer this specialty.

Hundreds of individuals have completed such training, but there's no requirement that coordinators and teachers of gifted students have such preparation, and no additional pay accompanies this work. Once again, it's up to the canton and school to decide whether to employ such specialists, if they're even available in the vicinity.

Though gifted education programs, insofar as they exist, are open to all pupils who qualify, we saw little evidence of extra effort by cantons to draw disadvantaged families into them. Everyone acknowledged that this is a problem for high-ability kids from Switzerland's growing immigrant population. (Some schools, especially in Zurich, are now majority-immigrant.[11]) Still, we were assured by Dr. Mueller-Oppliger that educators seldom ignore such children:

> A lot of schools are very aware of this problem of the so-called "Bildungsferne" (families with poor education background). But we don't have special programs for these kids. Nevertheless, I wouldn't say that the system is unaware, unnoticing or ignorant to this fact. It's part of Swiss thinking of integration and inclusion: To notice, to diagnose and to select responsibly but not to build up exclusive special programs.[12]

The middle grades (7–9) pose a sizable challenge for Swiss gifted education. This is where inclusion ends and education generally divides among three types of school, with children sorted into them largely on the basis of primary school grades.[13] There's a general belief that gifted kids get good grades and thus will win admission to the *Bezirkschule*, which is the traditional path into gymnasium and then university. Therefore, it is also believed, the traditional sorting mechanisms adequately meet the "gifted challenge." Yet while the *Bezirkschule* are accustomed to preparing high-scoring youngsters for gymnasium and university by following the standard curriculum, most have nothing special to offer pupils with exceptional ability—and the other two types of middle school, both more vocationally oriented, are unlikely to have specialized offerings for such students. Save for possible pupil acceleration, the middle level of Swiss education doesn't currently appear well suited to cultivating uncommon talent outside the traditional channels.

HIGH SCHOOL

At the upper secondary level, which typically lasts four years for the university-bound, the main provision for gifted students is the education provided by the regular gymnasium program. The Swiss assume that simply qualifying for these schools shows strong academic ability and achievement. Some gymnasia specialize, however—in sports, in music, in science, even in educating disadvantaged or immigrant students.[14] And a few schools operate programs for gifted pupils, including links with nearby universities that allow for early enrollment in their courses. But these are recent developments, grafted onto the traditional structure.

To quote our Swiss advisor again:

> In some cantons, we have time out for some kids to work with mentors (in professional research programs, with artists and writers) while being excused from regular classes; also early studies at universities during the final two years of gymnasium; also special ability groups for special interests (like philosophy) as additional courses. Some schools also offer students the opportunity to take regular courses in foreign languages. In Basel, for example, they can take two or three subjects in English or Spanish besides the regular learning in German.
>
> Also on offer are semesters at foreign gymnasia. There's a wide range of possibilities but, like everything, it depends on the gymnasium and canton.[15]

Switzerland does not, however, believe in gymnasia (or schools at other levels) that cater exclusively to high-ability students. That idea strikes them as elitist and separatist. As our advisor explains,

> What's not opportune for Switzerland is to create separate elite schools. . . . We have the idea that schools are the mirror of an inclusive society and that students have to learn to live and work together with all different capabilities.[16]

Meanwhile, Switzerland's expanding set of education offerings for young people who don't hike the gymnasium-to-university path furnish widening options for those who may be exceptionally able but not academically inclined. The Swiss have done better than most at developing high-quality alternatives to college, respected educational offerings (at both secondary and postsecondary levels) that lead people into satisfying and lucrative careers, and that are open to late deciders and course-changers. Here, more than in the primary grades (with their standardized curriculum) and the hidebound middle grades, is where Switzerland's attentiveness to human capital across the spectrum incorporates ways for one to be highly able in fields outside the traditional disciplines.

DIVERSITY AND DISADVANTAGE

Switzerland is exceptionally prosperous—regardless of the gauge, it never falls below sixth in the world in GDP per capita—so its lowest SES quartile isn't all that low.[17] Still, comparing its lowest and highest quartiles (using OECD metrics), Switzerland does just a little better than the OECD average on PISA math (though far better than the United States), with a ratio close to 1:4 for those who become high scorers. And 6 percent of its test takers with poorly educated parents reach those lofty ranks, compared with 26 percent (among the world's highest) of young people with at least one parent who completed college. The situation is bleaker in reading and science. In both, Switzerland's percentage of top-scoring kids from the lowest SES quartile falls below the OECD average, as does its ratio of top scorers from low and high SES. Overall, Switzerland does not appear to do very well when it comes to equity at the upper end of achievement. (See tables A.3 and A.4 in the appendix for more information.)

As Mueller-Oppliger writes, "Our school system produces an enormous heterogeneity of achievement and . . . our schools don't succeed sufficiently, when it comes to [advancing] the social-cultural disadvantaged. Too often, unrevealed giftedness from students from lower social-economic families or foreign-language speakers still is not going to be discovered and not appropriately fostered."[18]

The striking decentralization of Swiss education also means that access to opportunities for high-ability students depends heavily on both the circumstances of one's birth and where one goes to school.

And because cantons and schools tend to respond—direct-democracy style—to the priorities of residents and parents, a high-ability youngster from an immigrant or rural farming family, say, who attends school with others from similar circumstances, is apt to find herself with few opportunities beyond what her regular teacher provides.

DILEMMAS, CHALLENGES, AND TAKEAWAYS

Plenty of issues remain unresolved for gifted education in this mountainous land, which is also now implementing a challenging new national curriculum. Critics say the revised plan of study is too narrowly discipline-focused to be optimal for gifted kids with wide-ranging interests. The standards on which it's based, however, are organized into chunks, which make acceleration more practical than grade-specific standards.

Teacher preparation and qualifications remain problematic, too. Even as some universities provide quality preparation for educators of gifted pupils, many teacher-education programs pay scant heed to the topic, which—unlike special education—requires no extra certification.[19] Since it's optional for teachers, explicit training in gifted education happens mostly at the postgraduate level.

Mueller-Oppliger concisely summarizes six other major challenges that lie ahead for Switzerland:

- "Unevenness across the country in the absence of overarching policy or program. . . . Considering the . . . absence of enforcement or even evaluation from the cantonal level, we see that there's no systematic way for Switzerland's energetic gifted-education advocates to propagate awareness of the needs of high-ability children or to organize programs for them."
- Structural rigidities in the middle grades and limited awareness there that high-ability children might need additional learning opportunities.
- Insufficient attention to high-ability children from disadvantaged circumstances. "Compensation of social disadvantage and the promotion of kids from less educated families dawn more and more, but do not yet lead into specific programs for those who are both gifted and disadvantaged."

- Scant recognition of "special achievements within the regular school. Scholastic marks [and entry into the next school on the basis of those marks] are the only stimulus. No bonuses, no special diploma or announcements for special achievements. . . . Low promotion of high achievement implies negative consequences, such that families with income power and high expectations make use of their right to educate their children in private schools."
- Infrequent evaluation of gifted education programs to determine which approaches work best with which kinds of kids under what circumstances.
- Weak financial support in many parts of the country, and no extra help from the national level.[20]

That summary looks right to us. Meanwhile, however, American educators might profitably borrow not only from Switzerland's finely honed technical-vocational programs at the secondary level but also from the high-quality part-time pull-out and afterschool supplements provided to gifted primary pupils in some cantons as well as the universal student-screening practices employed in parts of the country. Although the unevenness of such practices around Switzerland distresses the country's gifted education partisans, K–12 education in the United States is almost as decentralized, and these promising approaches to schooling high-ability children are best undertaken by individual states or districts.

15

England:
Sifting Through
the Policy Rubble

GIFTED EDUCATION IN ENGLAND is in flux today—and has been for
quite a while. Starting with a White Paper in 2001 while Tony Blair was
prime minister, Labor governments mounted a multifaceted national
program to equalize opportunity for able poor kids who could not
attend the country's elite private schools—a problem that had wors-
ened in the 1970s when England turned almost all of its publicly
supported university-prep "grammar" schools into nonselective "comprehensive" high schools, and was exacerbated again in 1997 when
the same Labor government abolished a voucher-like program meant
to help poor but able children enter private schools. But the national
gifted and talented initiative was shut down in 2010 (also by Labor,
in the waning days of the Gordon Brown era), and the current coalition government is disinclined to revive anything of the sort, believing that the right response to almost every education challenge is to
give schools maximum freedom, then hold them to account for performance against rigorous standards by *all* their pupils. Some other
promising policy changes have recently been initiated, but these won't
show any effects for years to come.[1]

Based on the most recent data from PISA, TIMSS, and PIRLS,
the mishmash of reforms over the past fifteen years hasn't borne

much fruit for the United Kingdom at the high end.[2] (See table 15.1.) Although the country boasts slightly more top scorers than the United States in PISA's three subjects, it ranks a bit below the OECD average in math and just a little over in reading and science.[3]

England's own chief inspector of schools, Sir Michael Wilshaw, painted a dark picture in mid-2013, declaring, "Too many non-selective schools are failing to nurture scholastic excellence. While the best of these schools provide excellent opportunities, many of our most able students receive mediocre provision. Put simply, they are not doing well enough because their secondary schools fail to challenge and support them sufficiently from the beginning."[4]

As we write, the overall education policy situation in England is also uncertain. In summer 2014, as part of the run-up to the next national election, hard-charging education minister Michael Gove was relieved of his portfolio and replaced by Nicky Morgan, whose views on most major issues remain veiled. And with the election coming soon, nobody expects the Cameron team to do anything that could be framed as an example of "Tory elitism." Indeed, insofar as the prime minister (himself a product of Eton and Oxford) has recently had anything to say about education—and that hasn't been much—he's gone populist, as in, "This party is the trade union for children from the poorest estates and the most chaotic homes."[5]

Bear in mind, too, that while the occupant of 10 Downing Street is prime minister of the "United Kingdom," his government makes primary-secondary education policy only for England. Scotland, Wales, and Northern Ireland control their own schooling. The London-based Department for Education is thus directly responsible for educating about 85 percent of U.K. children—and is quite forcefully in charge of *their* education, as local control of schooling has been waning in England since the Thatcher years. Parliament makes the policies and provides most of the funding, while the Department sets the regulations and directly authorizes thousands of individual schools. An autonomous agency called Ofsted is responsible for inspecting schools and reporting on their performance, while a unit called Ofqual oversees an elaborate system of national exams at various "key stages" of a child's education, including the General Certificate of

TABLE 15.1   England average scale scores and percentages of high scorers on international assessments over time, with trend lines

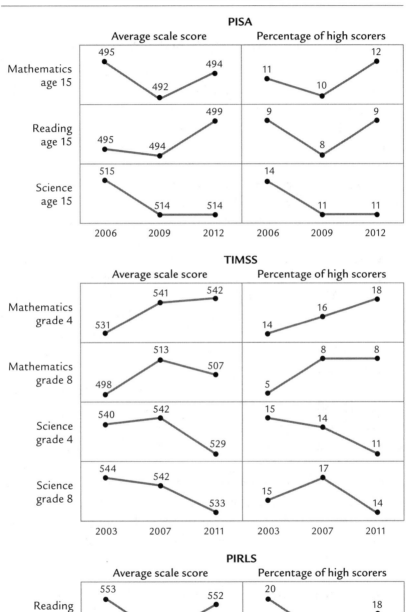

Secondary Education (GCSE) tests given around age sixteen and the A-levels that determine university admission two years later.[6]

GIFTED EDUCATION FUNDAMENTALS

British policy makers are chronically skittish about elitism. "What race is to the U.S.," one remarked to us, "social class is to the U.K." The overall direction of their postwar policies has been to reduce barriers, foster mobility, and enhance equality. Which also means those concerned with the education of high-ability children generally find themselves swimming upstream.

Class stratification in British education previously took several forms, beginning with a web of private schools that today educate about 7 percent of the country's pupils (but up to 20 percent in London), get many graduates into Oxford and Cambridge, and have produced many leaders of government, business, and other prominent fields. These schools—including such famous old names as Eton, Rugby, and Harrow—have played such a significant role in British history that for ages they were dubbed "public schools." (Today, they're more commonly termed "independent schools."[7]) While most offer financial aid to some pupils, they've traditionally been bastions of the upper classes.[8]

A second form of stratification was the "tripartite" system of secondary schooling in the public sector that prevailed from World War II to the 1970s. At the end of primary school (around age eleven), students sat for an aptitude test, the results of which determined whether they were then tracked into "grammar schools," "secondary modern" schools, or technical-vocational institutions. Only the first of these was dedicated to university preparation—and the whole arrangement ignited controversy as it became clear that most children entering the grammar schools came from the middle classes.[9] It began to look like a system designed to preserve privilege rather than to foster mobility and equality.

Although a smattering of grammar schools remains in parts of the country—164 among some 3,500 secondary schools—beginning in the 1960s most of England phased out the tripartite system. Today, the overwhelming majority of secondary pupils attend "comprehensive" schools akin to those that James B. Conant urged upon the United States in 1959.[10]

This and similar efforts to advance equity in education inevitably gave rise to the question of what (if anything) to do about high-ability youngsters, especially those whose family circumstances placed independent schools out of reach. Should they go to the same primary and comprehensive secondary schools as everyone else? Take the same classes from the same teachers?

In 1980, Margaret Thatcher's Conservative government offered a partial response by launching the "assisted places scheme," a scholarship program intended to enable high achievers from poor families to enroll in private schools alongside those whose parents paid full freight.[11] Over the ensuing seventeen years, some 80,000 kids benefited from this program, but Labor, once back in power, scrapped it on grounds that it was elitist, costly, and not reaching many truly needy students. (The teacher unions didn't like it, either.)

What to do instead? The Blair team was concerned with economic competitiveness, with assisting the poor—and with stemming the flight of middle-class families into private schooling. They also wanted to demonstrate that the public education sector could do right by students at every ability level. But they couldn't tolerate allegations of elitism. So they took several steps, including more flexible definitions of giftedness and talent and measures to enrich the education of poor children possessing such qualities. Much of the action took place within a broader initiative called "Excellence in Cities" and sought to introduce a distinctively British approach to gifted and talented education across the system. Schools were required to designate gifted education coordinators, Ofsted was charged with incorporating schools' handling of this issue into its reviews, and the Department for Education was tasked with ensuring that various national programs and funding streams incorporated this mission.

Included among those initiatives was the creation, at Warwick University, of a new Academy for Gifted and Talented Youth, consciously modeled in part (by Blair advisors Michael Barber and Andrew Adonis) on the Johns Hopkins Center for Talented Youth. It was led by an accomplished academic named Deborah Eyre and charged with running summer programs for high-ability youngsters, professional development for teachers, and various efforts at distance learning. Barber says the mandate of the new center and the larger initiative in which it was embedded was to get schools across England to pay attention to—and do more for—the highest-achieving 10 percent of their pupils.

Less than a decade later, however, as the Labor government was winding down, the center's plug was pulled.[12] The budget was tight, the contractor that took over from Warwick University had done a mediocre job, the new ministerial team had stopped paying attention, and nobody in the department was particularly fired up about the education of high-ability children. So the national gifted and talented initiative ground to a halt.

Shortly thereafter, David Cameron's coalition government placed Michael Gove in charge of education. He was convinced that, if standards were high, curricula robust, schools empowered to manage their own affairs and then held to account for results, and parents had plenty of quality school options for their children, then government would not need to prescribe an endless stream of one-off policies, categorical programs, limited initiatives, and restricted funding pipelines. Individual schools would have ample incentives to see to everybody's education, even that of high-ability youngsters.

Gove is gone now, but few in government seem keen on rekindling attention to high-ability children at this time. The one recent exception comes from Chief Inspector Wilshaw and Ofsted, which in July 2014 declared (in its *School Inspection Handbook*) that "Inspectors should pay particular attention to whether more able pupils in general and the most able pupils in particular are achieving as well as they should. . . . Inspectors should summarise the achievements of the most able pupils in a separate paragraph of the inspection report."[13]

Because the inspectors cycle through essentially every school in England, this admonition is potentially important to the education of high-ability children. But it still leaves activity in this realm to individual schools and private organizations such as the Sutton Trust (a large, energetic charity devoted to social mobility) rather than addressing the topic as a national policy challenge. Indeed, at the policy level, "erratic" might be the most polite way to describe England's handling of this challenge over the past several decades.

PRIMARY AND MIDDLE GRADES

Aside from the recent Ofsted initiative, at this time no systematic policy or practice guides the education of gifted youngsters in the early and middle years. Although some independent schools cater to such students, within the state-supported sector it's up to schools and local education authorities to determine whether students with exceptional ability receive anything but standard instruction in the standard curriculum. And it's largely up to teachers to spot such children.

As in many countries, British educators generally favor "mainstreaming" students and expect teachers to differentiate their classroom practice according to children's distinctive needs, capabilities, and prior achievement. Ability grouping is widely practiced, especially in math, but again, this is up to the school and instructor. Which might work better if teachers were systematically prepared to handle high-ability pupils. Yet little of that happens; it's simply nobody's top priority.

Schools in England have considerable freedom to select their own teams, manage their resources, and chart their own education course, although for most that freedom is bounded by a fairly prescriptive national curriculum and assessment system. In recent years, schools have been able to secure even greater autonomy by converting to—or starting as—"academies" and "free schools," akin to U.S. charter schools. They remain subject to national tests and inspections but can vary the curriculum and specialize in particular subjects or student populations. Although most such schools are secondary, as of 2013 almost 10 percent of English primary schools were operating as "academies."

The results, predictably, are uneven, especially for able kids from disadvantaged circumstances. As in the United States, middle-class families tend to find schools that do right by their children—with classmates who are often similar. Poor kids, however, are apt to attend the nearest school, usually in a poor neighborhood. As Dr. Eyre remarked to us, "If you're disadvantaged, you're more likely to attend a bad school than a kid from a higher-income background." Full of other disadvantaged girls and boys, such a school faces myriad challenges, and boosting able pupils is seldom its top priority.

The results show it. During the course of primary schooling, according to a 2014 study by the government's Social Mobility and Child Poverty Commission, "High-achieving children from the most deprived families fall behind lower-achieving children from the most affluent families, while low-achieving children from the most affluent families catch up with higher-achieving children from the most deprived families."[14]

HIGH SCHOOL

The secondary school scene in England is complex, like an archaeological dig with the remains of multiple civilizations layered atop one another, beginning in this case with independent (i.e., private) schools that date back many centuries.[15]

Also left over from earlier eras are some selective-admission secondary schools aimed at university admission and enrolling students who share that goal. Included in this handful of grammar schools (accounting for about 5 percent of England's secondary population) are single-sex institutions and schools with highly competitive admission, some of them in areas where the "eleven-plus" testing regime remains intact.[16] They may do fine at boosting high-ability pupils onward, but they're typically located in middle-class communities that declined to convert their schools to "comprehensive" status, and they typically enroll few youngsters from disadvantaged backgrounds. Nor will there be any more of them, as current law bars starting new ones (though existing schools may, and do, expand).[17] Because these schools are selective, a tutoring-and-cram-school industry exists to prepare youngsters for their entrance exams—and, because parents must ordinarily pay for such coaching, those who can manage this expense obviously enjoy an advantage.[18]

From the latest chapter of British education history, we find the fast-growing sector—already about four thousand schools, roughly two-thirds of all secondary institutions—consisting of the academies and free schools described above. These are government-financed but independent of local authorities and answerable directly to Whitehall. Many are run by "chains" such as ARK and the Harris Federation, some of which operate excellent schools, but others are dismal education failures, and still others some of both.[19]

Academies and free schools enjoy considerable curricular independence and can specialize—in the arts, in math and science, in English as a foreign language, for example. By law, they may not practice selective admission on the basis of "ability" (at least not before age sixteen), yet they can select pupils within demographic "bands," may operate as single-sex schools, may limit their students to particular religions, and may even choose students according to various "aptitudes."[20] By declaring their academic specialties, they can also shape the pool of likely applicants.[21]

Occupying a sizable if shrinking niche between independent and grammar schools on the one hand, and academies and free schools on the other, are England's "comprehensive" high schools—nonselective and open to all comers, but typically containing multiple curricular strands, including tracks aimed at university admission. Some do well at preparing students for the A-level exams, and some are praised in inspectors' reports for their success in educating highly able pupils. But such success is the exception, according to a biting 2013 Ofsted report on the entire nonselective sector of secondary schooling, including both academies and comprehensive schools. In just one-fifth of the 2000-plus lessons that inspectors observed were "the most able students . . . supported well. Moreover, in around 40 percent of the schools visited in the survey, the most able students were not making the progress of which they were capable. In a few of the schools visited, teachers did not even know who the most able students were."[22] The inspectors found that 65 percent of students who had achieved top marks in both English and math at the end of primary school did not go on to earn top grades in those subjects at age sixteen, although such grades "are a key predictor of success" in the A-levels that come later. In other words, there's a huge achievement fall-off between ages eleven and sixteen.

Among other major Ofsted findings:

- In many schools, expectations of what the most able students should achieve are too low.

- Schools do not routinely give the same attention to the most able as they do to low-attaining students or those who struggle at school.

- Transition arrangements from primary to secondary school are not effective enough to ensure that students maintain their academic momentum.

- Students said that too much work was repetitive and undemanding. . . . As a result, their progress faltered and their interest in school waned.

- Inequalities between different groups of the most able students are not being tackled satisfactorily. The attainment of the most able students who are eligible for free school meals, especially the most able boys, lags behind that of other groups.

- Assessment, tracking, and targeting are not used sufficiently well in many schools. Some of the schools visited paid scant attention to the progress of their most able students.[23]

Not only did many schools ill-prepare their strongest pupils for entry to competitive universities—20 percent of them produced *no* graduates with top A-level grades—but, as Hoxby has reported in the United States, Ofsted also found that many schools did a lackluster job of supplying such students with information and encouragement regarding what they could achieve after graduating. In American parlance, they were "undermatched," a shortfall particularly evident among young people whose family members had not attended university.

DIVERSITY AND DISADVANTAGE

The United Kingdom does only a little better than the United States—and considerably worse than the OECD average—in pulling disadvantaged students into the high-scoring ranks. (See appendix tables A.3 and A.4.) This holds whether "disadvantage" is defined by OECD's socioeconomic indicator or by levels of parents' education—and regardless of whether one looks at math, science, or reading.[24] In the 2012 PISA math round, for example, for every youngster from the lowest SES quartile who scored 5 or 6, more than six top-quartile students did so. When gauged by parents' education, the result is a bit better, on par with Australia and Finland—and better than the United States—but still not great: for every British fifteen-year-old whose parents had not completed high school but who reached the equivalent of NAEP's Advanced level in math, almost four youngsters with at least one college-graduate parent attained that level.

Here as elsewhere, it's not that children from disadvantaged backgrounds lack the ability. Many more do well in England at age seven, for example, than in high school—and more do well at age eleven than at eighteen. The Social Mobility and Child Poverty Commission reported in 2014: "[O]f the 7,853 children from the most deprived homes who achieve level 5 in English and maths at age 11, only 906 make it to an elite university. If they had the same trajectory as a child from one of the least deprived families, then 3,066 of these children would be likely to go to an elite university, suggesting that 2,160 children are falling behind."[25]

DILEMMAS, CHALLENGES, AND TAKEAWAYS

Education in England faces plenty of difficulties that resemble our own.[26] Overall academic performance is far lower than it should be and high-end performance far rarer. Although at some fine schools and celebrated universities outstanding education is possible for top students, those opportunities are fewer than they should be and are poorly distributed across the country's diverse population.

While England's broad education-policy thrusts have been fairly steady over several decades, with emphases (as in the United States) on higher standards, assessments and accountability, and school innovation, autonomy, and choice, the handling of high-ability youngsters has been sketchy and episodic. Whether one is looking at policy fluctuations or outcomes, especially for disadvantaged children, no reasonable observer could term this realm a great success.

Chief Inspector Wilshaw might have been referring to American education when he framed the major challenges that he sees for England:

First, we need to make sure that our most able students do as well academically as those of our main economic competitors. This means aiming for A* [A+] and A grades and not being satisfied with less.

The second challenge is to ensure, from early on, that students know what opportunities are open to them and develop the confidence to make the most of these. They need tutoring, guidance and encouragement, as well as a chance to meet other young people who have embraced higher education.

The third challenge is to ensure that all schools help students and families overcome cultural barriers to attending higher education. Many of our most able students come from homes where no parent or close relative has either experienced, or expects, progression to university.[27]

Wilshaw and Ofsted do not, however, run schools, prepare teachers, or test pupils. Those responsibilities rest with other government agencies and private organizations. And centralized control of schooling across such a large country turns out to be a mixed blessing. Initiative and innovation are surely possible—free schools are a fine example—but must be the kinds that the reigning government favors, and promising projects are vulnerable to the next election. Because new policies and programs are often layered on top of their predecessors, the "archaeological site" continues to accumulate. Particularly visible is England's lingering ambivalence regarding tight, uniform regulation on the one hand versus decentralization and choice on the other. Add to that the long-standing British sensitivity about elitism, class, and diversity, plus plenty of politics and preelection maneuvering, and it's no surprise that the education of gifted students presents a cloudy picture.

But all is not lost. Considering Ofsted's worthy push and the chief inspector's energetic use of his bully pulpit, as well as mounting concern over Britain's economic vitality, there's reason to suspect that the coming years may see more purposeful activity in this domain, including changes under way in the national exam structure, especially the GCSE tests. These are intended to raise standards, curb grade inflation, and reward schools for student gains across the board, including at the top.[28]

Private organizations—notably the Sutton Trust—are hard at work, too, with various blends of aspiration-raising, academic enrichment, and practical counseling. These include summer programs for low-income high achievers near the end of secondary school and others that identify such students early and work to keep them pointed toward eventual entry into top-flight universities.[29]

When it comes to public policy, however, England has had an NCLB-style emphasis on children below a minimum level of achievement, while neglecting those above it. The exam-scoring system has also produced a "ceiling effect" such that some students cannot get a high grade no matter how well they do.[30] Others get high marks regardless, leaving them with scant incentive to learn more. The refurbished exam structure is supposed to do better at gauging performance at the top, to incentivize schools to attend to their high achievers, and to reward them for moving such students upward. *How* to do this, however, will remain a school-level decision, not a uniform program. So if you're a smart kid in England, the school that you attend—and the place where you live and the parents who raise you—will probably continue to make a huge difference in the education that you get.

England and the United States have been exchanging education-reform ideas for decades now, and this is apt to continue, but in the gifted and talented realm we may not have a great deal to learn from the present muddled situation across the North Atlantic. It would, however, be worthwhile for states to consider school inspections akin to those conducted by Ofsted. This would broaden the focus of school performance beyond today's test score obsession while giving schools and districts constructive feedback on multiple fronts—and it would be a fine thing if one of those fronts turned out (as in England's case) to be how well schools are handling the education of their high-ability pupils.

16

Ontario:
How "Special"
Is "Gifted"?

AS IN THE UNITED STATES, Canada's primary-secondary education system is decentralized, with key decisions made by the thirteen provinces and territories. National programs and policies barely exist, save for the Pan-Canadian Assessment given to eighth graders.[1] There's no federal education department—and no common approach to educating high-ability children, which turns out to vary greatly across this vast land.

We focused on Ontario, the most populous province, as it's convenient, we found willing advisors there, and other aspects of Ontario's education system have drawn generous praise from contemporary analysts.[2]

Much of that acclaim was catalyzed by Canada's strong performance on the 2006 PISA assessment, combined with Ontario's openness to inquiry, its relatively calm history of education reform (including teacher-union relations that are often amicable, if sometimes intense), and the presence at the University of Toronto of Professor Michael Fullan, a lively booster of education as practiced in his province.[3]

In 2009 and 2012, however, Canada's PISA performance slipped a bit in all three subjects, setting off alarms among pundits and politicians.[4] (See table 16.1.) Yet at the high end, Canada still does

TABLE 16.1   Canada average scale scores and percentages of high scorers on international assessments over time, with trend lines

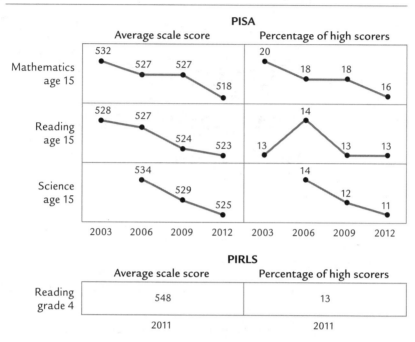

respectably, with 16 percent of test takers in math (13 percent in reading, and 11 percent in science) reaching the top two tiers in 2012.

Within Canada, Ontario students, at least the large majority whose primary language is English, score at or above the national average on most PISA gauges and also do well on the Pan-Canadian Assessment; they generally rank first or second among the provinces in all subjects and are well represented among those with top scores.[5]

Ontario is the size of Texas and Montana combined, with a population equivalent to Pennsylvania's and territory that ranges from metropolitan Toronto to a near-endless rural expanse stretching to Hudson's Bay. It has, unsurprisingly, decentralized the operation of its schools to some 125 local boards.[6] Although there's been recent creep toward uniformity—evident in teacher licensure, school finance, and a province-wide curriculum—many key decisions are still localized, in part because of the province's size and diversity, in part because its powerful teacher unions prefer it that way. Despite the uniform curriculum, for example, beyond a list of courses there's no province-wide high school graduation standard or exit requirement save for an undemanding literacy test. One's diploma otherwise depends entirely on teacher-conferred grades in the relevant courses—and there is mounting concern about the grade inflation that has ensued.

GIFTED EDUCATION FUNDAMENTALS

Ontario displays two approaches to educating high-ability students, not counting private schools and what parents may do on their own.

First, the special education version. In Ontario, giftedness is recognized as one of a dozen "exceptionalities" that entitle an "identified" student to have his/her individual needs met via the full-bore review and customized program more often associated with disabled youngsters. Giftedness—the only special ed category that does not involve a "deficit"—is currently defined as an "unusually advanced degree of general intellectual ability that requires differentiated learning experiences of a depth and breadth beyond those normally provided in the regular school program to satisfy the level of educational potential indicated."[7]

The law requires that local boards "serve" all kids who are so identified. But it's up to the boards to decide what's meant by "unusually advanced . . . intellectual ability," and how many such students wind up being served depends crucially on those local decisions, which may in turn be influenced by budgetary issues. As of 2012, about 15 percent of formally identified special ed pupils in Ontario were deemed gifted, which translated to 1.5 percent of all students in the province.

Special education funding amounts to about 10 percent of overall provincial support for primary-secondary schooling, but local boards have no obligation to spend any of it on gifted students. And while teachers must have an "additional qualification" before taking on special ed classes, there's no true specialization in gifted education. Indeed, we were told that Ontario universities, even the high-status University of Toronto, typically offer no regular courses in gifted education.[8]

The second approach to gifted education in Ontario lies outside the special ed framework. Because it's cumbersome, costly, and chancy to pursue that route, because some families eschew the label or want to select their child's school, and because of limits on how many children can be served that way, some boards operate their own magnet- or alternative-school programs for high-ability or high-achieving youngsters. As most of this takes place at the secondary level, we will return to it under the high school discussion.

PRIMARY AND MIDDLE GRADES

Despite the provincial mandate to serve all children with "exceptionalities," local boards determine *how* (and even whether) they'll be identified and served. Parents may initiate such an evaluation but they may have to contend with school system bureaucracies and, perhaps, the costs of private testing in order to pursue their claim.

The Ontario Association for Bright Children conducted a survey a few years back and found that five of sixty-two local boards had no programmatic options specifically for gifted students and a third of them did not "actively search" for such children.[9]

This unevenness is a mixed blessing. On the upside, it empowers communities to set their own priorities and hold their school systems to account. On the downside, it leads to discrepancies such that, for example, a youngster deemed to be gifted in one community might not be so classified in the adjoining community, and the education offerings and resources available to such a child would diverge widely.

We found enormous variability even within the same city. Toronto's Catholic school board screens *all* fourth graders via an IQ-type test and offers its version of gifted education to the top 2 percent—but not more. At the time of our visit, the Catholic schools had 2,300 students participating in some version of gifted ed.

By contrast, the Toronto District School Board (TDSB) tests only those who are "referred" by teachers or parents.[10] (It also limits participation to the top 2 percent on an IQ test.[11]) Here, grade 3 is the main testing year.[12]

Other local boards have various ways of identifying and serving gifted students. Some employ holistic evaluations. Some do little identification of any kind. It hinges greatly on parent and community pressures. Places where parents push for gifted education are apt to have more of it, which generally means that high-ability kids in educated, middle-class communities get more than their peers in less affluent places. It's also a problem in rural Ontario, for this sprawling province contains many small school systems that lack psychologists on staff and may also lack educators knowledgeable about gifted education.

Once children are identified within the 2 percent limit in Toronto, their board assigns them to schools. Families don't choose. Toronto's Catholic school program for grades 5–8 is concentrated in a handful of "withdrawal" centers that offer enrichment activities, usually once a week. (In the primary grades, it's completely up to individual teachers and "home" schools to handle.) In three locations, the Catholic school board also offers full-time separate ("congregated") classes for gifted learners in grades 6–8.[13]

Meanwhile, TDSB has separate full-time classes for gifted students in grades 4–8 but, again, only at designated schools.[14] Some other districts follow similar patterns, while some opt for supplementary programming after school or during summer vacation.[15] Enterprising teachers and parents may also seek out other sources, such as the variegated education offerings of the Ontario Science Center.[16] Options of this kind may be particularly valuable for those who don't make the cut in their districts or whose boards offer little.

Moving kids across town to an assigned school can be burdensome for parents. (Many boards do not provide transportation for gifted students, though they do for other special ed categories.) In rural Ontario, it's essentially impossible. Nor do all families with able kids want to leave their local schools to pursue a more challenging education somewhere else.

For these reasons, plus the cost and complexity of operating specialized classes and schools, Ontario in general (and Toronto in particular) emphasizes "differentiated instruction" within regular classrooms. This aligns with the wider push that the Ministry calls "learning for all," which seeks more individualized education delivered to all kids as well as heavier emphasis on mainstreaming students with exceptionalities.[17]

At every level of education in Ontario, we found deep faith in differentiation (including flexible, within-class groupings) and inquiry-based learning as ways of dealing with giftedness (and other exceptionalities). Leaders of Toronto's Catholic school board are particularly bullish on their success in preparing teachers to provide such instruction, and a senior Ministry official allowed that his strong preference is for that approach rather than "segregating" exceptional students.

Also sometimes possible within a child's home school or district is acceleration and "curriculum compacting," including early advancement in specific subjects, even skipping entire grades. However, this depends on where one goes to school. Some boards have elaborate acceleration policies.[18] Yet officials of the Toronto Catholic School Board say they never do it.

HIGH SCHOOL

As gifted students head into high school, their special ed placement changes, which means the committee apparatus to review and build their individualized education plans must again be convened. This presents a considerable burden when—as in the school we visited—as many as seven hundred gifted students study under the same roof. On the other hand, it creates opportunities for youngsters not previously deemed gifted to climb aboard.[19]

Between grades 8 and 9, the TDSB shifts its approach from self-contained programs to "partial integration." Now students identified as gifted are channeled—based on where they live—to one of a handful of high schools with special curricula and classes in core academic subjects. In the whole sprawling district, however, just six of one-hundred-plus high schools operate gifted programs, which speaks both to the tight limits that TDSB places on students who can be designated as "gifted" and, perhaps, to the low priority that this form of education holds for local officials. It also creates long commutes through a congested metropolis for many young people.[20]

Seemingly at cross-purposes with the creation of gifted education programs in a half-dozen high schools in one district is Ontario's policy push for inclusion and integration. Yet that's the approach adopted by Toronto's Catholic School Board, which operates no special programs for gifted students at the high school level, believing that each school can address their needs with suitable courses and activities, including AP and International Baccalaureate classes.

We visited the TDSB high school with the city's largest gifted ed enrollment and learned that its leaders, too, believe gifted learners should be integrated as much as possible with everybody else and should not turn into a separate society. That's a challenge, considering that one-third of this school is designated as gifted. The principal would favor shrinking that fraction. He understands that high-ability kids need challenging classes but doesn't want them to think of themselves as superior, or other students to view themselves as lacking.[21] We encountered similar sentiments in many places. Yet placements in schools such as this are much sought by parents, and tightly capping the gifted enrollment in this school would bring its own backlash.

Meanwhile, parallel to but separate from the special education version of giftedness, some Ontario boards operate—or allow individual secondary schools to initiate—magnet-type programs for high-ability, high-achieving, or highly motivated students who do not get "identified" as gifted or who may bail out of the special ed system. TDSB has a number of these, such as the TOPS science program and other offerings aimed at strong pupils in the Marc Garneau and Bloor Collegiate Institutes.[22] Admission to such schools and programs—including dual-enrollment options with universities—is selective, based on both grades and exam scores. But they're schools of choice: nobody is assigned to them.

This is part of yet another Toronto policy, which is to encourage specialized high schools and programs, some of them heavily academic (e.g., International Baccalaureate[23]), others focused on arts, sports, "cyber studies," and more special interests.[24] Many of these have their own prerequisites, sometimes academic, and applicants are often evaluated holistically—that is, very differently from the special education version of giftedness with its single-minded focus on IQ scores.

Toronto is not alone. The Halton district, for example, has International Baccalaureate high schools with selective admission. And independent private schools, such as the University of Toronto Schools, offer further options for educating high-ability kids—as long as parents can afford their stiff tuitions.[25]

Besides the flexibility and autonomy for both schools and students that comes with this approach—and the additional capacity to serve gifted pupils beyond the 2 percent limit—holistic admissions means schools can screen applicants not just for talent but also for prior achievement and motivation, thereby avoiding the problem of adept test takers who don't care to study hard. On the flip side, this approach may also mean that such programs are less apt to be sought by, or to admit, kids who depend on the education system to spot their abilities and cultivate them. In other words, school-developed programs combined with choice and holistic admission may give extra advantage to high-achieving kids with motivated parents and good elementary schools while doing less for equally able youngsters who haven't been encouraged by the system. (This approach may also leave out "double exceptionality" students who combine giftedness with, say, a learning or speech impediment. Such youngsters are more apt to be found in the special ed version of gifted education.[26])

DIVERSITY AND DISADVANTAGE

Other reviews have praised Ontario education for its progress in reducing achievement gaps. This has not, however, been a complete success, especially for the province's Francophone students, who do far worse on just about every assessment measure (including PISA) than its English-speaking pupils.

Ontario resembles Canada as a whole in the proportion of PISA takers who make it into the high-scoring ranks. While that accomplishment is distributed across the population more evenhandedly than in many countries, it remains less than fully equitable. For every Canadian fifteen-year-old from the lowest SES quartile who reaches levels 5 or 6 in math, science, or reading, nearly four students from the highest quartile get there—about the same ratio as in Finland and markedly more equal than the OECD average and the U.S. record. When viewed in relation to parental education, the percentage of high scorers in all three subjects among students with at least one college-graduate parent is thrice the percentage among those whose parents did not complete high school. Again, that ratio is among the world's lowest, if still a distance from true equality. (See appendix tables A.3 and A.4 for more information.)

DILEMMAS, CHALLENGES, AND TAKEAWAYS

That Canada's strong PISA results recently slipped has already catalyzed considerable concern, although the focus has been on how the average score compares with other countries, not the proportion of young Canadians earning top marks.

Much like the United States in the No Child Left Behind era, Canada has concentrated its education energies in recent years on boosting low achievers to a minimal level of proficiency in core subjects. Although Pan-Canadian Assessment results are reported at four levels of performance, most of the emphasis is given to the proportion of students who reach level 2, the "expected level." How many attain levels 3 ("above expected level") and 4 ("advanced") commands scant attention.

Ontario's own assessment program is keyed to grade-level standards and here, too, the results focus on how many students attain that standard—and then sustain it in later grades. On a four-tier scale, 3 is the "standard," and Ontario educators and policy leaders are keen to move at least 75 percent of students to that level in reading, writing, and math. (No mention of science.) The assessment results are explicit, even voluminous, in slicing and dicing data on how many are getting from 1 to 2 and 2 to 3. Yet those reports seldom even bother to distinguish how many students reach level 4. Nor is it clear, psychometrically, how well these tests measure gains among high achievers. They surely were not designed for that purpose. In sum, as in the United States, there's plenty of interest in getting kids up to a standard but not much attention paid to those already above it.[27]

Insofar as the education of high-ability students may one day become a more pressing concern in Ontario, a host of tough questions arises. Should giftedness continue to be treated as an "exceptionality" within special education—especially when districts such as Toronto then place a 2 percent limit on the student population that may qualify? (It's hard to picture such a limit being placed on an actual disability!) What does it mean to have a province-wide law that requires any youngsters identified as gifted to be served by the cognizant local board but fails to spell out how—or even whether—such identification will take place or what kinds of services must be provided? If giftedness is indeed a bona fide "exceptionality," how much sense does it make to wait until third or fourth grade to look for it? And to neglect the preparation of instructors for such students? Moreover, how sensible is it for local boards to operate selective-admission magnet schools that afford choices to high-ability students in tandem with a heavily regulated special ed version of gifted education that assigns students to schools?

As we write, much about special education is under review within Ontario's education ministry (including the very definition of "giftedness"), and new priorities may emerge in coming months. The Ministry's policy team understands that the traditional "separateness" of special ed for some kids makes less sense in an era of individualized instruction for every child. They're also aware that, if recent special ed trends continue, Ontario will soon find itself with 20 percent of all students deemed "exceptional." While some of those children, perhaps many, really do require additional support and resources, a special ed designation under current policies carries substantial administrative burdens and costs.

The same policy team also realizes, however, that any major overhaul faces heavy fire from multiple interests that believe they need and benefit from the "exceptionality" designation and the resources and accommodations that come with it. Prominent among these interests are parents of gifted learners. One veteran participant-observer predicts that if gifted education were removed from special education, it would rapidly vanish from Ontario schools. From his perspective, "exceptionality" helps protect gifted education. No doubt many parents see matters the same way and will fight anything that looks like a rollback of existing benefits—and they have plenty of political allies and could muster more if needed.

Pushing against them are budgetary considerations, the "learning for all" and "differentiated instruction" emphases that today are both faddish among educators and seemingly equitable in concept, plus widespread Canadian aversion to the "elitism" associated with distinctive education offerings for high-ability youngsters.

Time will of course tell how this plays out. Today in Ontario, however, whether a high-ability child ends up with a suitably challenging and supportive education hinges to a considerable extent on luck: having the right parents and enough money, being spotted by teachers, and living in a place with suitable opportunities. It works pretty well for the smart and fortunate, but the picture is dimmer for equally able youngsters from other circumstances.

Although Ontario cannot be said today to place much emphasis on the education of high-ability youngsters, it does illustrate both the up- and downsides of including giftedness within special education. On the one hand, children who qualify as gifted under the definitions used by local school boards (if indeed they use any at all) are thereafter entitled to individualized education that is supposed to be tailored to their learning needs. On the other hand, practices vary so widely from board to board that where a family lives within the province—and how aggressive the parents are—winds up mattering a lot. Moreover, limits on budget and program participation, and the concentration of gifted programs in a handful of schools, reduce the benefit of this version of gifted education—which also explains why Toronto, at least, has developed a number of secondary school options for high achievers outside the special ed framework. Instead of placing giftedness within that rigid framework (as a handful of U.S. states have done), we find greater merit in the broader individualization of children's education and progress through the K–12 system—a suggestion that we revisit in chapter 19.

17

Western Australia: In for the Long Haul

AUSTRALIA IS AWASH in education reforms at both the national and state levels, complicated by the fact that it has huge private and Catholic primary-secondary sectors, all government-subsidized and -regulated. Most of the responsibility for schooling—policies, regulations, teacher certifications, and much of the financing—rests with the country's six states, although, as in the United States, the federal government also plays a multifaceted and often-controversial role, now including a national curriculum and assessments aligned with it.[1]

Policies and practices concerning high-ability students at the primary-secondary level belong exclusively to the states, however, meaning that in order to look at gifted education Down Under we had to focus on one of them. We chose Western Australia (W.A.), the largest by area, fourth by population, and overwhelmingly rural outside the Perth metro area. W.A. takes gifted education seriously, at least in the public school sector, and does well on measures such as PISA—as does Australia generally—including a goodly proportion of high scorers. Its officials were also receptive to this study and proved quite helpful as we went about it.

Western Australia enrolls about 430,000 primary and secondary students (similar to Nevada), two-thirds of them in government-operated schools.[2] Unlike several countries in this study, enrollments here—both public and private—are rising along with the population, which is growing even faster in W.A. than in the country as a whole, due largely to the state's robust natural-resource-based economy.

Public education here is run centrally by the state education department, which operates schools in eight regions, though regionalization appears to be giving way to a burgeoning list of semiautonomous schools, each with considerable say over budget and personnel and directly answerable to department officials in Perth, not to a regional office.

In the 2012 round of PISA, Australia surpassed the OECD average (and the United States) in math, although it trailed eight other countries in our sample. (See figure 2.5.) Fifteen percent of test takers scored at the high end. (See table 17.1.) In Australia, as in America, individual states may also obtain PISA scores, and Western Australia did somewhat better than the nation, with 18 percent of its test takers earning math scores of 5 or 6. (The large states of New South Wales and Victoria came in at 17 and 12 percent, respectively.)[3]

Australia fared better still in reading, lagging only five other countries in this study (the four Asian nations plus Canada) and had 12 percent scoring at the high end, more than the United States and the OECD average.[4] Western Australia had the highest mean reading score among Australian states and tied (with New South Wales) for the top percentage of high-scoring pupils.[5]

Science, however, was the country's brightest spot on PISA, outdoing all but three of our dozen countries (including the United States) and getting 14 percent of students into PISA's top ranks. Australia's TIMSS and PIRLs scores show respectable but uneven results, particularly at the high end.

On Australia's own national assessment, W.A. students were about average in generating high scores, generally lagging New South Wales (and the Australian Capital Territory around Canberra), but about the same as Victoria and ahead of Queensland.[6]

In most of the countries that we examined, we paid scant attention to private schools because they do not occupy large chunks of

TABLE 17.1   Australia average scale scores and percentages of high scorers
on international assessments over time, with trend lines

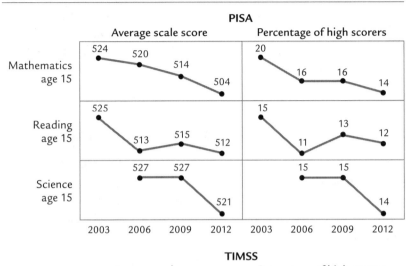

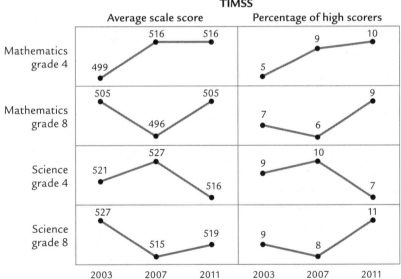

education real estate. In Australia, however, where they enroll one in three students, they're not to be dismissed.[7]

Countrywide, Australia's independent school pupils rack up substantially higher PISA scores than students in government schools, with those enrolled in Catholic schools approximately in the middle, although these differences shrink when scores are controlled for socioeconomic status.

GIFTED EDUCATION FUNDAMENTALS

Western Australia has sailed a fairly steady course in gifted and talented education since the mid 1970s. The program has weathered multiple political changes and policy cycles, although its managers have been moved hither and thither within the bureaucracy. They remain able, committed, and forward looking, albeit firmly attached to several core precepts that also function as constraints.

The government sector's Gifted and Talented Program is grounded in a commitment to social justice ("these kids have needs, too, and society has an obligation to meet them"). We heard less about human capital development or economic competitiveness as grounds for cultivating high-ability students. Consistent with their philosophical orientation, administrators strive to give every youngster a fair shot at entering the program, although it's bounded by exam-based admissions and fixed limits on numbers.

The Catholic schools of W.A. are more ambivalent about gifted education. They insist that they're meeting students' varied needs and they supply guidance to schools and teachers for how to do this with high-ability youngsters, but church doctrine generally declines to single out individuals or groups as special.[8] Still, these schools enjoy considerable autonomy, and market forces are nudging more of them to take seriously the education of gifted children.

The state's independent schools are all over the lot regarding gifted pupils. Some are expensive, high-status prep schools with traditions of lofty standards and successful university placements. Others are new, sometimes cheap (living more on government subsidy than parent fees), and espouse education views that range from "everyone is equal" to enthusiastic ability grouping and acceleration.

Because they receive public subsidies (though they can also charge additional fees), independent schools are not permitted to turn anyone away on the basis of ability. On the other hand, they give scholarships and other preferences to the students they want.

Western Australia isn't big on school choice, beyond the offerings of its robust Catholic and independent sectors. Gifted education is essentially the only realm within the state sector where choices exist. At the secondary level, the gifted program offers qualifying students their pick of schools. Otherwise, students not opting—and able to pay—for private schooling must attend the public school that corresponds to their place of residence.[9]

PRIMARY AND MIDDLE GRADES

Through grade 4, Western Australia has no organized statewide program or systematic policy for educating high-ability youngsters, leaving this up to individual schools and teachers to work out as they and children's parents see fit.

Some regions have experimented with gifted programs for young children and have pushed to widen awareness of the value of early identification and cultivation, such as the Early Years Extension program in the North Metro region.[10] Statewide, however, there's no extra funding for such activities, though the Education Department supplies instruments that teachers and parents can use to identify gifted kids at a young age. Generic policies definitely encourage individualization and differentiation to meet children's varied needs. But that seems to be the end of it. (Parents may, however, turn to several private sources of advice, support, and materials for determining whether their young children have exceptional talent and helping to nurture it.)[11]

In fourth grade (ages 9–10), all children in public schools—about 19,000 of them—sit for tests intended to identify candidates for the gifted education program that begins in fifth grade. Such testing is universal and free (though to keep costs within bounds, the Education Department recycles old multiple-choice tests that it knows should be replaced). This produces the population of children eligible for the statewide Primary Extension and Challenge (PEAC) Program.

It's limited to 2.5 percent of the pupil population, however, and that number includes artistic and "language" giftedness as well as the academic kind.

PEAC operates in the fifth, sixth, and seventh grades—although it's losing seventh grade, which in 2015 will move to the secondary level as part of Australia's new national curriculum.[12] Currently, PEAC consists of part-time pull-out classes that meet for half a day per week over ten weeks (with three such cycles annually). This takes place at various centers to which parents must bring their children.[13] The sprawling North Metro region, for example, with about two hundred elementary schools, has eight PEAC centers with an ever-changing menu of course offerings, devised by teachers but intended also to respond to children's interests.[14]

The Education Department makes extra staffing available to cover these offerings—teachers being the main cost—and a bit of cash as well. For example, a 180-school region gets 11.2 additional full-time-equivalent teachers to instruct and manage its PEAC classes.

Largely unchanged for two decades and lacking any systematic evaluation or other means of determining its efficacy, PEAC may be reshaped or replaced in the coming years. Department staff have proposed creating full-time gifted classes in some primary schools.

HIGH SCHOOL

Western Australia's secondary-level gifted program is more systematic, beginning with the fact that it's full time. Participants are again limited to 2.5 percent of all students in the public sector and are again selected via examination. (Those seeking to participate in arts- or language-focused schools must also audition or perform and be interviewed.)

Interested students—it's voluntary—take a four-part, half-day test, administered at a dozen sites around the state, and covering math and science, reading comprehension, nonverbal reasoning, and writing. The test is multiple-choice except for its writing portion.

About 2,500 sixth graders go through the exam process, and roughly one-third of them end up being placed in full-time gifted classes or schools. About 500 enter academic programs, which carry on through the full five—soon to be six—years of high school, and another 350 join art-centered programs.

Private cram schools and tutors are available to help students prep for the exams, and 10 to 15 percent of test takers patronize them, mainly middle-class youngsters whose families can afford it. Though W.A. doesn't release its old tests, other Australian states do, so it's possible to access materials with which to cram. We were told, however, that there's little evidence that such cramming does much good.

It takes about two months to get back the test results, and families may appeal the results if they're displeased. (About 150 to 200 do so each year, though few appeals lead to score changes.) Then begins a long, intricate "matching" process by which students' preferences and scores are rank-ordered to determine who gets into which programs.[15]

Seventeen W.A. high schools house gifted programs, all but one of them in the Perth metro area, and students may apply for—and rank their preferences among—up to three of these. Besides two gifted-only high schools, fifteen programs—eight academic, two concentrating on languages, and five on the arts—operate within comprehensive high schools. Collectively, they offer about 940 places a year to entering eighth (soon seventh) graders, of which about 850 slots get taken up. (Some programs aren't popular with high-scoring students or aren't conveniently located.)

Perth Modern—the gifted-only academic school—has been entirely selective for just a few years. The institution itself is a century old and was originally selective, but lost that status during the sixties and only recently, with much political Sturm und Drang, was it reborn as the equivalent of an American "exam school." It includes a dorm component so students from the "outback" can attend, although parents must cover most of that cost.[16]

The rest of the secondary Gifted and Talented Programs are integrated to varying degrees into their host schools, which get extra staff and some cash to accommodate them. (At one that we visited, that amounts to two FTE teachers and about A$13,500 annually.) Building leaders determine how best to manage the gifted students within a comprehensive setting. We visited one where separate classes vanish after tenth grade, as we saw in Germany, with courses during the final two years open to all of the school's pupils. The upshot is that gifted kids end up comprising a large fraction of the school's challenging academic classes but not many vocational classes.

By the end of high school, it can be hard to distinguish students who entered via the gifted route from able, ambitious youngsters who came to the school because they live nearby. Hence administrators at one school we visited estimated that "at year twelve, half the high achievers were never in the Gifted and Talented Program." Obviously, selection into it isn't predestination. (Of course, one might also wonder whether the gifted program was necessary and how much value it actually added. Due to the lack of credible external evaluations, it's impossible to know for sure.)

Not every teacher wants to teach gifted students or tangle with their "challenging" parents. At one secondary school, fifteen instructors each get paid A$1,500 extra to staff the gifted and talented classrooms. Referring to the challenge of finding enough teachers for the program, the principal sounded relieved when he said "We manage to fill it," but staff members aren't exactly rushing to volunteer. It takes extra effort to plan for and stay ahead of these young people and to deal with both their own idiosyncrasies (such as a know-it-all attitude) and their parents' ambitions and agitations.

DIVERSITY AND DISADVANTAGE

As we have seen almost everywhere, girls in Australia do better than boys at reading, while boys get higher scores in math. In the 2012 PISA math round, 12 percent of female Aussie test takers earned scores of 5 or 6, compared with 17 percent of males. On the reading test that year, 15 percent of females scored similarly, versus 9 percent of males. (W.A. displays a wider boy-girl gap in math than other Australian states, although its reading gap was the narrowest.)[17]

In terms of socioeconomic backgrounds, Australia produced slightly more equitable high-end results in math than the OECD average, with approximately six high scorers from the lowest SES quartile for every twenty-seven from the top quartile. That ratio of nearly 1:5 is substantially better than the 1:8 ratio recorded by the United

States. This general narrative holds for PISA reading and science, too. (See appendix table A.3.)

Comparisons based on parents' education show a similar pattern regardless of subject. On PISA math, for example, 5 percent of Australians without high school graduate parents reached the math score that corresponds to NAEP's Advanced level, versus almost 20 percent of those with at least one college-graduate parent. Corresponding figures for the United States are 2 percent and nearly 12 percent. (See appendix table A.4.)

Children from indigenous backgrounds score significantly lower than other children—but first-generation immigrants (many of them Asian) score higher than native-born Australians. Predictably, students attending school in metropolitan areas do better than those in small towns and rural communities.[18]

DILEMMAS, CHALLENGES, AND TAKEAWAYS

Plans are afoot to update gifted education in Western Australia. In late 2013, the Education Department's director general approved reforms developed by program staff, including some that her predecessors had avoided. It will take several years to implement them, however, and it's unclear whether the budgetary challenges will easily be surmounted. Key shifts at the primary level include creation of some full-time classes as well as part-time pull-out classes for gifted youngsters who eschew the full-time option. (New exams will also replace the antiquated qualification tests.) Supplemental programs will continue but will feature online options, particularly designed for children for whom transportation to another school or center is impractical.

Planned changes at the secondary level include new efforts at quality control and accountability, with performance criteria spelled out for programs and the schools that house them, regular evaluations, and grounds for terminating weak programs. That would be a worthy move, since the effectiveness of W.A.'s gifted education offerings is currently unknown. Absent worthwhile "value-added" metrics, the schools end up judging themselves, and being judged by the department, the press, and others on the basis of student scores on Australia's national assessments and, at the high school level, the country's common university entrance test.[19] There's some irony here, considering how some of the same school leaders railed in our presence about Australia's obsession with testing, the stress it creates in students, and the resulting inattention to the many things they do to develop the "whole child," gifted or otherwise.

Also in the works for gifted programs in W.A., as well as state schools in general, is a new, student-centered funding model—one effect of which is supposed to be budget neutrality with respect to changes in gifted education. In other words, planned program alterations aren't supposed to add to the state budget.[20]

Though most of the changes seem obvious, even overdue, they aren't easy to make. Principals of other schools, for example, hate to lose their smart kids to schools with gifted programs. That kind of political pushback, plus budget constraints, may be why we detected no stomach in W.A. for loosening the 2.5 percent cap, widening the definition of gifted and talented, or easing back on test-based selection.[21] But increasingly autonomous schools can take steps themselves to augment the state program. One high school that we visited, for example, operates its own program for "high performance learners," really a track within the school that flags a couple of classes for swifter pupils who don't qualify for the Gifted and Talented Program. This seems to function as a "second prize" that also helps the school compete for able pupils who live within its prosperous catchment area but might otherwise go to private schools.[22]

Thus what initially struck us as an arbitrary constraint on how many students can benefit from Western Australia's earnest efforts to do right by its high-ability children may not function as an insurmountable barrier after all. We admit, though, that it still seems odd for the state to assert (whether from conviction or budget realities or both) that its "official" program offerings will accept no more than twenty-five students out of a thousand.

Limiting pupil numbers in this way would not likely go over well in the United States, but we could profit by adopting W.A.'s practice of universal screening of fourth graders as well as its purposeful establishment of gifted-learner mini-schools (including some focused on the arts) inside a number of high schools. Also intriguing is the practice in some of those schools (as in Germany) of recombining the gifted pupils with the larger student population during the concluding years of secondary education.

PART III

Toward
the Future

18

What Have
We Learned?

PULLING TOGETHER what we have learned about the policies and practices of other countries, gained from on-the-ground informants and knowledgeable advisors as well as our site visits and other sources, we see five common threads that merit the attention of U.S. educators and policy makers.

First, not surprisingly, countries with education systems that generally do well on international measures also tend to do pretty well at producing high scorers. (Recall figure 2.5.) Unfortunately, that does not mean moving the whole U.S. curve to the right—important though this is—will "catch us up" in terms of high achievers. The rising-tide-lifts-all-boats formula won't work very well here. We also need to float some different boats. Too few young Americans make it into the ranks of high scorers today for curve-shifting to yield enough additional high scorers. (See figure 18.1.) As the hypothetical curve shows, shifting both the U.S. and Korean scores rightward by fifty points (while keeping the present cutoff for PISA level 5) actually widens the difference between the two countries in the percentage of test takers above that cutoff. And such a shift would accomplish even less for disadvantaged kids, because so few now fall within our modest proportion of high achievers. For the United States to do anywhere

FIGURE 18.1   PISA math 2012: Actual and hypothetical score
distributions for the United States and Korea

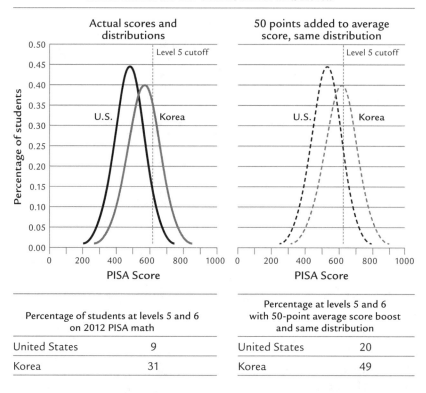

Percentage of students at levels 5 and 6 on 2012 PISA math		Percentage at levels 5 and 6 with 50-point average score boost and same distribution	
United States	9	United States	20
Korea	31	Korea	49

near well enough at the high end—particularly for poor kids—we must
do more than raise the average.

Second, although some countries do better than others—and most do
better than we do—at including disadvantaged kids among their high
scorers, not many bend over backward to draw such children into
their gifted education programs. So it remains murky just how much
the stronger high-end showings among disadvantaged youngsters are
culturally determined—in some societies even poor, ill-educated parents push their kids ahead—and how much they are the handiwork of
the education system itself. Most likely some of each.

We aren't the first to observe that the "Asian tigers" generally
put a premium on education. Parents in these lands see school (and

university) success as a path to the good life for their children. So, it appears, do parents who emigrate from Asian countries to America. For them and those back home who share their beliefs and values, competition is common, success is respected, and just about everyone—kids included—believes that hard work matters more than innate ability in determining who gets ahead.[1] In their communities, you seldom hear a child, parent, or teacher say of another student, "He's smarter." They're likelier to say, "He works harder" or "She studies more." Which is another way of saying "Maybe I could, too." It's as if they've been channeling Carol Dweck, Angela Duckworth, or Paul Tough.

Fierce competition is less common in Western cultures. Indeed, many educators deplore it and try to keep it out of their schools (as government officials are now struggling to do in several Asian countries, most visibly in Korea). More often encountered on our side of the Pacific are both a political and philosophical commitment to equality and the belief that exceptional achievement arises as much from immutable personal qualities (like innate intelligence), wealth, influence, and luck as from ambition and hard work.

Yet Asian competitiveness cannot adequately account for countries' success in propelling low-SES children and those with poorly educated parents into the ranks of high scorers on PISA and other international assessments. Examine appendix tables A.3 and A.4, notably the columns delineating high scorers from the bottom ESCS quartile and from families with "low-education" parents, and you will see several European and Anglophone nations holding their own near the top of the list—just as you will observe the United States at or near the bottom on every single table. We see that Asia isn't the only continent where schools are places one goes to learn and gain access to the opportunities that follow, and where advancing educational equity extends across the full achievement spectrum.

Third, almost everywhere we looked, today's gifted-student opportunities in the early and middle grades are uneven and often thin, sometimes almost haphazard. There may be an "underground" array of unusual schools, some of them private, that some families with high-ability children find their way into, but this is haphazard, too, often costly, and the schools are sometimes far from home. The regular public education system may make limited provision for individual pupils to accelerate by entering school a year earlier or skipping a grade. A few places (Ontario and Taiwan, as well as a handful of American states) regard the education of gifted children as part of "special education," which in principle should entitle such children to a panoply of instructional opportunities tailored to their individual needs. But it doesn't work out quite that way. Along with the familiar bureaucratic and procedural complexities of special education, seemingly arbitrary limits on children's participation and services get imposed by budget constraints, program caps, and rigid test-score cutoffs. A recurring example is the absence of transportation for gifted students to the schools and centers to which they're assigned.

Special education aside, what we found for high-ability students in the primary and middle grades generally sorts into three categories: (1) systems that espouse "differentiated instruction" in every school and want each classroom to be inclusive and uniform—and therefore offer nothing distinctive for smart kids beyond what regular teachers may provide;[2] (2) places that provide supplemental gifted ed programs of various kinds, such as part-time pull-out classes during the regular day or extra learning opportunities outside school; and (3) a few places with entirely separate classrooms or schools.

In our experience, the third approach most clearly signals a full commitment to developing these children to the max, although some versions of the second come close. In nearly all the countries that we looked at—little Singapore is the main exception—high-ability children without parents to navigate and supplement for them are pretty much at the mercy of a varied collection of districts, schools, and teachers to provide them with a little or a lot (or nothing) by way of learning opportunities that make the most of their potential. Some of those schools and teachers are better trained than others, some are more motivated, and some have greater resources to bring to bear. Even Singapore, systematic as it is from grade 4 onward, limits its offerings to a tiny fraction of children—and access appears at least somewhat vulnerable to private-pay cramming.[3] And while Western Australia is comprehensive in screening kids for giftedness, its program offerings in the primary and middle years are still patchy.

Fourth, in contrast to the earlier grades, every place we visited has some upper secondary schools attended primarily by high-ability, high-achieving young people. Because the supply of such schools never equals the demand, and because most schools of this sort want only top students to enroll, they typically practice selective admission. (One may fairly wonder whether they'd be as esteemed and coveted if they were *not* selective.) Unfortunately, both their mechanisms of selection and the limited availability (or high cost) of suitable preparation tend to dampen participation by able students from disadvantaged circumstances.

It seems unfair to such children—hypocritical, too—for an education system democratically to avow inclusion at the primary level but then practice selective admission at the secondary level. Yes, this may benefit children who start slow and then speed up their learning during the middle grades, but overall it ends up favoring kids from families that read stories at bedtime and go to museums and historic sites, that can pay for tutoring, juku, and other outside help, and that encourage their children to shoot for prestigious high schools. It also assumes, perhaps without thinking, that smart poor kids who rival their more prosperous peers in achievement at age eight will still be their equals at age fourteen. That's simply naïve—and contradicted by systematic data from England. We are not faulting selective admission at the secondary level. Rather, we're saying that, if the goal is to boost the prospects for able disadvantaged students to succeed in the high school admissions process (and then in the schools themselves and the universities that follow), it's important to start younger and stick with these kids along the way. And yes, unless a country's pupil population is plummeting, it's important also to expand the capacity of selective secondary schools—and move toward admission procedures that rely less on intelligence testing and more on a child's overall profile and track record. The point is to give effective primary and middle schools more opportunities to work with high-ability children from disadvantaged circumstances while increasing the system's capacity to educate more such youngsters in the best schools the society can create. This maximizes these kids' chances to excel academically, to gain admission to suitably challenging high schools and universities, and eventually to join the front ranks of a country's intellectual, scientific, and techno-logical leadership.

Fifth, there's no denying that culture, family, and personal qualities matter. As Amanda Ripley observed in the three countries (Korea, Finland, Poland) where she tracked the experiences of American high school students, attitudes toward the role of education and the function of schools have an enormous effect on what happens inside them. When a society sees schools as places for students to learn so as to get ahead, learning tends to occur there. But where young people view them as places to make friends, play ball, show off their duds, and plan for the prom, a lot less learning will occur.

One's own attributes also make a difference in one's educational performance. Whether we focus on self-control and "grit" à la Angela Duckworth, resilience à la Paul Tough, effort and "growth mindsets" à la Carol Dweck, "purpose" à la William Damon, or "conscientious-ness" à la Arthur Poropat, we have ample evidence that a person's beliefs, hopes, values, and behavior patterns affect his or her success. Some experts and observers—Dweck herself and Malcolm Gladwell both belong on this list—go so far as to pooh-pooh notions of "talent" and "ability," even to find them dysfunctional ("I'm smart so I don't have to work hard").[4]

We respond that while grit, goals, and gumption clearly influence what one accomplishes—and the more of these one possesses, the better off one is—it's also a fact that people differ in ways that such attributes often cannot trump. To insist otherwise is simply wishful and, for policy purposes, a kind of tranquilizer. Neither of us could become a concert pianist or great painter no matter how hard we might try. Some people can balance on roller skates sooner than others. Some sing better, perhaps because they have perfect pitch, or maybe just a beguiling voice. In academic matters, too, people differ. Some are born with learning disabilities. Others learn fast. They may read at age five or learn to multiply by second grade.[5] Some learn history faster than math or theoretical physics faster than poetry. Some win the Nobel Prize in economics—but most don't. That cannot, how-ever, be satisfactorily explained, much less predicted, by intelligence testing. Some people don't win the Nobel Prize because they want to be nurses, chefs, soccer players, or computer programmers rather than economists. And there's no denying the advantage of being "smart," just as it's a big help to have education-minded parents and the wherewithal to make more choices. It's wonderful to grow up in a home that also fosters resilience and ambition. But that's by no means the whole story.

There's also a policy risk in relying on a link between character attributes and individual accomplishment: that mode of thinking tends to let the education system and its schools and teachers off the hook, as if one's fate hinges mainly on factors quite beyond the reach of education policies, personnel, and practices.

We recognize limits on what schools in free societies can do to compensate for children's families and environments. We also understand the limits on what policies and programs can change when it comes to personal attributes, societal attitudes, and family priorities.[6] Yet that's no justification for fatalism—or for letting either the student or the school avoid responsibility. Schools governed by sound policies and decently resourced can definitely work on children's sense of self, helping them to understand what they are capable of accomplishing and what's needed to get there. Schools can move a speedy learner faster—and help a less-speedy child discover that slow-and-steady covers much terrain. Schools can obviously supply a rich buffet of skills and knowledge from the basic to the most advanced. And schools can do plenty to level playing fields such that better opportunities exist for students—both the speedy and the more deliberate kind—who want to learn more, and to help poor children get a fair shot at the best the system has to offer.

The United States has been working hard to level upward from the bottom, and that's a plus. We surely have it within us also to push upward at the top—and to bounce many more children into that territory. Our education system's porous, decentralized, forgiving, and "second-chance" qualities can help in this regard, as can our dual concerns with equity and international competitiveness. We have some good examples to point to—just not enough of them—and, while we ought to be embarrassed, even angry with ourselves, over the superior performance of other countries on many of the metrics that we've been examining, we ought not be intimidated. Nobody is doing this perfectly and nobody else's system lends itself to complete replication on American shores. In the next—and final—chapter, we offer our best thinking as to what the United States can and should do for itself.

19

Moves America Should Make

BASED ON PROMISING (and worrying) practices that we observed in other countries, as well as research by others and our own judgment, we suggest ten steps that would lead to better education for high-ability American youngsters while also adding more disadvantaged students to their ranks.

First and arguably most important, let's place this topic firmly on the policy agenda and rekindle the debate about how to have a society that prizes excellence as well as equity and pursues both—much as it deals with "pluribus" and "unum" simultaneously—and strives ceaselessly to calibrate the balance. Perhaps we need another blue-ribbon *Nation at Risk* commission to ring the bell once more for economic competitiveness, excellence, and equal opportunity, all at once. Let's work this challenge into the writings of pundits, the speeches of public officials, the chatter of talk shows, the priorities of philanthropists, the platforms of political parties, the studies of think tanks, and the deliberations of policy makers. Let's press them (and others) to understand that American prosperity depends on raising the education ceiling as well as lifting the floor, that it's unfair to smart kids to neglect their education or assume it will take care of itself, that it's imprudent for any country to settle for importing top talent rather than growing more of its own, and that it's downright un-American to let the ranks of tomorrow's scientists, innovators, and entrepreneurs fill primarily with those who grew up in privileged circumstances. Let's remind ourselves, too, that even the able and privileged—and their often-smug parents—need encouragement to pursue intellectually demanding paths and not settle for the lazy road to comfort and yet more privilege.

Second, let's strengthen our data systems and amplify our research agenda so that in time we can better understand what's happening to high-ability students and how well our policies, schools, and interventions are working for them. This recommendation, plus the next one, is where Washington could be most helpful. It can boost the capacity of the National Center for Education Statistics to do this better, augment the National Assessment's ability to track high-end achievement, sustain our participation in international measures like TIMSS and PISA, and encourage states, districts, and individual schools to participate directly in such measures.[1] Federal officials can also ensure that the research and evaluation agendas of the Department of Education and other agencies highlight the issues we've been flagging.[2]

Third, when Congress finally buckles down to reauthorizing the No Child Left Behind Act, the seminal law governing the biggest federal K-12 program whereby billions are disbursed each year to boost the education of disadvantaged youngsters, lawmakers ought not again settle for drawing a line called "proficiency" and tying school accountability solely to how many kids get across that line. Instead, federal incentives and sanctions—insofar as Congress retains these in the face of heavy fire directed against NCLB—should catalyze growth by students across the achievement spectrum, including its upper end. Schools should be judged by how well they optimize the attainments of all their pupils. Parallel shifts should be made in every state- or locally crafted system of standards, assessments, and results-based accountability. But for this to work as it should, the standards must be ambitious, the assessment system must not clamp a low psychometric ceiling on its measuring tools—computer-adaptive testing holds great promise here—and the resulting data must be disaggregated so it's clear which kids and groups are achieving at the high end as well as at the low.

Those three suggestions ought to be relatively easy and not expensive. Transparency matters across the spectrum, as do incentives. Much as NCLB drew belated attention (via its demand for data disaggregation) to gaps that people were unaware of (or had chosen to ignore), so will clearer data on gifted students—how many there are, how they are educated, how well they achieve, and which among them fare better than others. This will illumine a corner of American education that today is lamentably dark. It will enable policy makers to monitor schools and districts to make sure they're doing right by all kids.[3] And it will eventually benefit high-ability students, especially those whose potential—and performance—is most apt to be hidden today.

Now we turn to some heavier lifts.

Fourth, take advantage of universal screening. The United States—and millions of its young people—would benefit if we systematically identified children whose education could and should be beefed up. So let's exploit the fact that almost every public school student in the land now takes state exams in (at least) reading and math from third grade onward, and that this practice is likely to continue. Let's identify, say, the 5 percent with highest scores in a school, district, or state.[4] Do this in third or fourth grade, much as Singapore and Western Australia do, but don't use IQ or aptitude tests. Use existing—and universal—achievement metrics.[5] This will, with decent reliability, ferret out the high achievers who, there's good evidence to show, are the kids likeliest to benefit from opportunities to move faster and learn more.[6]

Do this at the school level, the district level, or (in big districts) the subdistrict level so as to spread the top 5 percent across communities, diversify the qualifying population, and not just favor upper-middle-class kids. (That's why Texas offers university admission to the top 10 percent of graduates of every high school rather than the top 10 percent of graduates statewide.[7])

Then ask teachers in every elementary school to nominate another 5 percent who may not be top scorers on state tests but who get excellent grades or simply, in the teachers' view, have unusual potential. Encourage them to look with extra care for children from poor, minority, and immigrant families, and to look holistically, not just on the basis of grades and scores. Equip them with screening tools to help with such identifications.[8] Invite students and parents to come forward if they would like to be considered. But also admonish principals to develop schoolwide methods for dealing with parental pressures, outside influencers, and allegations of favoritism or discrimination.

Combine these two steps and we've identified about 10 percent of students who, by the age of nine or ten, are already high achievers or, in their teachers' eyes, could be. This is a generous-enough definition of the gifted population to mitigate charges of elitism and dampen the competition to participate that is apt to work against those lacking educated or driven parents. We understand that this plan is based primarily on early signs of academic prowess and potential, especially in reading and math, and does not do justice to other forms of giftedness, such as musical or athletic talents. So be it, at least for now. These other challenges need tackling, too, but not as urgently.

Mindful that a child's achievement in the early grades has relatively more to do with background and upbringing and less to do with school effects than is the case with older students, it's important for the education system also to maintain later on-ramps to the options we describe below (as well as face-saving off-ramps for students who turn out to be ill-suited to such options or lack interest in them). Between grades 6 and 9, schools and teachers should look for additional kids who by then have emerged as high achievers. Scores on state tests are universally available through grade 8, but so, at this stage, are a host of other metrics and signals, some of them objective (such as the different tests already in use by "talent search" programs[9]) and some in the form of judgments by teachers, counselors, and others who have regular contact with young people, in school and out.

Still more strong learners will emerge during high school. As Hoxby and others have shown, thousands of disadvantaged students manage to excel all the way through today's K–12 system, and do so in spite of the shortcomings of that system, thus giving rise to the challenge of helping match them to a suitable college.[10] But spotting them ought not wait until their senior year! (See recommendations seven and eight, below.)

Our intention is not to limit this quest to 10 percent (or any arbitrary number) of young people. It's more like *begin* with 10 percent. The changes suggested above in assessment and accountability systems apply to everyone. And the changes suggested below should eventually reach every child in America. But we ought not let that goal deter us from starting.

Fifth, allow progress based on mastery. Once identified, the single best thing our education systems could do for high-ability students—and everybody else—is make it possible for them to progress through the curriculum at their own pace. Instead of age-based grade levels—all eleven-year-olds belong in fifth grade, where they're all held to the same performance standards—have kids proceed on the basis of mastery, one unit or module at a time, subject by subject, with no expectation that all children will move through all units at the same rate. Most should probably remain with their fellow eleven-year-olds for social reasons, and therefore we should probably continue to group kids by age for "homeroom," phys ed, maybe art and music. But move them through the core academic curriculum as expeditiously as they master units of math, reading, science, or history.

Speedy learners are apt to move faster, of course, but everyone goes at his or her own pace, monitored and encouraged—and prodded and tutored when necessary—by teachers. One way this might work is to physically relocate children during the school day to classrooms in particular subjects that are grouped according to the achievement of the kids in them rather than by grade. Another way is to keep students of the same age or grade together but, with ample help from technology, enable each child to proceed at her own speed through the subject at hand, seeking the teacher's help when needed and going on to the next module when ready.

Think of this suggestion as the apotheosis of differentiated learning. For it to succeed, however—indeed, for any version to work—schools must alter time-honored structures and familiar schedules, make smart use of technology, encourage team teaching, use tutors and aides as well as teachers, and wean themselves from grade-level textbooks. They'll also have to wean parents from stubbornly insisting that "my child is eleven so she must be in fifth grade." State standards and assessments will have to flex, too. Today, they're organized by grade level within subjects. They should instead be organized into subject modules or units.

Suppose—to take an easy case—that the K–12 math curriculum contains fifty units. Maybe a student must master units 1 through 35 to graduate. Maybe unit 42 signifies readiness for college-level work in math. Modules 43 through 50 *consist* of college-level work (like AP math today). How far beyond 35 a given student goes depends on him (though the school should nudge, coax, and advise). How fast he progresses depends on how quickly he masters the relevant skills and content and, of course, how far he wants to get. The kids we've been focusing on will likely move faster and go farther. But perhaps only in certain subjects—and over time they (and others) may speed up or slow down.[11] Some might pause to delve deeper into a unit that intrigues them. Doing so might change their life.

Sixth, acceleration (implicit in the previous suggestion) is a valuable option for high achievers even under current school structures. It can take different forms: skipping a grade, or allowing the fifth grader to study math with sixth or seventh graders. But subject-matter acceleration is not the only adaptation that would benefit such learners (as well as others) and their instructors. Schools and districts should also encourage flexible ability grouping within classrooms, multiage/ grade groupings, uses of technology for "blended-learning" and "flipped classrooms," and whatever else they can do to facilitate the educational individualization that we already demand for disabled youngsters and in time should provide to everyone.[12] Until that time comes, however, few students would benefit more from customization than high achievers.

Seventh, offer more learning opportunities *outside* the regular age-based classroom and conventional school curriculum. These are pricier and probably more contentious because they give extra options and resources to some children, yet a variety of them already exist in some U.S. districts, as well as most of the countries we examined. These are just a few examples:

- Particularly for younger students, offer afterschool or weekend enrichment classes, plus online options so that high-ability pupils (and others) can engage in independent study beyond the standard curriculum. A kid keenly interested in history, for example, might dive deep into the Civil War, while classmates eager to learn more about birds or glaciers or map making can dig into those topics. The instructor's role in these situations is to stimulate, suggest, supply learning resources, help guide children's own investigations, and occasionally redirect or rein in one that's going awry, not to teach didactically. In other settings, the enrichment instructor's mandate is to offer a mini-course on, say, topography, the history of jazz, or the causes and effects of sunspots.

- Because high school pupils are better able to study on their own, "blended" and "virtual" learning options make sense here, too, akin to the fast-changing offerings we see in higher education.[13] That doesn't mean teachers disappear. The "MOOC" (massive open online course) experience has already shown that students are likelier to stick with and learn from an online course if there are also discussion groups, advising sessions, even tutorials.

- Also at the secondary level, develop dual-enrollment plans (with access to bona fide university courses), honors programs, schools-within-schools, and beefed-up AP and International Baccalaureate sequences.

- Full-time, stand-alone options are needed, too, such as specialized magnets, "exam schools," early-college high schools, gifted-centric charter schools, and scholarships to bring opportunities such as Nevada's Davidson Academy and the Illinois Math and Science Academy within reach of more families.[14]

- Outreach is essential if more low-income families and their schools are to learn about fine summer supplements such as the "talented youth" programs at Johns Hopkins and the University of Iowa, the humanities institute at Stanford, and summer schools at Phillips Exeter and Hunter College. Numerous opportunities like these exist for able students (mainly after sixth grade), and middle-class families with bright kids often find them. Others would benefit from being steered—and given financial help when needed.

Eighth, adapt college-access programs so that they start younger. Many nonprofit organizations and philanthropies (such as Quest-Bridge, the College Board, the Jack Kent Cooke Foundation, Posse Foundation, and Bloomberg Philanthropies) already help low-income high achievers to make their way from high school into, then succeed in, selective universities.[15] This is important work and we need more of it. But—as with Hungary's Arany Janos program—waiting until high school risks losing a lot of talent along the way, as able poor kids in fourth or seventh grade get little encouragement or help and thus enter high school behind where they could be. Programs that begin earlier in children's lives would keep more of them on track.

Ninth, philanthropists as well as governments should support curricular and pedagogical innovation to benefit high-ability and fast-learning students—and the research and evaluation that will shed clearer light on what works best for which kids under what circumstances, and at what cost. This isn't just about raising test scores. Well-designed gifted programs—like quality education in general—also offer chances to engage in independent inquiry, cultivate creativity, and pursue other enrichment opportunities. But many questions remain unanswered in this realm.[16]

Tenth (and perhaps most obviously), schools need staff who are knowledgeable about educating high-ability learners, just as they need special ed teachers, math specialists, and others with targeted skills. Teachers of gifted pupils may not require separate certification but they need access to suitable preparation. We don't share the belief that professional development can cure every education ill, but getting, let's say, one teacher and administrator per school up to speed on the challenges and opportunities that we've flagged in this book would be a worthy step and would benefit a great many young people. Even better would be to get this issue incorporated into conventional teacher preparation—which means universities must recognize the need and acquire the expertise. After all, it's not just policy makers and pundits who need their consciousness raised and their understanding deepened! Although few teachers will encounter many future Mozarts or Einsteins in their classrooms, almost all of them will routinely contend with some students who learn faster and achieve more than others. Which means that such students—and the nation that they're part of—will be best served if almost every teacher knows how to spot them and has an arsenal of strategies for helping them.

AFTERWORD

WE TRUST that readers who have stuck with us, whether or not they agree with our recommendations—perhaps we've persuaded a few—are exiting this volume with this quintet of clearer understandings:

- There's overwhelming evidence that the United States is not doing as well as it could and should to maximize the educational accomplishments of its high-ability students, that other grown-up countries are doing it better, and that it's folly to think we can wait for a rising education tide to lift enough of these boats.
- For two big reasons, we should wrestle with this challenge, particularly for youngsters from disadvantaged circumstances. First, they need and deserve our help. Second, the country needs them as essential elements of its growth agenda if it's to compete successfully in the global marketplace and secure our grandchildren's future.
- We also need to restore the equality-excellence balance in our public policies and education priorities, not to focus exclusively on the former and thus leave the excellence path open mainly to lucky kids with savvy, prosperous parents.
- Getting this done means unseating the four horsemen of the gifted ed apocalypse: ideology and political correctness, fallacious theories of education, disagreements over who qualifies, and vagueness about what exactly to do for them.
- Getting this done also calls for investing attention, imagination, resources, and political capital. Government (at every level) needs to engage, but so do advocacy groups, philanthropists, educators, analysts, leaders of business and academe, those who are passionate about the country's prosperity, and those who understand that true equity includes *these* neglected youngsters, too.

No country we know has got this exactly right—some are scarcely better off than we are—and in any case the United States must tread its own path, honoring our values, building on our strengths, working within (while adapting) our structures, and minding our sensitivities. The examples we found in other lands would not necessarily all work here, even if they produce better outcomes in their own contexts. But some themes and strategies from abroad are worth adapting. They take different forms but have this in common: recognition that doing right by high-ability pupils, even when some people call it elitist, is essential for reasons of both equity and national self-interest. The crucial corollary: recognizing that none of this is self-propelled, particularly for disadvantaged children. It must be embedded in purposeful policy, professional practice, constant monitoring, and periodic retooling.

Retooling is under way in many of the countries that we visited. Indeed, we're struck by the extent to which the education of high-ability children—and sometimes the education of all children—is in flux around the world. Curricula are being overhauled, white papers issued, policies reconsidered, definitions revisited, school structures reshaped, and longstanding practices rethought. Almost nowhere is the situation static. While not every change on the horizon strikes us as positive, most places are in flux because their movers and shakers are striving to make their education system work better for high-ability children as well as for their country—and they're doing this despite tight budgets and competing needs. There's a lesson here for the United States: although much in our K–12 system is also in flux (new standards and assessments, for example, new ways of evaluating teachers, emerging uses of technology, widening forms of school choice), you'd be hard pressed to look around America today and find movers and shakers struggling to improve the education of high-ability children. Almost nowhere is it even on their radar. Yet this, too, is a realm where change is needed. The kids deserve it. And the country needs them.

APPENDIX

THE TABLES AND FIGURES included here supplement the analyses and data in chapter 2 and are presented in rough parallel with it, including domestic and international sections with achievement-gap data in both.

HIGH ACHIEVEMENT: DOMESTIC DATA

Low versus high achievers

Figure A.1 shows NAEP math and reading scores from 1996 through 2013 at the 10th and 90th percentiles in grades 4 and 8. Accompanying the figures are small tables showing how steeply the relevant score has risen or fallen over the period shown.[1] For example, the upper right of the table accompanying the math trend lines shows that the line for eighth graders at the 90th percentile has a slope of 2.04, meaning that, from one test year to the next (e.g., 1996 to 2000), this score went up—on average—approximately two points on the 500-point scale. But the lower right on the same table shows that the 10th percentile line rose more steeply: an average of nearly two and a half points between test administrations.[2] In all four pairs, the increase at the 10th percentile is steeper than the corresponding increase at the 90th percentile.

ACHIEVEMENT GAPS: DOMESTIC

Figures A.2 and A.3 and table A.1 examine the intersection of three factors that generally correlate with lower achievement in the United

FIGURE A.1   High- and low-scoring students, by NAEP percentile score,
subject, and grade level, 1996–2013

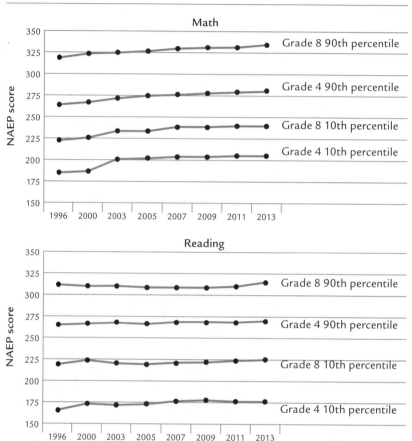

Math					Reading			
4th grade	Slope	8th grade	Slope		4th grade	Slope	8th grade	Slope
90th percentile	2.23	90th percentile	2.04		90th percentile	0.32	90th percentile	0.42
10th percentile	3.03	10th percentile	2.43		10th percentile	1.41	10th percentile	0.73

Note: Although both subjects and grades are on 0–500 scales, NAEP scores cannot be compared across subjects or grade levels. See appendix note 1 and the text referencing this figure for an explanation of what the slopes in the tables denote. Note, too, that this figure omits twelfth-grade data because those scores are reported on a different scale.

Eighth-grade students at/above NAEP Advanced level in math, by race and parents' education, 2013

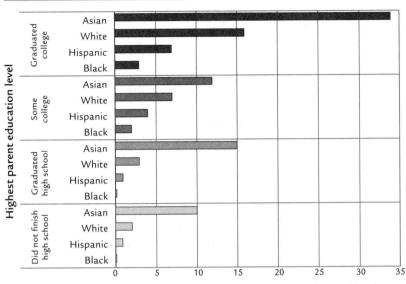

Note: Each category on the *y*-axis represents the highest level of education that either parent achieved, as reported by the test taker.

FIGURE A.3 Eighth-grade students at/above NAEP Advanced level in math, by race and FRPL eligibility, 2013

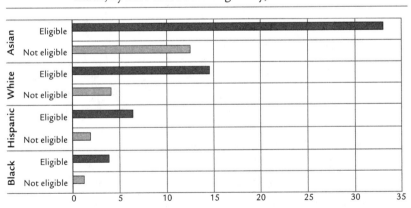

Note: A student is eligible for free or reduced-price lunch if his/her household income falls below 185 percent of the federal poverty line.

We also looked at these data for reading and found similar trends, although the proportions of high scorers were approximately half those in math across the board.

TABLE A.1   Percentage of eighth-grade students at/above NAEP Advanced level in math, by race, parents' education, and FRPL eligibility, 2013

Parents' education level	Race	Eligible for FRPL (%)	Not eligible for FRPL (%)
Graduated college	Asian	15	40
	White	6	18
	Hispanic	3	9
	Black	1	5
Some college	Asian	12	12
	White	5	9
	Hispanic	3	5
	Black	2	2
Graduated high school	Asian	15	15
	White	2	4
	Hispanic	1	2
	Black	0	0
Did not finish high school	Asian	10	7
	White	1	3
	Hispanic	1	2
	Black	1	0

States: race, parents' education level, and poverty (represented here by eligibility for the federal subsidized lunch program, or FRPL).

State differences

As in figure A.1, figure A.4 incorporates mini-tables showing how steeply the relevant score has risen or fallen over time.[3] For example, we see that, in math, the Massachusetts line has a slope of 3.5, by far the steepest of the four states. (In reading, Massachusetts is tied with Maryland for gains—and no line is very steep across the eight years.)

Figure A.5 charts the same metric as the math portion of figure A.4 but breaks down the percentages of high scorers by racial group. Here, Maryland's numbers are far closer to Massachusetts's,

Eighth-grade students at/above NAEP Advanced level, by subject and state, 2005–2013

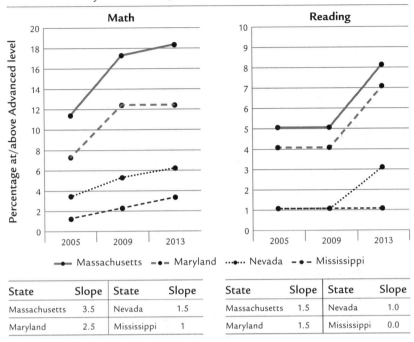

State	Slope	State	Slope
Massachusetts	3.5	Nevada	1.5
Maryland	2.5	Mississippi	1

State	Slope	State	Slope
Massachusetts	1.5	Nevada	1.0
Maryland	1.5	Mississippi	0.0

FIGURE A.5 Eighth-grade students at/above NAEP Advanced level in math, by state and race, 2005–2013

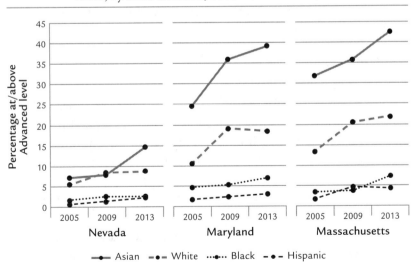

Note: Figure A.4 also included Mississippi, which is omitted here because that state's scores are so low that there aren't enough black and Hispanic students at the Advanced level to make the data reliable.

FIGURE A.6   Eighth-grade students at/above NAEP Advanced level, by gender and subject, 2005–2013

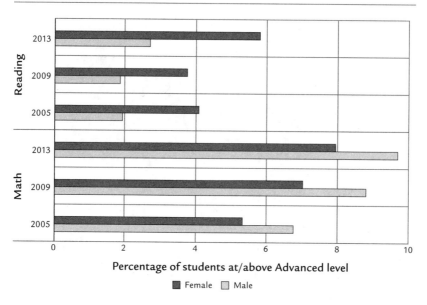

Percentage of students at/above Advanced level

■ Female   ☐ Male

indicating that lower-scoring racial groups make up a greater proportion of Maryland's population.

Gender

Figure A.6 charts the percentage of eighth-grade students at or above NAEP's Advanced level by gender for both math and reading from 2005 through 2013. The pattern is essentially the same throughout: boys do better in math, girls in reading. In all six combinations of subject and year, the gap between the higher- and lower-scoring genders is two to three points, not insignificant considering that just 10 percent of the best-performing group (boys in math in 2013) reached the Advanced level.

Note, too, as in figure 2.1 in chapter 2, that, while any increase is to be applauded, math scores are increasing faster than reading. Since 2005, the proportion of students reaching Advanced in math is up three points across both genders; in reading, we see a paltry 1 percent gain.

HIGH ACHIEVEMENT:
INTERNATIONAL EVIDENCE

Table A.2 shows how much the sample countries' proportions of high scorers on each international assessment have changed over time. For example, in 2003, 10.1 percent of U.S. fifteen-year-olds scored at PISA levels 5 and 6 in math. In 2012, only 8.8 percent of U.S. test takers placed in that score range, making for a 1.3 point decline. On TIMSS eighth-grade math, by contrast, the proportion of high scorers in the United States did not change between 2003 and 2011, even as fourth graders added 5.4 points to their high scorers (in math) over the same period.

ACHIEVEMENT GAPS:
INTERNATIONAL

Socioeconomic status

Table A.3 compares the top and bottom socioeconomic quartiles in our sample countries for math, science, and reading, using the OECD's Index of Economic, Social, and Cultural Status (ESCS).[4] For each subject, the first data column shows the percentage of children in the country's bottom quartile that scored at levels 5 and 6. The next column shows the percentage of those in the top quartile. The last column is the ratio of the top quartile percentage divided by the bottom quartile percentage.

Parents' education

Figures A.7 and A.8 resemble figure 2.7 (chapter 2), which related the education of students' parents to high achievement in math as gauged on PISA. Figures A.7 and A.8 do the same for the other two subjects, reading and science, respectively.

Table A.4 compares high achievement rates by parents' education levels. The "low" column is the percentage of high scorers among students whose parents didn't graduate high school. The "high" is that rate for test takers with college-educated parents. The ratio column shows the "high" percentage divided by the "low" percentage.

TABLE A.2   Percentage-point change over time in proportion of high scorers on PISA, TIMSS, and PIRLS, by country and assessment

	PISA			TIMSS				PIRLS
	Math 2003–2012	Reading 2003–2012	Science 2006–2012	Math Grade 4 2003–2011	Math Grade 8 2003–2011	Science Grade 4 2003–2011	Science Grade 8 2003–2011	Reading Grade 4 2001–2011
United States	**−1.3**	**−1.3**	**−1.7**	**+5.4**	**0.0**	**+1.7**	**−0.7**	**+2.7**
Australia	−5.0	−2.9	−1.1	+4.8	+2.1	−1.1	+1.9	—
Canada	−3.9	+0.2	−3.1	—	—	—	—	—
Finland	−8.1	−1.2	−3.9	—	—	—	—	—
Germany	+1.2	−0.6	+0.3	−0.5[c]	—	−2.5[c]	—	+1.0
Hungary	−1.4	+0.8	−1.0	−0.1	−3.6	+2.9	−5.0	+2.6
Japan	−0.6	+8.8	+3.2	+9.1	+2.8	+2.1	+3.8	—
Korea	+6.1	+2.0	+1.4	—	+11.9	—	+3.7	—
Singapore	+4.4[a]	+5.5[a]	+2.8[a]	+5.1	+3.2	+8.5	+6.8	+12.1
Switzerland	+0.2	+1.3	−1.2	—	—	—	—	—
Taiwan	+5.3[b]	+7.1[b]	−6.3	+17.5	+11.1	+1.4	−2.2	+5.9[d]
United Kingdom	+0.7[b]	−0.3[b]	−2.6	+4.1	+2.7	−3.6	−1.3	−1.8
OECD Average[e]	−2.0	−0.5	+0.2	+0.9	+1.0	+0.9	+1.4	+1.0

Note: For PISA and TIMSS, each cell represents the percentage-point change from 2003 (except where otherwise indicated) to the most recent administration of that test. In the case of PISA science, changes are shown only from 2006 because OECD changed the test between 2003 and 2006. For PIRLS, the change is shown from 2001 to 2011.

a Singapore did not participate in any PISA assessment until 2009, so these cells represent changes only between 2009 and 2012.

b Taiwan and the United Kingdom did not participate in any PISA assessment until 2006, so these cells represent changes only between 2006 and 2012.

c Germany did not participate in fourth-grade TIMSS assessments until 2007, so these cells represent percentage-point changes only between 2007 and 2012.

d Taiwan did not participate in the PIRLS assessment until 2006, so these cells represent percentage-point changes only between 2006 and 2012.

e "OECD average" is the average percentage-point change of high scorers in the test-taking populations of all OECD countries that took part in that particular assessment over the time periods shown at the top of each column.

TABLE A.3 Percentage of students at levels 5 or 6 on PISA assessments, by ESCS quartile and subject, with ratio, 2012

Math	Bottom	Top	Ratio	Reading	Bottom	Top	Ratio	Science	Bottom	Top	Ratio
Singapore	21.4	61.4	2.9:1	Japan	9.8	30.0	3.1:1	Finland	9.8	28.5	2.9:1
Korea	16.3	48.2	3.0:1	Finland	7.0	22.4	3.2:1	Japan	9.5	28.9	3.0:1
Taiwan	19.0	60.7	3.2:1	Canada	6.1	22.9	3.7:1	Canada	5.5	20.2	3.6:1
Japan	11.8	38.0	3.2:1	Korea	5.9	24.7	4.2:1	Korea	5.1	19.4	3.8:1
Finland	8.1	27.0	3.4:1	Singapore	8.8	39.3	4.5:1	Singapore	8.8	41.4	4.7:1
Canada	7.7	28.5	3.7:1	Australia	4.2	22.5	5.3:1	Australia	5.2	24.6	4.8:1
Switzerland	9.2	38.0	4.1:1	Germany	3.0	18.4	6.2:1	Germany	4.1	25.7	6.3:1
Australia	5.8	26.5	4.6:1	Taiwan	3.6	24.5	6.9:1	United Kingdom	3.2	23.9	7.5:1
Germany	6.6	36.0	5.5:1	Switzerland	2.5	19.0	7.5:1	Switzerland	2.5	19.8	8.0:1
United Kingdom	4.0	25.0	6.3:1	United Kingdom	2.2	19.0	8.5:1	**United States**	**2.0**	**17.3**	**8.8:1**
United States	**2.4**	**19.7**	**8.0:1**	**United States**	**1.6**	**18.1**	**11.1:1**	Taiwan	1.9	19.0	10.1:1
Hungary	1.5	22.6	14.8:1	Hungary	1.1	14.0	13.2:1	Hungary	0.8	15.2	18.0:1
OECD average	4.6	24.6	5.3:1	OECD average	2.9	17.0	5.9:1	OECD average	2.8	17.0	6.0:1

Source: The quartile data were computed and provided by OECD analyst Pablo Zoido.

Note: These data are based on OECD's ESCS socioeconomic indicator. (See chapter 2, note 18 for an explanation.) The first number of the ratio is the percentage in the "Top" column divided by the percentage in the "Bottom" column. "OECD average" denotes these data and ratio for all OECD countries in 2012 in each subject.

FIGURE A.7   High scorers on PISA reading, 2012, by parents' education

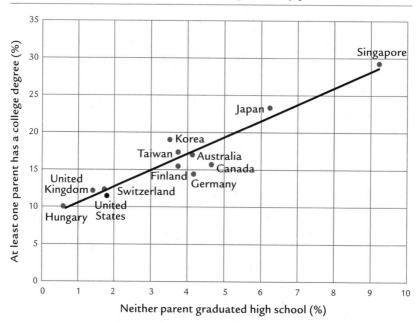

Source: "International Data Explorer," U.S. Department of Education, Institute of Education Sciences, National Center for Education Statistics, accessed November 29, 2014, http://nces.ed.gov/surveys/international/ide/. Unlike chapter 2, figure 2.7, which uses NAEP data for the United States, this figure uses only PISA data.

FIGURE A.8   High scorers on PISA science, 2012, by parents' education

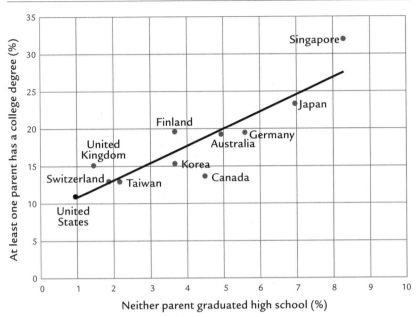

Source: "International Data Explorer," U.S. Department of Education, Institute of Education Sciences, National Center for Education Statistics, accessed November 29, 2014, http://nces.ed.gov/surveys/international/ide/. Unlike chapter 2, figure 2.7, which uses NAEP data for the United States, this figure uses only PISA data.

Note: Data on science are unavailable for test takers with poorly educated parents in Hungary and are, therefore, omitted.

TABLE A.4 Percentage of students at levels 5 or 6 on PISA assessments, by subject tested and parents' education level, with ratio, 2012

Math	Low	High	Ratio
Korea	15.4	38.1	2.5:1
Germany	8.3	25.2	3.0:1
Japan	9.5	29.2	3.1:1
Canada	5.8	18.4	3.2:1
United Kingdom	4.1	14.7	3.6:1
Finland	4.6	16.5	3.6:1
Australia	5.4	19.7	3.6:1
Switzerland	6.0	26.4	4.4:1
United States	**2.0**	**11.8**	**5.9:1**
Hungary	0.7	15.5	22.1:1

Reading	Low	High	Ratio
Singapore	9.2	29.3	3.2:1
Canada	4.6	15.6	3.4:1
Germany	4.2	14.5	3.5:1
Japan	6.2	23.3	3.7:1
Finland	3.7	15.4	4.2:1
Australia	4.1	17.2	4.2:1
Taiwan	3.8	17.2	4.6:1
Korea	3.5	19.0	5.4:1
United States	**1.8**	**11.5**	**6.6:1**
Switzerland	1.7	12.1	7.1:1
United Kingdom	1.4	12.1	8.7:1
Hungary	0.6	10.0	18.1:1

Science	Low	High	Ratio
Canada	4.5	13.5	3.0:1
Japan	7.0	23.2	3.3:1
Germany	5.6	19.4	3.5:1
Singapore	8.3	31.9	3.8:1
Australia	4.9	19.2	3.9:1
Korea	3.7	15.2	4.1:1
Finland	3.7	19.5	5.3:1
Taiwan	2.2	12.8	5.9:1
Switzerland	1.9	12.9	6.9:1
United Kingdom	1.5	15.0	10.3:1
United States	**0.9**	**10.8**	**11.5:1**

Sources: See chapter 2, notes 22 and 23.

Note: The first number of the ratio is the percentage in the "High" column divided by the percentage in the "Low" column.

Language

Figure A.9 compares the scores of test takers whose home language is also the test language with those whose home language is different, and does this for PISA math and reading for 2012.[5] As explained in chapter 2, students are likelier to be high scorers if their home language is the same as the language of the test, which, generally speaking, is also the language of instruction in their schools. Obvious exceptions are Canada and Australia, both of which have been admitting significant numbers of relatively well-off Asian immigrants. Canada is also a dual-language country with both Anglophone and Francophone school systems. PISA was administered in either English or French, based on the language of the respective school system. Toronto, for example, has both English and French systems, and each has PISA administered in its language of instruction. Also interesting in these data is Singapore, where the language of the test—and of the schools— is English, but a great many children live in homes where the primary language is Chinese, Tamil, or Malay.

FIGURE A.9   Percentage of students at PISA level 5 or 6, by subject tested and language spoken at home, 2012

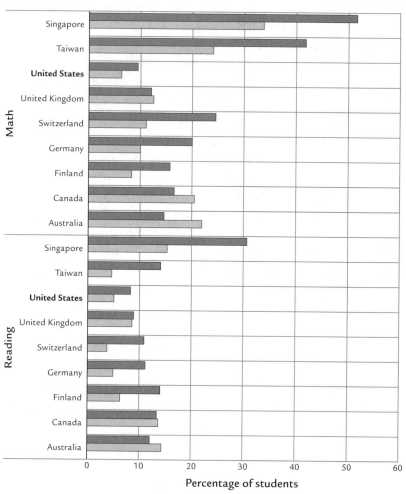

Percentage of students

Language spoken at home: ■ Language of test ☐ Other

Note: The dark bars indicate that the language spoken at home is the language in which the test is administered. The light bars indicate that the language spoken at home is different from the language in which the test is administered.

NOTES

INTRODUCTION

1. Frederick M. Hess, "America's Future Depends on Gifted Students," *New York Times*, June 4, 2014, http://www.nytimes.com/roomfordebate/2014/06/03/are-new-york-citys-gifted-classrooms-useful-or-harmful/americas-future-depends-on-gifted-students.
2. Chester Finn's father attended that school in Dayton around 1932.
3. John W. Gardner, *Excellence: Can We Be Equal and Excellent Too?* (New York: W. W. Norton & Company, 1961).
4. S. P. Marland, "Education of the Gifted and Talented: Report to the Congress of the United States by the U.S. Commissioner of Education and Background Papers Submitted to the U.S. Office of Education," 92d Congress, 2d Session (Washington, DC: U.S. Government Printing Office, March 1972).
5. *A Nation at Risk: The Imperative for Educational Reform*, National Commission on Excellence in Education, April 1983, http://www2.ed.gov/pubs/NatAtRisk/index.html.
6. David Leonhardt, "Better Colleges Failing to Lure Talented Poor," *New York Times*, March 16, 2013, http://www.nytimes.com/2013/03/17/education/scholarly-poor-often-overlook-better-colleges.html?pagewanted=all&_r=0.
7. Mikhail Zinshteyn, "A Brief Look at America's Gifted Students," *Ed Beat* (blog), Education Writers Association, January 27, 2015, http://www.ewa.org/blog-ed-beat/brief-look-americas-gifted-students.

CHAPTER 1

1. "National Excellence: A Case for Developing America's Talent," U.S. Department of Education, October 1993, https://www.ocps.net/cs/ese/programs/gifted/Documents/National%20Excellence_%20A%20Case%20for%20Developing%20America%27s%20Talent_%20Introduction.pdf.
2. It's no secret that some exceptionally able and creative individuals lack conventional education credentials. Harvard dropouts Bill Gates, Steve Jobs, and Mark Zuckerberg are famous recent examples. But they are also rare exceptions. (And all three had educated parents—and got into Harvard.)
3. "10 Reasons the Tech Industry Will Break Down Without Immigration Reform," Partnership for a New American Economy Action Fund, accessed November 29, 2014, http://www.renewoureconomy.org/issues/entrepreneurship/10-reasons-tech-industry-will-break-without-immigration-reform/.

4. Lindsay Gellman, "On B-School Test, Americans Fail to Measure Up," *Wall Street Journal*, November 5, 2014, http://online.wsj.com/articles/on-b-school-test-americans-fail-to-measure-up-1415236311.

5. Eric A. Hanushek and Ludger Woessmann, *The Knowledge Capital of Nations: Education and the Economics of Growth* (Cambridge, MA: MIT Press, 2015).

6. Philip Galanes, "Elton John and Darren Walker on Race, Sexual Identity and Leaving the Past Behind," *New York Times*, November 28, 2014, http://www.nytimes.com/2014/11/30/fashion/elton-john-and-darren-walker-on-race-sexual-identity-and-leaving-the-past-behind.html?_r=0.

7. Jonathan Plucker et al., "Equal Talents, Unequal Opportunities: A Report Card on State Support for Academically Talented Low-Income Students," Jack Kent Cooke Foundation (March 2015), http://www.excellencegap.org/assets/files/JKCF_ETUO_Report.pdf.

8. "AAP: Frequently Asked Questions," Fairfax County Public Schools, accessed December 4, 2014, http://www.fcps.edu/is/aap/faqs.shtml.

9. See appendix table A.3.

10. "National Excellence: A Case for Developing America's Talent."

11. Nicholas Colangelo, Susan G. Assouline, and Miraca Gross, "A Nation Deceived: How Schools Hold Back America's Brightest Students, Volume I," Templeton National Report on Acceleration, John Templeton Foundation, 2004, http://www.accelerationinstitute.org/Nation_Deceived/ND_v1.pdf.

12. Steve Farkas, Ann Duffett, and Tom Loveless, "High-Achieving Students in the Era of No Child Left Behind," Thomas B. Fordham Institute, June 18, 2008, http://edexcellence.net/publications/high-achieving-students-in.html.

13. Jonathan A. Plucker, Nathan Burroughs, and Ruiting Song, "Mind the (Other) Gap! The Growing Excellence Gap in K–12 Education," Center for Evaluation & Education Policy, February 4, 2010, http://www.jkcf.org/assets/1/7/ExcellenceGapBrief_-_Plucker.pdf. The authors acknowledged that most student groups had made modest high-end gains "at some grade levels in some content areas," but the gains made by middle-class and white youngsters surpassed those of disadvantaged and minority youngsters. Hence the widening gap.

14. Paula Olszewski-Kubilius and Jane Clarenbach, "Unlocking Emergent Talent: Supporting High Achievement of Low-Income, High-Ability Students," National Association for Gifted Children, 2012, http://www.jkcf.org/assets/1/7/Unlocking_Emergent_Talent.pdf. We update these figures in chapter 2.

15. Caroline Hoxby and Christopher Avery, "The Missing 'One-Offs': The Hidden Supply of High-Achieving, Low-Income Students," Brookings Institution, 2013, http://www.brookings.edu/~/media/Projects/BPEA/Spring%202013/2013a_hoxby.pdf.

16. Jonathan Plucker, Jacob Hardesty, and Nathan Burroughs, "Talent on the Sidelines: Excellence Gaps and America's Persistent Talent Underclass," University of Connecticut Center for Education Policy Analysis, October 2013,

http://webdev.education.uconn.edu/static/sites/cepa/AG/excellence2013/Excellence-Gap-10-18-13_JP_LK.pdf.

17. Plucker et al., "Equal Talents, Unequal Opportunities: A Report Card on State Support for Academically Talented Low-Income Students."

18. Steve Farkas, Ann Duffett, and Tom Loveless, "High-Achieving Students in the Era of No Child Left Behind," Part II, Thomas B. Fordham Institute, June 18, 2008, http://edexcellence.net/publications/high-achieving-students-in.html.

19. Individual schools, of course, get visibility and credit when one or another of their pupils excels on the National Spelling Bee, the Intel Science Talent Search, or other high-profile competitions, but most such accolades have nothing to do with public policy priorities.

CHAPTER 2

1. Eric A. Hanushek, Paul E. Peterson, and Ludger Woessmann, "Not Just the Problem of Other People's Children: U.S. Student Performance in Global Perspective," PEPG Report 14-01, Harvard Kennedy School, Program on Education Policy and Governance and *Education Next*, May 2014, 9 (citing John H. Bishop, "The Impact of Academic Competencies on Wages, Unemployment, and Job Performance," *Carnegie-Rochester Conference Series on Public Policy* 37 (December 1992): 127–194; Richard J. Murnane, John B. Willett, and Frank Levy, "The Growing Importance of Cognitive Skills in Wage Determination," *Review of Economics and Statistics* 77, no. 2 (May 1995): 251–266; and Eric A Hanushek, Guido Schwerdt, Simon Wiederhold, and Ludger Woessmann, "Returns to Skills Around the World" (NBER Working Paper 19762, Cambridge, MA: National Bureau of Economic Research, December 2013)).

2. "Basic" is defined as "Partial mastery of prerequisite knowledge and skills that are fundamental for proficient work at each grade." "Proficient" is defined as "Solid academic performance for each grade assessed. Students reaching this level have demonstrated competency over challenging subject matter, including subject-matter knowledge, application of such knowledge to real-world situations, and analytical skills appropriate to the subject matter." "Advanced" is defined as "superior performance" in general, then refined for each grade and subject. In twelfth-grade math, for example, students at this level "should demonstrate in-depth knowledge of the mathematical concepts and procedures represented in the framework. Students should be able to integrate knowledge to solve complex problems and justify and explain their thinking. These students should be able to analyze, make and justify mathematical arguments, and communicate their ideas clearly." See "NAEP Achievement Levels," National Center for Education Statistics, accessed November 29, 2014, http://nces.ed.gov/nationsreportcard/achievement.aspx, and "The NAEP Mathematics Achievement Levels by Grade," National Center

for Education Statistics, accessed November 29, 2014, http://nces.ed.gov/
nationsreportcard/mathematics/achieveall.asp.

3. Here and throughout the book, except as indicated, NAEP data—including
demographic data—were obtained via the NCES "NAEP Data Explorer." See
"NAEP Data Explorer," U.S. Department of Education, Institute of Education
Sciences, National Center for Education Statistics, accessed November 29, 2014,
http://nces.ed.gov/nationsreportcard/naepdata/dataset.aspx.

4. "The ACT College Readiness Benchmarks . . . represent the level of achievement required for students to have a 50% chance of obtaining a B or higher or
about a 75% chance of obtaining a C or higher in corresponding credit-bearing
first-year college courses." "The Condition of College & Career Readiness
2014: National," ACT, Inc., 2014, http://www.act.org/newsroom/data/2014/
pdf/CCCR14-NationalReadinessRpt.pdf.

5. Ibid. Note, however, that only 57 percent of the graduating class took the ACT
because some students took other exams, such as the SAT, or eschewed college
entrance tests entirely.

6. At least as depressing as widespread unreadiness for college academics, which
typically leads students into remedial classes, is evidence that some
40 percent of college *graduates* still lack the reasoning skills needed to
succeed in typical "white-collar" jobs. Douglas Belkin, "Test Finds College
Graduates Lack Skills for White-Collar Jobs," *Wall Street Journal*, January 16, 2015, http://www.wsj.com/articles/test-finds-many-students-ill-
prepared-to-enter-work-force-1421432744.

7. "NAEP as an Indicator of Students' Academic Preparedness for College," U.S.
Department of Education, accessed November 29, 2013, http://www.nations
reportcard.gov/reading_math_g12_2013/#/preparedness.

8. "Explore AP," The College Board, accessed November 29, 2014, https://apstudent
.collegeboard.org/exploreap.

9. Ibid. Many colleges and universities, however, require scores of 4 or 5 before
actually awarding credit to entering students. See, e.g., "AP, IB Credit and
Other Pre-College Credit," Undergraduate Admissions, Vanderbilt University,
accessed November 29, 2014, http://admissions.vanderbilt.edu/academics/
ap-ib.php.

10. 2011 is the most recent year for which NCES provides grade 12 enrollment
data by race and ethnicity. Because these proportions don't fluctuate significantly from year to year, we use the 2011 data as denominators when estimat-
ing the proportions of high school seniors in 2014 for each racial group. See
"Table 1.–Grade 12 Enrollment, by Race/Ethnicity, Gender, and State: Years
1992-93 Through 2010-11," U.S. Department of Education, Institute of Education Sciences, National Center for Education Statistics, accessed April 13,
2015, https://nces.ed.gov/ccd/tables/ESSIN_Task5_f1.asp.

11. This discrepancy is widely known. See, e.g., "Civil Rights Data Collection: Data Snapshot: College and Career Readiness," Issue Brief No. 3, U.S. Department of Education, Office for Civil Rights, March 21, 2014, http://www2 .ed.gov/about/offices/list/ocr/docs/crdc-college-and-career-readiness-snapshot .pdf.

12. There are also lingering gender-related gaps, as we show in appendix figure A.6. Boys have long produced more high scorers in math (and science), while girls have done so in reading (and other "humanities" subjects.)

13. "NAEP Data Explorer."

14. If a student reports on two parents, the datum used is the education level of the parent with more.

15. We also looked at these data for reading and found similar trends, although the proportions of high scorers were approximately half those in math across the board.

16. Among eighth-grade math test takers in 2013, Maryland was 45 percent white and 35 percent black, while the corresponding percentages in Massachusetts were 67 and 9. (Hispanic and Asian figures were more similar between the two jurisdictions.) See "NAEP Data Explorer."

17. See Mark Schneider, "The International PISA Test," *Education Next* 9, no. 4 (Fall 2004), and "Program for International Student Assessment (PISA), Frequently Asked Questions," U.S. Department of Education, Institute of Education Sciences, National Center for Education Statistics, accessed November 29, 2014, http://nces.ed.gov/surveys/pisa/faq.asp.

18. The line shown in the figure is called the "best fit" trend line because, of all possible lines that one could draw through the data points, this one has the least possible combined distance between it and each point. It is used to indicate trends, such as the rate at which something is increasing or decreasing over time. In this chapter, all best-fit trendlines were calculated using Microsoft Excel.

19. ESCS was derived from three other OECD indices: highest occupational status of parents, highest educational level of parents gauged by years of education, and home possessions (which, in turn, is derived from indices based on wealth, cultural possessions, home education resources, and the number of books in the home). OECD also performs a separate analysis to see how ESCS components operate across countries. They found the patterns similar and state that all three parts of the index contribute similarly. See OECD, *PISA 2012 Results: Excellence Through Equity: Giving Every Student the Chance to Succeed (Volume II)*, OECD Publishing, 2013, http://www.oecd.org/pisa/keyfindings/ pisa-2012-results-volume-II.pdf.

20. Cross-national comparisons of socioeconomic status are difficult. What disadvantage means in any country is a complicated question—and what it means in sixty of them, and how to compare them, is exceptionally challenging. See,

e.g., Robert M. Hauser, "Some Methodological Issues in Cross-National Educational Research—Quality and Equity in Student Achievement," *EurAmerica* 43, no. 4 (December 2013).

21. "World Factbook," U.S. Central Intelligence Agency, accessed November 29, 2014, https://www.cia.gov/library/publications/the-world-factbook/fields/ 2172.html. "This index measures the degree of inequality in the distribution of family income in a country.... The more nearly equal a country's income distribution ... the lower its Gini index.... The more unequal a country's income distribution ... the higher its Gini index.... If income were distributed with perfect equality ... the index would be zero; if income were distributed with perfect inequality ... the index would be 100."

22. In the domestic analysis in this chapter, we split parent education levels into four categories: the three shown here plus a category where "at least one parent has taken some college courses, but neither has a degree." Here, however, we rely on Hanushek et al., who used just three categories and looked at all thirty-four OECD countries. They found the United States surpassing just nine on the low-education metric and besting a woeful six when looking at the percentage of high achievers among kids with well-educated parents. Hanushek, Peterson, and Woessmann, "Not Just the Problem of Other People's Children."

23. Here and throughout the book, except where otherwise indicated, PISA, TIMSS, and PIRLS data—including demographic data—were obtained via the NCES "International Data Explorer." See "International Data Explorer," U.S. Department of Education, Institute of Education Sciences, National Center for Education Statistics, accessed November 29, 2014, http://nces.ed.gov/ surveys/international/ide/.

CHAPTER 3

1. North Carolina's (residential) science and math high school, for example, begun in 1980 by former Democratic governor James Hunt, "was built on the premise that regions which invest in the creation of human and intellectual capital will receive global economic returns, the key to success in a world-wide economy." See "History and Mission," North Carolina School of Science and Mathematics, accessed on November 29, 2014, http://www.ncssm.edu/ about-ncssm/history-and-mission.

2. We've also seen late bloomers (the senior author's son was one), high-potential individuals who were unmotivated for years but later got their acts together and made something significant of themselves.

3. Australian psychologist Arthur Poropat favors "conscientiousness" and "openness" as the dimensions of personality that correlate more closely with achievement than does intelligence. Arthur E. Poropat, "Other-Rated

Personality and Academic Performance: Evidence and Implications," *Learning and Individual Differences* 34 (August 2014): 24–32.

4. The University of Connecticut's Joseph Renzulli developed a "three-ring model" of giftedness, used in a number of countries and focused on the intersection within an individual of "above average ability," "task commitment," and "creativity." See Joseph S. Renzulli, "Three-Ring Conception of Giftedness," University of Connecticut Nead Center for Gifted Education and Talent Development, accessed November 29, 2014, http://www.gifted.uconn.edu/sem/semart13.html. The University of Quebec's François Gagné, also highly regarded in the field, offers a "differentiated model of giftedness and talent" that combines the former (based on natural aptitudes) with the latter ("outstanding mastery of systematically developed abilities, called competencies [knowledge and skills], in at least one field of human activity"). He estimates that about 10 percent of the population warrants such a designation. See François Gagné, "Building Gifts into Talents: Brief Overview of the DMGT 2.0," *Gifted* 152 (April 2009): 5–9, http://www.eurotalent.org/Gagne_DMGT_Model.pdf. A third respected theorist, psychologist Robert Sternberg, fuses "analytical, creative and practical abilities" into a definition of intelligence that works differently in specific contexts. "Robert J. Sternberg: (1949–) Cognitive Psychologist," *Human Intelligence*, accessed November 29, 2013, http://www.intelltheory.com/sternberg.shtml. And the valuable work of Rena F. Subotnik, often working with Paula Olszewski-Kubilius and Frank C. Worrell, has stressed the importance of identifying and addressing domain-specific rather than generic talents, with an eye toward maximizing later success in those fields. See, e.g., Rena F. Subotnik, Paula Olszewski-Kubilius, and Frank C. Worrell, "Rethinking Giftedness and Gifted Education: A Proposed Direction Forward Based on Psychological Science," *Psychological Science in the Public Interest* 12, no. 1 (2011), https://www.apa.org/ed/schools/gifted/rethinking-giftedness.pdf, and Rena F. Subotnik, Paula Olszewski-Kubilius, and Frank C. Worrell, "Nurturing the Young Genius," *Scientific American* 23, no. 5s (2015), http://www.scientificamerican.com/article/nurturing-the-young-genius/.

5. A veteran policy analyst in California told us that this widening of categories meant his state's modest categorical funding for "GATE" programs began to look like a small sum spread across a potentially limitless set of dissimilar activities with unmeasurable results—which contributed to those dollars being amalgamated in 2009 into a general funding stream that districts could thereafter apportion pretty much as they saw fit. That change surely contributed to the present situation in which many California districts now report to the Office for Civil Rights that they have *no* students enrolled in gifted education programs.

6. Title XI § 9101 (22), http://www2.ed.gov/policy/elsec/leg/esea02/pg107.html.

7. "Gifted Education in Ohio, Facts for Parents," Ohio Department of Education, accessed November 29, 2014, http://education.ohio.gov/getattachment/ Topics/Other-Resources/Gifted-Education-(1)/Resources-for-Parents/Gifted-Education-Fact-Sheet/Parent-Factsheet.pdf.aspx.

8. "General State Information," National Association for Gifted Children, accessed November 29, 2014, http://www.nagc.org/sites/default/files/Gifted-by-State/Table%20%20A%20%28general%29.pdf.

9. "Local Plan for the Education of the Gifted, 2011–2016," Fairfax County Public Schools, accessed November 29, 2014, http://www.fcps.edu/is/aap/pdfs/localplan/FinalLocalPlan.pdf.

10. "Gifted Education," Virginia Beach City Public Schools, accessed November 29, 2014, http://www.vbschools.com/curriculum/gifted/.

11. We don't deal here with the infinitely trickier issues that arise in realms such as the arts. How is it decided which child is a gifted painter, dancer, or pianist? Portfolios and auditions will play a role, of course, but who judges them? Do those judgments "hold up in court"? And how well do they recognize potential as well as accomplishment?

12. "Specialized High School Admissions Test (SHSAT)," New York City Department of Education, accessed January 17, 2015, http://schools.nyc.gov/accountability/resources/testing/shsat.htm.

13. "Gifted Services," Sarasota County Schools, accessed November 29, 2014, http://www.sarasotacountyschools.net/departments/pupilsupportservices/default.aspx?id=44336.

14. "Gifted/Talented Programs Introduction," Los Angeles Unified School District, accessed November 29, 2014, http://www.lausd.net/lausd/offices/GATE/intro-2.html.

CHAPTER 4

1. The website of the National Association for Gifted Children also identifies five types of programs or treatments, although they're not quite the same as the quintet described here. See "Gifted Education Practices," National Association for Gifted Children, accessed November 29, 2014, http://www.nagc.org/resources-publications/gifted-education-practices.

2. "A Nation Deceived: How Schools Hold Back America's Brightest Students, Volume II," John Templeton Foundation, 2004, http://www.accelerationinstitute.org/Nation_Deceived/ND_v2.pdf.

3. Chester E. Finn Jr. and Jessica Hockett, *Exam Schools: Inside America's Most Selective Public High Schools* (Princeton, NJ: Princeton University Press, 2012).

4. Jonathan Plucker et al., "Equal Talents, Unequal Opportunities: A Report Card on State Support for Academically Talented Low-Income Students," Jack Kent Cooke Foundation (March 2015), http://www.excellencegap.org/assets/files/JKCF_ETUO_Report.pdf.

5. "Table 52. Number of Gifted and Talented Students in Public Elementary and Secondary Schools, by Sex, Race/Ethnicity, and State: 2004 and 2006," U.S. Department of Education, Institute of Education Sciences, National Center for Education Statistics, accessed November 29, 2014, http://nces.ed.gov/programs/digest/d12/tables/dt12_052.asp.

6. "Civil Rights Data Collection: 2009–10 National and State Estimations," U.S Department of Education, accessed November 29, 2014, http://ocrdata.ed.gov/StateNationalEstimations/Projections_2009_10.

7. As we discuss in chapters 10 and 16, Taiwan and Ontario (and some other places, including a handful of U.S. states) have defined giftedness as a condition that entitles a student to "special education," which creates a semblance of a legal right to some version of gifted education, although such identification may bring complexities and drawbacks of its own, and programmatic or budgetary limits on student participation generally dampen the value of this arrangement.

8. "2013–2014, Gifted Indicator, Gifted Indicator Data File," Ohio Department of Education, accessed December 4, 2014, http://reportcard.education.ohio.gov/Download%20Data/2013-2014/Gifted%20Indicator/Gifted_Indicator_2014.xls.

9. Sa Bui, Steven Craig, and Scott Imberman, "Poor Results for High Achievers," *Education Next* 12, no. 1 (2012), and Sa Bui, Steven Craig, and Scott Imberman, "Is Gifted Education a Bright Idea? Assessing the Impact of Gifted and Talented Programs on Students," *American Economic Journal: Economic Policy* 6, no. 3 (August 2014).

10. David Card and Laura Giuliano, "Does Gifted Education Work? For Which Students?" (NBER Working Paper 20453, National Bureau of Economic Research, September 2014), http://www.nber.org/papers/w20453.

11. Linda Gorman, "Who Benefits from Education for the Gifted?" National Bureau of Economic Research, accessed January 17, 2015, http://www.nber.org/digest/jan15/w20453.html.

12. See Carolyn M. Callahan and Holly L. Hertberg-Davis, *Fundamentals of Gifted Education: Considering Multiple Perspectives* (New York: Routledge, 2013); Saiying Steenbergen-Hu and Sidney M. Moon, "The Effects of Acceleration on High-Ability Learners: A Meta-Analysis," *Gifted Child Quarterly* 55, no. 1 (January 2011); and "A Nation Deceived: How Schools Hold Back America's Brightest Students, Volume II."

13. Plucker et al., "Equal Talents, Unequal Opportunities: A Report Card on State Support for Academically Talented Low-Income Students."

CHAPTER 5

1. Tracy A. Huebner, "What Research Says About . . . / Year-Round Schooling," *Education Leadership* 67, no. 7 (April 2010).

2. "Homepage," Carol Tomlinson Ed.D., accessed November 29, 2014, http://www.caroltomlinson.com/.

3. We found nine states in which gifted education has most of the trappings of special ed, including student identification and "individual education plans." As with other special ed categories, however, the percentage of students actually *served* by gifted education programs varies widely among these states, as in places where it's not treated like special education.

4. Carol L. Tieso of the College of William and Mary does a nice job of summarizing the multiple ingredients that go into effective differentiation. See, e.g., Carol L. Tieso, "Differentiation Made Easy: An Oxymoron?," Catholic Schools Forum, Archdiocese of Washington, October 10, 2008, http://crins07 .wmwikis.net/file/view/Dr%20Tieso%20Differentiated,%20Gifted%20Students .pdf, and Carol L. Tieso, "The Effects of Grouping Practices and Curricular Adjustments on Achievement," *Journal for the Education of the Gifted* 29, no. 1 (2005): 60–89.

5. There is evidence that "high flyers" who attend schools with lots of "low flyers" are likely to start algebra later than eighth grade. Considering the extent to which algebra prior to ninth grade is a gateway to successful grappling with calculus during high school—and then to more advanced math in college—such a delay (presumably caused by the school's need to concentrate its math resources on low achievers) is not inconsequential for high-ability youngsters who might otherwise speed through mathematics. See Eric Parsons, "The Icarus Syndrome: Why Do Some High Flyers Soar While Others Fall?," Economic and Policy Analysis Research Center, University of Missouri, July 2013, http://economics.missouri.edu/working-papers/2013/WP1308_parsons.pdf.

6. As the senior author has observed in his grandchildren's classrooms, this can happen even in elite private schools with small classes and highly educated veteran teachers.

7. Holly Hertberg-Davis, "Myth 7: Differentiation in the Regular Classroom Is Equivalent to Gifted Programs and Is Sufficient: Classroom Teachers Have the Time, the Skill, and the Will to Differentiate Adequately," *Gifted Child Quarterly* 53, no. 4 (October 2009).

8. James R. Delisle, "Differentiation Doesn't Work," *Education Week*, January 6, 2015, http://www.edweek.org/ew/articles/2015/01/07/differentiation-doesnt-work.html?plckFindCommentKey=CommentKey:dda01338-e20a-4e89-bceb-3cacd98db7fe. See also James R. Delisle, *Dumbing Down America: The War on Our Nation's Brightest Young Minds (And What We Can Do to Fight Back)* (Waco, TX: Prufrock Press, 2014).

9. Michael J. Petrilli, "All Together Now?," *Education Next* 11, no. 1 (Winter 2011).

10. Tracy A. Huebner, "What Research Says About . . . / Differentiated Learning," *Educational Leadership*. 60, no. 5 (February 2010).

CHAPTER 6

1. As effective as acceleration may be, it's seldom practiced in U.S. schools nowadays and, when it consists only of getting through the standard curriculum faster, it does not necessarily bring the benefits of deeper inquiry, independent study, and freedom to pursue wider-ranging interests.

2. Note, though, that the comparative international performance data (from PISA, TIMSS, and PIRLS) that appear in the book are for the entire countries of Australia, Canada, and Germany.

3. As shown in the case studies, parents in a number of countries (particularly in Asia) may incur sizable out-of-pocket expenses by sending their children to "cram schools" of various kinds in order to gain entry to a gifted education program or selective high school. Other parent expenses include transportation for their children in the (many) situations where the government-financed gifted program does not cover this.

CHAPTER 7

1. "International Data Explorer," U.S. Department of Education, Institute of Education Sciences, National Center for Education Statistics, accessed November 29, 2014, http://nces.ed.gov/surveys/international/ide/.

2. Recent PISA data suggest, however, that this agony may not be justified: Japan's fifteen-year-olds came in third in the world—after Singapore and Korea—in "creative problem-solving." "Programme for International Student Assessment (PISA) Results from PISA 2012 Problem Solving: Japan," OECD, accessed November 29, 2014, http://www.oecd.org/pisa/keyfindings/PISA-2012-PS-results-eng-JAPAN.pdf.

3. The concept of inclusion is, however, making headway in Japanese special education. A 2012 survey found that 6.5 percent of the students in regular classrooms had learning or developmental disorders. See "Special Needs Education in Japan," National Institute for Educational Policy Research, accessed November 29, 2014, http://www.nier.go.jp/English/educationjapan/pdf/201209SEN.pdf.

4. Interview by J. Mark Bade, "A Conversation with Nobutaka Matsumura," *Twice Exceptional Newsletter*, Issue 39, March/April 2010, http://www.2enewsletter.com/2e_Newsletter_Issue_39.pdf.

5. Ibid.

6. Private school tuition is not terribly pricey in Japan—rarely more than $10,000—and financial aid is increasingly available for students from low-income families.

7. Almost as highly esteemed (and dating to the nineteenth century) are the private Keio and Waseda universities.

8. A Japanese advisor explains it this way: "Students may apply to two national and multiple private universities. Universities that compete against each other

often align their exam dates to ease the difficulty of predicting which success-ful applicant will actually enroll. Kyoto University accepts applications only once, and University of Tokyo has declared that it will do the same starting in 2015. These universities are also experimenting with a new type of admission that will look for gifted students based less on test scores and more on per-formance, such as winning International Science Olympiads." (Personal com-munication to authors.)

9. About seventy gain admission directly from high school; the other thirty get in later, after a year or more spent in special cram schools for secondary grad-uates who didn't make it on the first round.

10. Nationwide, 72 percent of Japanese high school pupils attend academic-track schools, while the rest enroll in vocational or "comprehensive" institutions. Some 57 percent of graduates go on to two- or four-year colleges (and another 17 percent to specialized vocational or technical institutions).

11. Others might contend that Japan has figured out how to have the best of both worlds, egalitarian and communitarian through grade 6, competitive and meritocratic thereafter.

12. The high school admission process is intricate. Private and national high schools administer their exams on a single date, while schools run by the pre-fecture administer theirs on a single later date. (Nobody could satisfactorily explain to us this fixation on one-shot exams, other than to say it's been done this way for ages and various interests want to keep it that way.) The upshot: a youngster may be able to apply to a total of two high schools.

13. School officials estimated that, among 160 students admitted to Koishikawa, only ten had not attended juku to boost their chance of getting in.

14. Schools with the "super science" designation did not display much of the sophisticated technology that high-performing STEM schools in other coun-tries often show visitors. Nor did we see much by way of independent research projects, field trips, internships, mentorships, or early access to college-level courses.

15. Jeffrey Hays, "Schools in Japan: The Culture, Peer Groups and Juku," Facts and Details, accessed January 24, 2015, http://factsanddetails.com/japan/cat23/sub150/item832.html.

16. Yuka Hayashi, "Piketty on Japan: Wealth Gap Likely to Rise," *Wall Street Journal*, May 13, 2014, http://blogs.wsj.com/japanrealtime/2014/05/13/piketty-on-japan-wealth-gap-likely-to-rise/.

17. Some juku also offer scholarships and free exams. Nevertheless, the costs of juku can rival those of full-time private schooling.

18. Personal communication with authors.

19. One boy nearing graduation from Tokyo's most exclusive private high school spoke wistfully to us of wanting to attend CalTech but did not seem to know what that would entail, nor was it evident that anyone on the school staff was able to help him.

20. "University of Tokyo, Kyoto University Move to Reform Exam-Based Admission Process," *Mainichi*, June 22, 2014, http://mainichi.jp/english/english/features/news/20140622p2a00m0na006000c.html.

21. Robert Leestma et al., "Japanese Education Today: A Report from the U.S. Study of Education in Japan," U.S. Department of Education, January 1987, 73, http://files.eric.ed.gov/fulltext/ED275620.pdf.

CHAPTER 8

1. "International Data Explorer," U.S. Department of Education, Institute of Education Sciences, National Center for Education Statistics, accessed November 29, 2014, http://nces.ed.gov/surveys/international/ide/.

2. As we were conducting this research, Singapore's gifted ed policies were under review—part of a six-year cycle—and it appears likely that the result will point toward broader access for more students. This review, we were told, is based in part on extensive surveys of various constituencies regarding present policies and programs for gifted students. For a country as analytic and uncomplacent as Singapore, however, we were struck by how little seems to have been done to develop formal evaluations of the existing programs. Efforts to track graduates longitudinally have proven inconclusive and in recent years there's been little by way of external review.

3. "Gifted Education Programme: Development and Growth," Singapore Ministry of Education, accessed November 29, 2014, http://www.moe .gov.sg/education/programmes/gifted-education-programme/development-and-growth/.

4. The Ministry has a lucid description of present policies and programs. See "Gifted Education Programme," Singapore Ministry of Education, accessed November 29, 2014, http://www.moe.gov.sg/education/programmes/gifted-education-programme/

5. "The Phoenix: Vocational Education and Training in Singapore," Center on International Education Benchmarking, October 2012, http://www.ncee.org/wp-content/uploads/2014/01/The-Phoenix1-7.pdf, and "Aspire Committee Report: 6 Ways to Improve Polytechnic and ITE Education," *The Straits Times*, August 25, 2014, http://www.straitstimes.com/news/singapore/education/story/aspire-committee-report-6-ways-improve-polytechnic-and-ite-education-.

6. We asked "70 percent of what number?" and learned that this varies with signs of the Zodiac! Singapore parents, at least the Chinese parents, would, for example, try for a baby to arrive in the year of the dragon or tiger but not the year of the snake or rat.

7. Though Singapore's total population is stable or growing slightly, its fertility rate is way down and there are fewer school-age kids every year. In 2010, there were about 216,000 kids in the five-to-nine age group.

8. See "Primary School Curriculum," Singapore Ministry of Education, accessed November 29, 2014, http://www.moe.gov.sg/education/primary/curriculum/.

9. Because regular primary classrooms in Singapore schools have up to 40 students, teachers would face significant challenges if there were no ability grouping.

10. "Enrichment Activities and Programmes for High-Ability Learners (HAL)," Singapore Ministry of Education, accessed November 29, 2014, http://www.moe.gov.sg/education/programmes/gifted-education-programme/high-ability-learners/.

11. As in many policy realms, Singapore's approach to gifted education reveals some tension regarding what to mandate centrally and what to leave to local discretion and initiative. (We actually heard officials use the phrase "centralized decentralization"!)

12. The University of Cambridge International Examinations program asserts that more than nine thousand schools in 160 countries use its tests.

13. Three hundred Singapore dollars equals about US$240, which would be deemed a bargain by even the least-expensive American private schools. Hefty government subsidy of private schools' basic operating costs (for Singapore students, not foreign kids) makes a big difference.

14. We saw an interesting exception in the Raffles Institution's impressive instructional-materials center, where teachers are helped by IT experts to develop their own curricular materials.

15. The Ministry of Education, we were told, does not keep data on student ethnicity or poverty, at least in relation to participation in specific programs, so they were unable to give us information on how ethnically or socioeconomically "equitable" is actual participation in the GEP. They did note that it serves more boys than girls.

16. "Is the Gifted Stream Still Relevant," All Singapore Stuff, October 26, 2014, http://www.allsingaporestuff.com/article/gifted-stream-still-relevant.

17. SMILETutor is an example of such a tutoring school. See "Homepage," SMILETutor, accessed November 29, 2014, http://www.findhometuition.com/.

CHAPTER 9

1. "International Data Explorer," U.S. Department of Education, Institute of Education Sciences, National Center for Education Statistics, accessed November 29, 2014, http://nces.ed.gov/surveys/international/ide/.

2. Cuiling Su, "The Other Arms Race: South Korea's Education Fever Needs Cooling," *The Economist*, November 6, 2013, http://www.economist.com/news/special-report/21588204-south-koreas-education-fever-needs-cooling-other-arms-race.

3. "A Shift Toward 'Education for Happiness,'" *Korea Herald*, March 27, 2013, http://www.koreaherald.com/view.php?ud=20130327000679.

4. Another such school, located in Busan and perhaps the highest-status secondary school in the land, also enjoys a close affiliation with KAIST. See "Homepage," Korea Science Academy of KAIST, accessed November 29, 2014, http://www.ksa.hs.kr/english/.

5. Evan Ramstad, "Studying Too Much Is a New No-No in Upwardly Mobile South Korea," *Wall Street Journal*, October 6, 2011, http://online.wsj.com/news/articles/SB10001424052970204612504576608680528108152.

6. Se-Woong Koo, "An Assault Upon Our Children: South Korea's Education System Hurts Students," *New York Times*, August 1, 2014, http://www.nytimes.com/2014/08/02/opinion/sunday/south-koreas-education-system-hurts-students.html?_r=0, and "A Pram Too Far," *The Economist*, October 23, 2014, http://www.economist.com/news/special-report/21588207-faced-overwhelming-pressures-south-korean-women-have-gone-baby-strike-pram-too.

7. Evan Ramstad, "Studying Too Much Is a New No-No in Upwardly Mobile South Korea."

8. Late on test day 2013, we found ourselves outside the Daejeon municipal education office as the completed student exam papers arrived with a police escort! A few leading universities, however, are de-emphasizing test scores in their admissions decisions; some are relying entirely on school records, interviews, and other "holistic" measures.

9. A fine account of the early history can be found in Seokhee Cho, "Gifted and Talented Education in Korea: Its Problems and Visions," *KEDI Journal of Educational Policy* 1, no. 1 (2004).

10. The specific domains are "general intelligence," "specific academic aptitude" (i.e., in a particular discipline), "creative thinking ability," "artistic ability" and "physical talents."

11. See Tim Dracup, "Gifted Education in South Korea—Part One," *Gifted Phoenix* (blog), March 1, 2012, https://giftedphoenix.wordpress.com/2012/03/01/gifted-education-in-south-korea-part-one/.

12. "How Does Class Size Vary Around the World?" OECD, November 2012, http://www.oecd.org/edu/skills-beyond-school/EDIF%202012—N9%20FINAL.pdf.

13. A good English-language description of such high schools can be found in Kyong Mi Choi and Dae Sik Hon, "Gifted Education in Korea: Three Korean High Schools for the Mathematically Gifted," *Gifted Child Today* 32, no. 2 (2009), http://files.eric.ed.gov/fulltext/EJ835841.pdf.

14. Many seek entry to multiple schools. School leaders estimated that, altogether, three thousand students applied to the national science high schools and fewer than one in four gained access.

15. On the other hand, commented one observer, a child's marks in a gifted high school are apt to be lower than what the same child would earn in a regular high school, which in parents' eyes may be a disadvantage when it comes to college admission.

16. An example is the Korean Minjok Leadership Academy, a boarding school open to students from across the country. It admits students via a multitiered selection process—but charges $15,000 or more.

17. "The Widening Educational Divide," *Education in Korea* (blog), May 21, 2011, http://educationinkorea.blogspot.com/2011/05/widening-educational-divide.html.

18. This varies greatly by province, from 1.0 in Gangwon to 8.0 in Chungbuk.

19. We also heard of schools that provide extra help for disadvantaged children with high ability.

20. "International Data Explorer."

21. Amanda Ripley, *The Smartest Kids in the World: And How They Got That Way* (New York: Simon & Schuster, 2013), 192.

22. Korea (and other Asian nations) may flagellate itself more than is warranted regarding student "creativity." The 2012 PISA assessments included a special look at "creative problem solving," said to measure "students' capacity to respond to non-routine situations." Korean fifteen-year-olds did exceptionally well, yet this accomplishment did not come at the expense of Korea's performance on the traditional math and science measures. See *PISA 2012 Results: Creative Problem Solving: Students' Skills in Tackling Real-Life Problems (Volume V)*, OECD, accessed November 29, 2014, http://www.oecd.org/pisa/keyfindings/PISA-2012-results-volume-V.pdf.

23. "Home page," Illinois Mathematics and Science Academy, accessed January 17, 2015, https://www.imsa.edu/.

CHAPTER 10

1. Children under fourteen composed 32 percent of the total population in 1980 but just half that in 2010.

2. Ting-feng Wu and Chia Lun Huang, "Taiwan's Dire Brain Drain," *Common-Wealth Magazine*, June 27, 2014, http://english.cw.com.tw/article.do?action=show&id=14807&offset=0.

3. "The World Factbook: East & Southeast Asia: Taiwan," Central Intelligence Agency, accessed November 30, 2014, https://www.cia.gov/library/publications/the-world-factbook/geos/tw.html.

4. Tom Loveless, "Lessons from the PISA-Shanghai Controversy," Brookings Institution, March 18, 2014, http://www.brookings.edu/research/reports/2014/03/18-pisa-shanghai-loveless, and "International Data Explorer," U.S. Department of Education, Institute of Education Sciences, National Center for Education Statistics, accessed November 29, 2014, http://nces.ed.gov/surveys/international/ide/.

5. "Key Measures for Special Education," Republic of China (Taiwan) Ministry of Education, accessed November 30, 2014, http://english.moe.gov.tw/ct.asp?xItem=14754&ctNode=11435&mp=11.

6. "The White Book of Gifted Education," Republic of China (Taiwan) Ministry of Education, accessed November 30, 2014, http://english.moe.gov.tw/public/Attachment/2959202371.pdf.

7. The fact that teachers generally get to choose their schools and, once there, cannot easily be removed or reassigned, means overstaffing of gifted education is visible in some places, particularly in schools with shrinking enrollments or where many students have moved to programs at other schools. We visited a primary school that was staffed by six gifted education specialists but enrolled just eighteen pupils in the gifted program.

8. We visited a Taichung elementary school with such a program. School staff were vague about actual curricula but asserted that they provide enrichment in creativity, leadership, independent study, "emotional giftedness," and "career planning."

9. We met students who were able to gain admission to gifted programs in primary school but not in junior high, and vice versa, as well as some who could find space only in subjects that didn't interest them.

10. Pat Gao, "Learning Free and Fair," *Taiwan Review*, July 1, 2012, http://taiwan review.nat.gov.tw/ct.asp?xItem=191992&CtNode=1222.

11. Joy Lee, "12-Year Compulsory Education Law Passed," *China Post*, June 28, 2013, http://www.chinapost.com.tw/taiwan/national/national-news/2013/0 6/28/382303/12-year-compulsory.htm. The private school subsidy evidently applies to all who enroll in vocational high schools. In academic high schools, it apparently does not extend to children from high-income families.

12. "About the National Federation of Teachers Unions," National Federation of Teachers Unions, R.O.C., accessed November 30, 2014, http://en.nftu.org.tw/AboutUs/AboutUs.aspx.

13. Taiwan also has several "experimental" high schools that operate under the aegis of the National Science Council rather than the education ministry; these also include gifted classes. See, e.g., "About NEHS: Brief History," National Experimental High School at Hsinchu Science Park, accessed November 30, 2014, http://www.nehs.hc.edu.tw/index_e.html.

14. The 2012 numbers are markedly different from 1999, when Taipei City high schools with gifted classes in academic subjects numbered just four, alongside twenty-six with gifted classes in the arts. What's evident, at least in the capital city, is growth in the academic program and shrinkage in the arts. But the total number of students in these classes, combining all fields, was slightly down—although not as much as Taiwan's total high school enrollment.

15. Results on the 2011 PIRLS test were similar. Note, too, that while Taiwan is by no means a world leader in reading (nor a superstar in science), its 12 percent of students scoring in the top two PISA tiers places it ahead of the United States and the OECD average (both about 8 percent) as well as most European countries. See "International Data Explorer."

16. "Buxiban in Taiwan," *The Newsletter* 56 (Spring 2011), http://www.iias.nl/sites/default/files/IIAS_NL56_15_0.pdf.

17. Elise Potaka and Benjamin Yeh, "Book Dragons: Inside Taiwan's Cram Schools," *Taipei Times*, June 8, 2011, http://www.taipeitimes.com/News/taiwan/archives/2011/06/08/2003505264.

18. Lee Seok Hwai, "Cram Schools Face Ban on English and Maths Tuition," *Straits Times*, Asia Report, August 31, 2013, http://www.straitstimes.com/the-big-story/asia-report/taiwan/story/cram-schools-face-ban-english-and-maths-tuition-20130831.

19. "The White Paper on Talent Training and Development of the Ministry of Education," Republic of China (Taiwan) Ministry of Education, December 2013, http://www.edu.tw/userfiles/url/20131209094223/%E6%95%99%E8%82%B2%E9%83%A8%E4%BA%BA%E6%89%8D%E5%9F%B9%E8%82%B2%E7%99%BD%E7%9A%AE%E6%9B%B81.pdf. There is no English version, so we arranged privately for relevant portions to be translated for us, including the title, publishing entity, and date shown here.

CHAPTER 11

1. "Finland: Slow and Steady Reform for Consistently High Results," OECD, accessed November 30, 2014, http://www.oecd.org/pisa/pisaproducts/46581035.pdf.

2. Pasi Sahlberg, "Finnish Students' Achievement Declined," *PasiSahlberg.com* (blog), November 14, 2013, http://pasisahlberg.com/news/new-study-finnish-students-achievement-declined-significantly/.

3. Christine Gross-Loh, "Finnish Education Chief: 'We Created a School System Based on Equality,'" *The Atlantic*, March 17, 2014, http://www.theatlantic.com/education/archive/2014/03/finnish-education-chief-we-created-a-school-system-based-on-equality/284427/.

4. Quoted in Valerie Strauss, "Are Finland's Vaunted Schools Slipping?," *Washington Post*, December 3, 2013, http://www.washingtonpost.com/blogs/answer-sheet/wp/2013/12/03/are-finlands-vaunted-schools-slipping/.

5. "Curriculum Reform 2016: Renewal of the Core Curriculum for Pre-Primary and Basic Education," Finnish National Board of Education, accessed November 30, 2014, http://www.oph.fi/english/education_development/current_reforms/curriculum_reform_2016.

6. Finland previously had a tracked system, like England's old "11-plus" exam, that sorted kids into those who went to an academic school and those who got a vocational education or just headed to work. Not so today, at least not through ninth grade.

7. The twelve-year-old national curriculum was undergoing revision in 2014 and those working on it expect the next version to pay a bit more attention to

high-ability learners, although such terminology may again be banished. See "Curriculum Reform 2016."

8. Practicing teachers, we were told, hunger for more in-service help with gifted pupils but little is available, even though Finnish schools and universities are awash in in-service education on myriad other topics.

9. Vast tracts of Finland are rural and many "urban settlements"—the national statistics report 745 of them!—are tiny. Yet the population (5.4 million, almost identical to Singapore's) is quite concentrated. Some 85 percent of Finns live on 2.2 percent of the landscape.

10. Principals of "receiving" schools also have discretion to weigh factors such as siblings already attending the school.

11. "Special Schools, Basic Education," City of Helsinki Education Department, accessed November 30, 2014, http://www.hel.fi/hki/opev/en/school+search/school+categories/special+schools%2C+basic+education.

12. "Helsingin Normaalilyseo (The Normal Lyceum of Helsinki)," Helsingin Yliopisto, accessed November 30, 2014, http://www.norssi.helsinki.fi/index.php?page=in-english.

13. It works for religious education, too: if there are three or more children of a particular faith in a school, instruction must be provided in that religion.

14. It's possible to map some sample-based assessment results onto communities to determine which areas within them have "good" or "bad" schools. And demographic data make it possible to see which neighborhoods are, say, heavy with immigrants.

15. For general descriptions and statistics, see "General Upper Secondary Education in Finland," Finnish Ministry of Education and Culture, accessed November 30, 2014, http://www.minedu.fi/OPM/Koulutus/lukiokoulutus/?lang=en, and "Upper Secondary and Post-Secondary Non-Tertiary Education," European Commission, accessed November 30, 2014, https://webgate.ec.europa.eu/fpfis/mwikis/eurydice/index.php/Finland:Upper_Secondary_and_Post-Secondary_Non-Tertiary_Education.

16. "Front Page," Studyinfo.fi, accessed November 30, 2014, https://opintopolku.fi/wp2/en/. Teachers determine the grades that go into students' GPA calculations and these may differ greatly by teacher. The grading scale is 4 to 10, but only at level 8 ("good performance") does the National Board of Education provide any sort of grading rubric, and it's pretty nebulous. This means that individual teachers mostly use their own criteria, even though the numerical average of these marks is hugely important to a student's future.

17. Kirsi Tirri and Elina Kuusisto, "How Finland Serves Gifted and Talented Pupils," *Journal for the Education of the Gifted* 36, no. 1 (2013), http://jeg.sagepub.com/content/36/1/84.

18. "Upper Secondary Schools," Espoo Esbo, accessed November 30, 2014, http://www.espoo.fi/en-US/Childcare_and_education/Upper_Secondary_Schools.

19. "The IB Programme at Mattlidens," Mattilidens Gymnasium, accessed November 30, 2014, http://www.mattliden.fi/gym/index.php/en/ib-section. For other examples of specialized high schools in Finland, see, e.g., "General Upper Secondary Education in Finland," Finnish Ministry of Education and Culture, accessed November 30, 2014, http://www.minedu.fi/OPM/Koulutus/lukiokoulutus/?lang=en; "Englanti," Kuopion Yhteiskoulun Musiikkilukio, accessed November 30, 2014, https://musiikkilukio.onedu.fi/web/englanti/; "Information," Sotunki Upper Secondary School, accessed November 30, 2014, http://www.sotunki.edu.vantaa.fi/koulu/info/english/; and "Etela-Tapiola High School," The OPEDUCA Project, accessed November 30, 2014, http://www.opeduca.eu/Etela-Tapiola_High_School.html.

20. "Millennium Youth Camp," Technology Academy Finland, accessed November 30, 2014, http://taf.fi/en/events/millennium-youth-camp/.

21. As in most countries, there's a status hierarchy, with the University of Helsinki ranking sixty-seventh in the world, just below Carnegie-Mellon on some international gauges. "QS World University Rankings 2014/15: Finland," Quacquarelli Symonds, accessed November 30, 2014, http://www.topuniversities.com/university-rankings/world-university-rankings/2014#sorting=rank+region=140+country=156+faculty=+stars=false+search=.

22. See Amanda Ripley, *The Smartest Kids in the World: And How They Got That Way* (New York: Simon & Schuster, 2013), 192, and "Entrance Exams," Study in Finland, accessed November 30, 2014, http://www.studyinfinland.fi/how_to_apply/eligibility_criteria/entrance_examinations.

23. "International Data Explorer," U.S. Department of Education, Institute of Education Sciences, National Center for Education Statistics, accessed November 29, 2014, http://nces.ed.gov/surveys/international/ide/.

24. Math scores are more equal, with males doing slightly better than females. The reading gap, however, is profound, as discussed in Tom Loveless, "2015 Brown Center Report on American Education: How Well Are American Students Learning? Part I: Girls, Boys, and Reading," Brookings Institution, March 24, 2015, http://www.brookings.edu/research/reports/2015/03/24-gender-gap-loveless. This sizable difference in reading prowess is paralleled by a large female-male gap in higher education. Although more men than women enter Finnish polytechnics—perhaps because of boys' edge in math—new university entrants in 2012 consisted of almost 13,000 women compared with 10,000 men. This despite the fact that 32 percent of male applicants were admitted versus 28 percent of females.

CHAPTER 12

1. "Education in Bavaria," Bayerisches Staatsministerium für Bildung und Kultus, Wissenschaft und Kunst, accessed November 30, 2014, http://www.km.bayern.de/education-in-bavaria.html, and "Basic Structure of the Education System in the Federal Republic of Germany—Diagram," Ständige Konferenz

der Kultusminister der Länder in der Bundesrepublik Deutschland (KMK), accessed November 30, 2014, http://www.kmk.org/fileadmin/doc/Dokumentation/Bildungswesen_en_pdfs/en-2014.pdf.

2. The traditional university-prep sequence lasted thirteen years and in places still does, as some parents worry that children will be overloaded if obliged to learn all the same material in one less year.

3. "Strong Performers and Successful Reformers in Education: Germany," Pearson Foundation, accessed November 30, 2014, http://www.pearsonfoundation.org/oecd/germany.html.

4. "Germany: Once Weak International Standing Prompts Strong Nationwide Reforms for Rapid Improvement," OECD, 2010, http://www.oecd.org/pisa/pisaproducts/46581323.pdf.

5. "Germany to Introduce Federal School Standards," DW, December 5, 2003, http://www.dw.de/germany-to-introduce-federal-school-standards/a-1050915.

6. Moving onto the gymnasium path, however, usually requires additional years of catch-up study.

7. "International Data Explorer," U.S. Department of Education, Institute of Education Sciences, National Center for Education Statistics, accessed November 29, 2014, http://nces.ed.gov/surveys/international/ide/.

8. Ibid.

9. This gap is ubiquitous in Germany. The various states' education laws address promoting ability among students but their teacher-training laws do not deal with specialized preparation of instructors in this realm. See, e.g., Christian Fischer and Kerstin Müller, "Gifted Education and Talent Support in Germany," *CEPS Journal* 4, no. 3 (2014), http://www.cepsj.si/pdfs/cepsj_4_3/CEPSj_4_3_Fischer_Muller_pp_31-54.pdf.

10. They're well qualified academically, however. Gymnasium teachers in Bavaria must possess at least two master's degrees, sometimes three!

11. Students have a limited choice of subjects in which to be examined, usually four or five in all, because they must span three major fields of learning. The structure and rules of the Abitur also vary by state.

12. Despite its generally leftist politics, Berlin has long subsidized private school attendance. As we write, however, lawmakers are weighing a reduction in the subsidy level and the addition of more frequent performance reviews to determine which schools will continue to receive the subsidy.

13. Berlin parents who think their child may be gifted can also turn to several private organizations and counselors for advice regarding the best school placements.

14. Regular gymnasium admission into grade 7 is based entirely on the marks a student earned in primary school. Everyone seems aware that such marks are not necessarily comparable from teacher to teacher or school to school, but that does not appear to be a big concern.

15. There are also a few schools that specialize in arts, sports, even dance. See, e.g., "Welcome to the Homepage of the State Ballet School of Berlin," State Ballet School of Berlin, accessed November 30, 2014, http://www.ballettschule-berlin.de/cids/englisch/.

16. If a child wants to attend gymnasium outside his town or city, the "sending" community must pay for transportation, though not for school tuition.

17. It did not, however, appear that churches, NGOs, or other social agencies play much of a role in this recruitment and referral process.

18. That evaluation showed positive program effects, but the absence of random assignment and a proper control group makes the comparisons suspect.

CHAPTER 13

1. As discussed in chapter 2, Hungary's Gini coefficient is the smallest among the dozen countries we examined, including the United States. See "World Factbook," U.S. Central Intelligence Agency, accessed November 29, 2014, https://www.cia.gov/library/publications/the-world-factbook/fields/2172 .html.

2. "International Data Explorer," U.S. Department of Education, Institute of Education Sciences, National Center for Education Statistics, accessed November 29, 2014, http://nces.ed.gov/surveys/international/ide/.

3. Ibid.

4. "Pupils and Students in Full-Time and Part-Time Education (1990-)," Hungarian Central Statistical Office, accessed November 30, 2014, https://www .ksh.hu/docs/eng/xstadat/xstadat_annual/i_wdsi001b.html.

5. Ágnes Vinkovits, "On Their Way—Hungarian Worker Migration Threats," *Budapest Business Journal*, October 18, 2002, http://www.bbj.hu/bbj/on-their-way—hungarian-worker-migration-threats_64200.

6. "Hungary Economy Profile 2014," Index Mundi, accessed November 30, 2014, http://www.indexmundi.com/hungary/economy_profile.html.

7. One unhappy observer also suggested to us that "the prime minister doesn't like data." See "Orban the Unstoppable," *The Economist*, September 27, 2014, http:// www.economist.com/news/europe/21620246-criticised-abroad-viktor-orban-going-strength-strength-home-orban-unstoppable?zid=309&ah=80dcf288b 8561b012f603b9fd9577f0e, and "Hungary's Divisive Prime Minister," *The Economist*, April 2, 2014, http://www.economist.com/blogs/economist-explains/2014/04/economist-explains-0?zid=309&ah=80dcf288b8561b012 f603b9fd9577f0e.

8. "Public Education Act Centralizes Hungary's Schools," Open Equal Free, accessed November 30, 2014, http://www.openequalfree.org/ed-news/public-education-act-centralizes-hungarys-schools, and "Hungary," Freedom House, accessed November 30, 2014, http://www.freedomhouse.org/report/nations-transit/2013/hungary#.VC2nxBYXJ88.

9. Official data say the Roma population is 3 percent, but knowledgeable Hungarians estimate it to be twice that.

10. Educator salaries in Hungary, university faculty included, are the subject of strongly held opinions and differing realities, depending on whom one speaks to. But they definitely appear lower than elsewhere in Western Europe. "Professor Salaries—International Comparison," World Salaries, accessed November 30, 2014, http://www.worldsalaries.org/professor.shtml, and "Teachers' and School Heads' Salaries and Allowances in Europe, 2013/14," European Commission, accessed November 30, 2014, http://eacea.ec.europa.eu/education/eurydice/documents/facts_and_figures/salaries.pdf.

11. Benô Csapó, "The Second Stage of Public Education and the Matura," in *Green Book: For the Renewal of Public Education in Hungary*, eds. Károly Fazekas, János Köllô, and Júlia Varga (Budapest: Prime Minister's Office, 2009), 81–104, http://econ.core.hu/file/download/greenbook/chapter3.pdf.

12. The history is admirably recounted by Eva Gyarmathy of the Hungarian Academy for Sciences in "The Gifted and Gifted Education in Hungary," *Journal for the Education of the Gifted* 36, no. 1 (2013).

13. See "Previous Issues," *KöMaL—Mathematical and Physics Journal for Secondary Schools*, accessed November 30, 2014, http://www.komal.hu/lap/korabbilapok.e.shtml, and "Overview," USA Mathematical Talent Search, accessed November 30, 2014, http://www.usamts.org/About/U_AbOverview.php.

14. "On the Activities of Scientific Students' Associations, on the Council of National Scientific Students' Associations, and on the National Scientific Students' Associations Conference," Professzorok Háza, accessed November 30, 2014, http://www.prof.iif.hu/otdt/otdteng.htm.

15. Tim Dracup, "What Has Become of the European Talent Network? Part One," *Gifted Phoenix* (blog), March 28, 2014, http://giftedphoenix.wordpress.com/2014/03/28/what-has-become-of-the-european-talent-network-part-one/.

16. "News on High Ability," European Council for High Ability, accessed November 30, 2014, http://www.echa.info/, and "TalentMap of Europe," European Talent Centre Budapest, accessed November 30, 2014, http://www.talentcentrebudapest.eu/talentmap.

17. "What Is the National Talent Program?," Nemzeti Tehetség Program, accessed November 30, 2014, http://www.tehetsegprogram.hu/node/54; "Parliamentary Resolution Number 126/2008. (XII. 4.) OGY," accessed November 30, 2014, available at http://www.tehetsegpont.hu/dokumentumok/hungarian_talent_programme_charts.pdf; and Zsuzsa M. Szilágyi, "Talent Support in Hungary: Policy and Practice in the New Millennium," European Talent Centre Budapest, October 24, 2012, http://www.talentcentrebudapest.eu/sites/default/files/MSzilagyi_Szeged_2012oct.pdf.

18. "From the Hungarian Genius Programme to the Talent Bridges Project," Magyar Genius Portal, accessed November 30, 2014, http://geniuszportal.hu/node/7853, "Secondary Schools in Hungary," Matching in Practice, May 3,

2013, http://www.matching-in-practice.eu/secondary-schools-in-hungary/.

19. "Secondary Schools in Hungary," Matching in Practice, May 3, 2013, http://www.matching-in-practice.eu/secondary-schools-in-hungary/.

20. "Arany János Program for Developing Talents of Socially Disadvantaged Students," Arany János Tehetséggondozó Program, accessed November 30, 2014, http://www.ajtp.hu/digitalcity/homepage.jsp?dom=AAAACWTC&fmn=AAAAVNWU&prt=AAAANXBF&men=AAAAVNWV.

21. Secondary-school dorms, we learned, are a long-standing practice in Eastern Europe, with origins as far back as the eighteenth century. In 2010, some 450 of them, mostly state operated, housed some 70,000 students in Hungary, although three-quarters of these young people were enrolled in vocational-technical schools, not university-prep gymnasia.

22. Subprogram 1, we were told, has a 90 percent completion rate. Subprograms 2 and 3 have completion rates of 70 and 50 percent respectively.

23. "International Data Explorer."

24. Eric A. Hanushek, Paul E. Peterson, and Ludger Woessmann, "Not Just the Problem of Other People's Children: U.S. Student Performance in Global Perspective," PEPG Report 14-01, Harvard Kennedy School, Program on Education Policy and Governance and Education Next, May 2014.

25. Gyarmathy, "The Gifted and Gifted Education in Hungary."

26. "Education in Hungary: Past, Present, Future—An Overview," Hungary Ministry of Education and Culture, 2008, http://www.nefmi.gov.hu/letolt/english/education_in_hungary_080805.pdf.

27. This figure (which omits schools' direct expenditures on their students) would rise considerably if calculated per pupil or "per talented pupil." See Tim Dracup, "What Has Become of the European Talent Network? Part One," and Dracup, "What Has Become of the European Talent Network? Part Two," Gifted Phoenix (blog), March 28, 2014, http://giftedphoenix.wordpress.com/2014/03/30/what-has-become-of-the-european-talent-network-part-two/.

CHAPTER 14

1. Victor Mueller-Oppliger, "Gifted Education in Switzerland: Widely Acknowledged, but Obstacles Still Exist in Implementation," CEPS Journal 4, no. 3 (2014), http://www.cepsj.si/pdfs/cepsj_4_3/CEPSj_4_3_Mueller-Oppliger_pp_89-110.pdf.

2. "Schools and Education in Switzerland," ETH Zurich, accessed November 30, 2014, http://www.facultyaffairs.ethz.ch/dualcareer/bildung_EN, and "Global Perspectives: Lessons from Switzerland's VET System," Center on International Education Benchmarking, accessed November 30, 2014, http://www.ncee.org/2013/10/global-perspectives-lessons-from-switzerlands-vet-system/.

3. "International Data Explorer," U.S. Department of Education, Institute of Education Sciences, National Center for Education Statistics, accessed

November 29, 2014, http://nces.ed.gov/surveys/international/ide/.

4. Ibid.

5. Ibid.

6. We heard estimates that about half of Swiss gymnasia base admission on exam scores and about half rely on grades and individual evaluations.

7. Mueller-Oppliger, "Gifted Education in Switzerland."

8. Joseph S. Renzulli, "Three-Ring Conception of Giftedness," University of Connecticut Nead Center for Gifted Education and Talent Development, accessed November 29, 2014, http://www.gifted.uconn.edu/sem/semart13.html.

9. Center-based programs are also open to students in the lower secondary grades.

10. Switzerland's deep tradition of "direct democracy," with many cantonal decisions made by voters who may come to the polls several times a year, is echoed in the participatory nature of school-level governance.

11. In 2013, 28 percent of Swiss over age fifteen were first-generation residents; almost 20 percent were citizens of other countries. See "Migration and Integration—Data, Indicators: Population with a Migration Background," Switzerland Federal Statistical Office, accessed November 30, 2014, http://www.bfs.admin.ch/bfs/portal/en/index/themen/01/07/blank/key/04.html.

12. Victor Mueller-Oppliger, personal communication with the authors.

13. We detected no evidence that the Swiss worry much about the subjectivity and noncomparability of teacher-conferred grades, despite the absence of common rubrics.

14. See, e.g., "ChagALL," Jacobs Foundation, accessed November 30, 2014, http://jacobsfoundation.org/project/chagall/.

15. Mueller-Oppliger, personal communication with the authors.

16. Ibid.

17. "List of Countries by GDP (Nominal) per Capita," *Wikipedia*, accessed November 30, 2014, http://en.wikipedia.org/wiki/List_of_countries_by_GDP_%28nominal%29_per_capita.

18. Mueller-Oppliger, "Gifted Education in Switzerland."

19. Teachers of the gifted are not paid anything extra, either, although special education teachers are.

20. Mueller-Oppliger, "Gifted Education in Switzerland."

CHAPTER 15

1. For example, significant—and promising—alterations in the exams given toward the end of high school will not be in place before 2017.

2. We've tried throughout the book to standardize the names of countries in our sample, but this is not always possible with regard to England because TIMSS and PIRLS provide data for "England," while PISA data are for the "United

Kingdom," which includes Wales, Scotland, and Northern Ireland, although England contains about 85 percent of the U.K. population.

3. "International Data Explorer," U.S. Department of Education, Institute of Education Sciences, National Center for Education Statistics, accessed November 29, 2014, http://nces.ed.gov/surveys/international/ide/.

4. Heather Saul, "Underachieving Pupils More Susceptible to Joining EDL, Says Ofsted Chief Sir Michael Wilshaw," *The Independent*, June 15, 2013, http://www.independent.co.uk/news/education/education-news/underachieving-pupils-more-susceptible-to-joining-edl-says-ofsted-chief-sir-michael-wilshaw-8660051.html.

5. "David Cameron's Speech to the Conservative Conference—Full Text and Audio," *The Spectator*, October 1, 2014, http://blogs.spectator.co.uk/coffee house/2014/10/david-camerons-speech-to-the-conservative-conference-full-text/.

6. "Home," Ofsted, accessed November 30, 2014, http://www.ofsted.gov.uk/, and "Home," Ofqual, accessed November 30, 2014, http://ofqual.gov.uk/.

7. "Independent Schools," Eleven Plus Exams, accessed November 30, 2014, http://www.elevenplusexams.co.uk/schools/independent-schools.

8. Judith Burns, "Deeply Elitist UK Locks Out Diversity at Top," *BBC News*, Education and Family, August 28, 2014, http://www.bbc.com/news/education-28953881.

9. "History of the 11+," The 11 Plus, accessed November 30, 2014, http://www.the11pluswebsite.co.uk/history-of-the-11/.

10. "Comprehensive Schools: The History," *Times Higher Education*, January 15, 1986, http://www.timeshighereducation.co.uk/news/comprehensive-schools-the-history/92186.article, and William A. Proefriedt, "Revisiting James Bryant Conant," *Education Week*, May 17, 2005, http://www.edweek.org/ew/articles/2005/05/18/37proefriedt.h24.html.

11. This was part of a comprehensive suite of education reforms undertaken by the Thatcher team that also included national academic standards, curricula, and exams, as well as curbs on the power of (mostly Labor-dominated) "local education authorities" in favor of building-level control and more parental choices.

12. Janet Murray, "Farewell to the Gifted and Talented Scheme," *The Guardian*, February 1, 2010, http://www.theguardian.com/education/2010/feb/02/gifted-talented-scrapped-funds-redirected, and Julie Henry, "Ministers Pull the Plug on Gifted and Talented Academy," *The Telegraph*, January 23, 2010, http://www.telegraph.co.uk/education/educationnews/7062061/Ministers-pull-the-plug-on-gifted-and-talented-academy.html.

13. "School Inspection Handbook," Ofsted, September 19, 2014, http://www.ofsted.gov.uk/resources/school-inspection-handbook.

14. Claire Crawford, Lindsey Macmillan, and Anna Vignoles, "Progress Made by High-Attaining Children from Disadvantaged Backgrounds," Social Mobility and Child Poverty Commission, June 2014, https://www.gov.uk/government/

uploads/system/uploads/attachment_data/file/324501/High_attainers_progress_report_final.pdf. The analysts looked closely at changes in student achievement between what England calls "Key Stage 1," usually age seven, and "Key Stage 4," age fourteen or fifteen.

15. "Types of School," Gov.UK, accessed November 30, 2014, https://www.gov.uk/types-of-school/overview. Indeed, one of our British advisors notes that the complexity and variety of education policies and practices across England makes almost all generalizations suspect. "Most assertions about the English system," he explained to us, "really refer to 'tendencies' in the system rather than universal truths about that system. There are just so many accumulated exceptions." (Personal communication to the authors.)

16. Angela Harrison, "New Battles Loom Over Grammar Schools," *BBC News*, March 29, 2012, http://www.bbc.com/news/education-17551611.

17. Selective grammar schools turn out to be especially popular among working-class families that see them as paths to upward mobility for their children, though there's controversy over whether such schools actually help to effect such mobility.

18. Tess Reidy, "New Grammar School Test Thwarts 'Pushy Parents,'" *The Guardian*, February 8, 2014, http://www.theguardian.com/education/2014/feb/08/grammar-selective-schools-exam-tutors.

19. "The New School Rules," *The Economist*, October 9, 2014, http://www.economist.com/news/britain/21623766-academies-programme-has-transformed-englands-educational-landscape-new-school-rules.

20. See, e.g., "Admissions," Stockley Academy, accessed November 30, 2014, http://www.stockleyacademy.com/page/?title=Admissions&pid=19, and "Admissions," Twyford C of E High School, accessed November 30, 2014, http://www.twyford.ealing.sch.uk/admissions/.

21. Some also have permission to select up to 10 percent of their entering students on the basis of test scores, auditions, and other qualifications. And in perhaps the strangest example of selectivity that we encountered in England, one highly regarded academy in east London plans to base some of its student admissions on applicants' potential to become outstanding oarsmen in the school's rowing program, judging them by physical characteristics such as height, arm span, and strength. See Lucy Ward, "Calling Budding Olympians: State School to Pick Pupils on Rowing Ability," *The Guardian*, November 24, 2014, http://www.theguardian.com/education/2014/nov/24/london-school-select-pupils-rowing-admissions-mossbourne. Still, most academies in England are multipurpose secondary schools without particular specializations.

22. "The Most Able Students: Are They Doing as Well as They Should in Our Non-Selective Secondary Schools?," Ofsted, June 13, 2013, http://www.ofsted.gov.uk/resources/most-able-students-are-they-doing-well-they-should-our-non-

selective-secondary-schools.

23. Ibid.

24. Although England was the subject of our study, the PISA sample is drawn from the United Kingdom as a whole. (TIMSS and PIRLS focus on England itself.)

25. Crawford, Macmillan, and Vignoles, "Progress Made by High-Attaining Children from Disadvantaged Backgrounds."

26. One that's different is weakness in the attainments of white boys, a shortfall that seems to draw more attention in England than either excellence issues or minority concerns.

27. Ofsted, "The Most Able Students."

28. "Reforming GCSEs: The Changing Landscape: A Summary of What's Planned for GCSEs from 2015," Oxford Cambridge and RSA, accessed November 30, 2014, http://www.ocr.org.uk/Images/141803-guide-to-the-gcse-changes.pdf. One of our advisors explains that current tests have "been dominated by threshold measures (target of level 4 in national tests at 11, and a student's need to earn at least five grades of C or better on the GCSE) for over a decade, despite the fact that research showed early that this led to a neglect of the most and least attaining pupils."

29. "Home," Sutton Trust, accessed November 30, 2014, http://www.suttontrust .com/. Another valuable resource is the lively *Gifted Phoenix* blog, written by the former lead official for the national gifted program, which offers analyses of the impact of education policy on high-ability learners in England—and also provides useful insights on gifted education policies and programs in other countries. See "Home," *Gifted Phoenix* (blog), accessed November 30, 2014, https://giftedphoenix.wordpress.com/.

30. "2 Key Design Features: Tiering," Ofqual, accessed November 30, 2014, http:// webarchive.nationalarchives.gov.uk/20140813100319/http://comment.ofqual .gov.uk/gcse-reform-june-2013/category/2-key-design-features-tiering/.

CHAPTER 16

1. The national government does attend to the education of Canada's indigenous peoples and language minorities.

2. See, e.g., "Ontario, Canada: Reform to Support High Achievement in a Diverse Context," OECD, 2010, http://www.oecd.org/pisa/pisaproducts/46580959.pdf, and Michael Fullan, "What America Can Learn from Ontario's Education Success," *The Atlantic*, May 4, 2012, http://www.theatlantic.com/national/ archive/2012/05/what-america-can-learn-from-ontarios-education-success/ 256654/.

3. See, e.g., Martin Regg Cohn, "Falling Math Scores Shake Up Ontario's Political Calculus: Cohn," *The Star*, January 25, 2014, http://www.thestar.com/ news/canada/2014/01/25/falling_math_scores_shake_up_ontarios_political_

calculus_cohn.html, and Steve Kupferman, "Is Public Funding for Ontario Catholic Schools Back on the Political Agenda?," *Toronto Life*, January 23, 2014, http://www.torontolife.com/informer/toronto-politics/2014/01/23/public-funding-catholic-schools-ontario/.

4. Caroline Alphonso, "Canada's Fall in Math-Education Ranking Sets Off Alarm Bells," *Globe and Mail*, December 3, 2013, http://www.the globeandmail.com/news/national/education/canadas-fall-in-math-education-ranking-sets-off-red-flags/article15730663/.

5. Ontario's French speakers do significantly worse. See "Pan-Canadian Assessment Program (PCAP)," Council of Ministers of Education, Canada, accessed November 30, 2014, http://cmec.ca/240/Programs-and-Initiatives/Assessment/Pan-Canadian-Assessment-Program-%28PCAP%29/Overview/index.html.

6. This structure is not based solely on geography. A community may have as many as four education boards: English and French, public and Catholic, all of them supported by the province. (Roman Catholicism is the only faith whose schools receive government financing.)

7. "Special Education: A Guide for Educators," Ontario Ministry of Education, 2001, http://www.edu.gov.on.ca/eng/general/elemsec/speced/guide/speced handbooke.pdf. As we write, an expert task force is working on recommendations for the Ministry that will include a revised definition of giftedness.

8. Other Canadian postsecondary institutions, such as the University of British Columbia, do offer a few such courses. And the Ontario situation is expected to change as initial teacher preparation shifts from a one- to a two-year program. See "Giving New Teachers the Tools for Success: Ontario Enhancing Teacher Education, Supporting Greater Student Achievement," Ontario Ministry of Education, June 5, 2013, http://news.ontario.ca/edu/en/2013/06/giving-new-teachers-the-tools-for-success.html.

9. "A Look at Gifted Education Across Ontario," Association for Bright Children of Ontario, February 2011, http://www.abcontario.ca/images/pdfs/A_Look_at_Gifted_Education_Across_Ontario.pdf.

10. TDSB declined to meet with us but officials at Toronto's Catholic school board were hospitable and informative.

11. TDSB was created in 1998 by merging half a dozen preexisting districts, several of which used holistic criteria for determining which students belong in gifted ed programs. In the name of fairness and equity, postmerger they shifted to IQ-based admission only.

12. There are "tribunals" in Ontario where parents can appeal if they believe their child has not been properly "identified" or have concerns about the school placement or learning program that the district has devised for that child. See "Welcome Message from the Vice-Chair," Ontario Special Education (English) Tribunal, accessed November 30, 2014, http://oset-tedo.ca/eng/index.html.

13. "Gifted Programme Elementary Schools," Toronto Catholic District School

Board, accessed November 30, 2014, https://www.tcdsb.org/ProgramsServices/SpecialEducation/gifted/Elementary/Pages/default.aspx.

14. "Schools with Gifted and Primary Gifted Programs, 2014–2015," Toronto District School Board, September 2014, http://www.tdsb.on.ca/Portals/0/Elementary/docs/SpecED/SpEd%20Gifted%20Programs2014.pdf.

15. "Programs, Gifted Programming," Kawartha Pine Ridge District School Board, accessed November 30, 2014, http://www.kprschools.ca/Programs/GiftedProgramming.html#.Uv_UhM5fTSg.

16. "Programs & Films," Ontario Science Centre, accessed November 30, 2014, http://www.ontariosciencecentre.ca/School/Curriculum/Grade/.

17. "Learning for All: K to 12—Ministry of Education Policy Document," Community Living Ontario, accessed November 30, 2014, http://www.communitylivingontario.ca/learning-all-k-12-ministry-education-policy-document.

18. "Acceleration: An Effective Intervention, Grades 4–12," Thames Valley District School Board, 2010, http://www.vaderandson.com/joomla/images/stories/pdf/acceleration%202010%20tvdsb.pdf.

19. Only 80 percent of students enrolled in TDSB high school gifted programs had participated in such programs in earlier grades. Evidently the other 20 percent are newly identified for high school.

20. Whether transportation is subsidized again depends on the district. TDSB covers such costs—a considerable drain on its budget—for special-ed pupils residing far from the school to which they're assigned. Toronto's Catholic School Board, however, expects parents to transport their children.

21. The principal also remarked that teaching only gifted students is hard on teachers because they have to work hard to keep up!

22. "Marc Garneau C.I. News & Events," Marc Garneau Collegiate Institute, accessed November 30, 2014, http://schools.tdsb.on.ca/marcgarneau/, and "Bloor Collegiate Institute (GR. 09-12)," Toronto District School Board, accessed November 30, 2014, http://schoolweb.tdsb.on.ca/bloorci/AboutUs.aspx.

23. "Application Package, 2014–2015," Monarch Park Collegiate, accessed November 30, 2014, http://monarchparkcollegiate.ca/programs/Application_Package_2014_2015.pdf.

24. "Specialized Schools and Programs," Toronto District School Board, accessed November 30, 2014, http://www.tdsb.on.ca/HighSchool/GoingtoHighSchool/SpecializedSchoolsandPrograms.aspx.

25. "Welcome to UTS," University of Toronto Schools, accessed November 30, 2014, http://www.utschools.ca/.

26. At the TDSB high school that we visited, 20 percent of the "gifted" students have "dual exceptionalities." (In the United States, the more common term is "twice exceptional.")

27. It's also notable that, while NCLB set the unattainable goal of 100 percent proficiency at least in part because anything less would have catalyzed controversy

("Which kids do you not care about becoming proficient?"), Ontario policy makers seem copacetic with a more realistic target of 75 percent.

CHAPTER 17

1. Australia also has ten territories, three of which enjoy partial self-government. The others—all small and thinly populated—are run from Canberra.

2. "Table 1.01: Summary Statistics of Schools and Full-Time Students," Western Australia Department of Education, accessed November 30, 2104, http://www.det.wa.edu.au/redirect/?oid=com.arsdigita.cms.contenttypes.FileStorage Item-id-15491064&title=Table+101-20142&stream_asset=true.

3. Sue Thomson, Lisa De Bortoli, and Sarah Buckley, "PISA in Brief: Highlights from the Full Australian Report: *PISA 2012: How Australia Measures Up*," Australian Council for Economic Research, accessed January 25, 2014, http://www.acer.edu.au/files/PISA-2012-In-Brief.pdf.

4. "International Data Explorer," U.S. Department of Education, Institute of Education Sciences, National Center for Education Statistics, accessed November 29, 2014, http://nces.ed.gov/surveys/international/ide/.

5. Thomson, De Bortoli, and Buckley, "PISA in Brief."

6. "Home," National Assessment Program, accessed November 30, 2014, http://www.nap.edu.au/.

7. "A Guide for Parents: Non-government Schools in Western Australia," Department of Education Services, Non-government Schools, 2014, http://www.des .wa.gov.au/schooleducation/nongovernmentschools/parents_and_communities/ Documents/Non-Government%20Schools%20of%20Western%20Australia% 20-%20Guide%20for%20Parents%202014.PDF.

8. "Catering for Diversity," Catholic Education Office of Western Australia, accessed November 30, 2014, http://internet.ceo.wa.edu.au/Religious EducationCurriculum/CurriculumK-12/Pages/Catering-for-Diversity.aspx; "Processes and Procedures for the Identification and Support of Gifted and Talented Students in Catholic Schools in Western Australia," Catholic Education Office of Western Australia, October 2012, http://internet .ceo.wa.edu.au/ReligiousEducationCurriculum/CurriculumK-12/Documents/ Processes%20and%20Procedures%20for%20the%20Identification%20and%20 Support%20of%20Gifted%20and%20Talented%20Students%20in%20Catholic %20Schools.pdf; and "Gifted and Talented Education in Catholic Schools," Catholic Education Office of Western Australia, 2014, http://internet.ceo.wa .edu.au/ReligiousEducationCurriculum/CurriculumK-12/Documents/Gifted %20and%20Talented%20Education%20in%20Catholic%20Schools.pdf.

9. See, e.g., "Catchment Area," Shenton College, accessed November 30, 2014, http://www.shenton.wa.edu.au/prospective/catchment.

10. The Early Years Extension (EYE) Program is an example of such a program.

See "Early Years Extension (EYE) Program," North Metro Education Region PEAC, accessed November 30, 2014, http://www.northmetropeac.wa.edu.au/early_years.htm.

11. "Parent Courses—Gifted Kids Keys to Academic Success: Parent Intervention Programs," Gifted & Talented Children's Association of WA, Inc., accessed November 30, 2104, http://www.gatcawa.org/index.php/courses, and "Home," Mermaids and Mermen, accessed November 30, 2014, http://www.mermaidsandmermen.com.au/.

12. Most Australian states already treat seventh grade as part of high school. Western Australia's public schools are joining them, both because that's how the national curriculum is structured and because the state's Catholic and independent schools have already made the shift. In such a competitive student market, the government schools don't want to be left behind.

13. There are online offerings for gifted students outside the metro area, mostly synchronous classes with school-based teachers, not asynchronous "do it on your own whenever you like" classes.

14. See, e.g., "Courses & Work Samples," North Metro Education Region PEAC, accessed November 30, 2014, http://www.northmetropeac.wa.edu.au/work%20samples.htm.

15. The screening, appeals, and matching processes take so long that students are tested at the end of sixth grade for a program that (currently) doesn't start until eighth. This will presumably change as a consequence of moving seventh grade into high school.

16. "City Boarding," Western Australia Department of Education, accessed November 30, 2014, http://det.wa.edu.au/boarding/city/detcms/portal/. Parents of children in gifted education programs in W.A. also incur direct costs for field trips, materials and, especially, transportation. But these are not big surprises, as government schools themselves have "voluntary" fees simply to attend them, and high school parents must often pay for uniforms and textbooks. Private schools usually charge fees on top of their government subsidies. Graeme Powell, "Call to Review WA Voluntary School Fees System," *ABC (Australian Broadcast Corporation) News*, May 5, 2013, http://www.abc.net.au/news/2013-05-06/call-to-review-wa-voluntary-school-fee-system/4671392.

17. "International Data Explorer."

18. Sue Thomson, Lisa De Bortoli, and Sarah Buckley, *PISA 2012: How Australia Measures Up*, Australian Council for Economic Research, 2013, http://www.acer.edu.au/documents/PISA-2012-Report.pdf.

19. "2014 Australian Tertiary Admission Rank (ATAR) release," Universities Admissions Centre, accessed November 30, 2014, http://www.uac.edu.au/undergraduate/atar/.

20. Program staff insist that savings produced by the new funding model will be sufficient to offset the program enhancements.

21. Of course, the number of eligible participants within that percentage keeps rising as enrollments do.

22. Several people mentioned that other Australian states have gone overboard on selective-admission schools and programs such that they're now having to reach "far into the barrel" to fill their enrollments and (as with some American AP classes) may end up with students who are less than truly gifted.

CHAPTER 18

1. The psychologist Harold Stevenson began investigating Asian attitudes toward schooling in the 1970s, and he and James Stigler published the first influential book on the topic in 1992. See Harold W. Stevenson and James W. Stigler, *The Learning Gap: Why Our Schools Are Failing and What We Can Learn from Japanese and Chinese Education* (New York: Touchstone, 1992).

2. Relying on differentiation in ordinary classrooms is even shakier in locales that make scant provision for teachers to be specially trained to work with high-ability children. It's often possible for interested teachers to obtain some such training but—in sharp contrast to special education—almost nowhere is it mandatory.

3. Western Australia and some local boards within Ontario and Switzerland also engage in universal screening via tests given to all third or fourth graders, but the actual instructional opportunities that follow are spottier than Singapore's Gifted Education Program.

4. See Po Bronson, "How Not to Talk to Your Kids," *New York*, August 3, 2007, http://nymag.com/news/features/27840/, and Malcolm Gladwell, "The Talent Myth," *The New Yorker*, July 22, 2002, http://www.newyorker.com/magazine/2002/07/22/the-talent-myth.

5. We don't deal here with the extraordinary challenge of educating the rare "genius." See, e.g., June Kronholz, "Challenging the Gifted," *Education Next* 22, no. 2 (2011).

6. Angela Duckworth believes not only that perseverance can be taught—though nobody is yet quite sure how—but also that it has genetic elements that schools cannot readily alter. See Angela Duckworth, "Can Perseverance Be Taught?," Big Questions Online, August 5, 2013, https://www.bigquestionsonline.com/content/can-perseverance-be-taught.

CHAPTER 19

1. Some states and districts already obtain their own scores from PISA and TIMSS, and it has recently become possible for individual high schools to administer a PISA-equivalent test to their students, thus making international comparisons possible. The cost of such participation can be a problem, however, suggesting another useful role for philanthropy. See, e.g., "PISA-Based Test for Schools," Organisation for Economic Co-operation and

Development, Program for International Student Assessment, accessed April 13, 2015, http://www.oecd.org/pisa/aboutpisa/pisa-based-test-for-schools.htm, and "State and District Participation in TIMSS," U.S. Department of Education, Institute of Education Sciences, National Center for Education Statistics, accessed April 13, 2015, http://nces.ed.gov/timss/benchmark.asp.

2. A small but positive step to beef up research in this realm was taken in autumn 2014 when the federal Institute of Education Sciences, availing itself of a small appropriation of "Javits money" supplied by Congress that year (after three years of zero funding), made a modest grant to the University of Connecticut and several partner campuses to revive a National Center for Research on Gifted Education. See Del Siegle, "IES Awards National Center for Research on Gifted Education," University of Connecticut, October 22, 2014, http://ncrge.uconn.edu/2014/10/22/ies-awards-national-center-for-research-on-gifted-education/, and IES Grant: National Center for Research on Gifted, 2014, Award Number: R305C140018, U.S. Department of Education, Institute of Education Sciences, accessed January 21, 2014, http://ies.ed.gov/funding/grantsearch/details.asp?ID=1564.

3. A simple example: Ohio's school reporting system now tracks—and school report cards must display—the achievement of gifted students and the "value-added" that they make each year. Certainly a step in the right direction! See "2014 Gifted Rankings," Ohio Department of Education, accessed November 29, 2014, http://education.ohio.gov/getattachment/Topics/Data/Accountability-Resources/Ohio-Report-Cards/Report-Card-Lists-and-Rankings/Copy-of-2014_Gifted_Rankings_v_1-1_External.xlsx.aspx.

4. Severely disabled youngsters may be excused from participation in these assessments, but charter school students take part in them, as do growing numbers of private school pupils.

5. Some in the gifted education world contend that, if tests are used at all, they should not be IQ or achievement tests but, rather, efforts to get at "creativity," "problem solving," "critical thinking," and such. A worthy impulse, indeed, and one that PISA has endeavored to employ for its sample, but the cognitive psychologists for whom we have greatest respect have serious reservations about the accuracy and reliability of such measures when applied to individuals rather than large populations. See *PISA 2012 Results: Creative Problem Solving: Students' Skills in Tackling Real-Life Problems (Volume V)*, OECD, accessed November 29, 2014, http://www.oecd.org/pisa/keyfindings/pisa-2012-results-volume-v.htm.

6. David Card and Laura Giuliano, "Does Gifted Education Work? For Which Students?," (NBER Working Paper 20453, National Bureau of Economic Research, September 2014), http://www.nber.org/papers/w20453.

7. Mindful of too many anecdotes about high school valedictorians who turn out to need remediation in college, we must understand that a child scoring

near the top of a very weak school may not, in fact, be very high achieving—or well prepared for greater education challenges.

8. Any number of "rating scales" and checklists exist, some of them carefully validated. See, e.g., Joseph S. Renzulli, "A Practical System for Identifying Gifted and Talented Students," University of Connecticut Neag Center for Gifted Education and Talent Development, accessed November 29, 2014, http://www.gifted.uconn.edu/sem/semart04.html, and "Common Behavioral Characteristics of Gifted and Talented Students," *Exceptionally Able Children*, 1996, http://toolbox4gifted.wikispaces.com/file/view/ID_Checklist_Characteristics.doc/196379458/ID_Checklist_Characteristics.doc. See also Emmanuel Felton, "Can Schools Create Gifted Students?," *The Hechinger Report*, January 26, 2015, http://hechingerreport.org/can-schools-create-gifted-students/, for an example of a Louisiana school district that asks teachers to identify students who might have high ability by looking for traits such as being "highly imaginative, highly opinionated, being able to speak persuasively and having a good sense of humor." The district's objective is to bring more high-ability minority children into its gifted and talented program than is currently possible using test results alone.

9. See, for example, "About the Tests," Johns Hopkins Center for Talented Youth, accessed January 24, 2015, http://cty.jhu.edu/talent/testing/about/index.html.

10. Caroline Hoxby and Christopher Avery, "The Missing 'One-Offs': The Hidden Supply of High-Achieving, Low-Income Students," Brookings Institution, 2013, http://www.brookings.edu/~/media/Projects/BPEA/Spring%202013/2013a_hoxby.pdf.

11. We understand that mastery-based assessment would confound the "universal screening" that we suggest for grades 3 or 4, but an equivalent screening scheme could be built into a modularized assessment system.

12. We would not follow Taiwan's and Ontario's lead and define giftedness as an "exceptionality" deserving of inclusion under "special education." But America's current approach to special education—little changed since 1975—is itself being eclipsed by the recognition that every child deserves an individualized education and by technologies and practices that are gradually moving the entire K–12 system in that direction.

13. MOOCs are rapidly becoming available for high school students. See, e.g., "All High School Courses," edX Inc., accessed November 29, 2014, https://www.edx.org/course-list/allschools/high-school-courses/allcourses.

14. These are examples of selective public schools that are ordinarily free to residents of their states but often carry ancillary costs for families, such as university-course tuition fees and boarding expenses. Nevada's Davidson Academy illustrates the former cost and the Illinois Math and Science Academy illustrates the latter. See "Home page," Davidson Academy of Nevada,

accessed November 29, 2014, http://www.davidsonacademy.unr.edu/, and "Home page," Illinois Mathematics and Science Academy, accessed November 29, 2014, https://www.imsa.edu/.

15. "Bloomberg Philanthropies Launches New Initiative to Help High-Achieving, Low- and Moderate- Income Students Apply to and Enroll in Top Colleges and Universities," Bloomberg Philanthropies, October 28, 2014, http://www .bloomberg.org/press/releases/bloomberg-philanthropies-launches-new-initiative-help-high-achieving-low-moderate-income-students-apply-enroll-top-colleges-universities/.

16. The Philanthropy Roundtable has provided excellent guidance for philanthropists seeking to narrow the "high-achievement gap." See Andy Smarick, *Closing America's High-Achievement Gap* (Washington, DC: The Philanthropy Roundtable), 2013.

APPENDIX

1. The slope data reported in these tables are based on "best-fit trend lines," not shown in the accompanying figure. Such a line is used to indicate trends, such as the rate at which something is increasing or decreasing over time. In this appendix, all best-fit trend lines were calculated using Microsoft Excel.

2. The 10th percentile score is the score for that year above which 90 percent of students scored. And the 90th percentile is the score *below* which 90 percent of students scored. Changes in these lines are a way of tracking whether low and high scorers within the population are gaining or losing over time on these assessments.

3. See note 1 and the accompanying text that references figure A.1 for an explanation of the slope calculation in these tables.

4. For information on this measure, see chapter 2, note 19.

5. These data aren't available for Japan, Hungary, and South Korea. The reason given by PISA is that its reporting standards weren't met.

ABOUT THE AUTHORS

CHESTER E. FINN, JR. is the distinguished senior fellow and president emeritus at the Thomas B. Fordham Institute and a senior fellow at Stanford's Hoover Institution. His previous positions include Professor of Education and Public Policy at Vanderbilt University, counsel to the U.S. ambassador to India, legislative director for Senator Daniel Patrick Moynihan, and Assistant U.S. Secretary of Education for Research and Improvement. He has also been on the research staffs of the Brookings Institution, the Hudson Institute, and the Manhattan Institute, and has taught high school social studies in Massachusetts. He is the author, coauthor, or editor of more than twenty books and has written more than four hundred articles in a wide array of scholarly and popular publications. He is a regular contributor to Fordham's *Education Gadfly Weekly*, a contributing editor of *Education Next*, and a contributor to such online outlets as *NationalReview.com*, *Politico*, and *Atlantic.com*. He serves on the Maryland State Board of Education and the boards of the National Council on Teacher Quality and the Core Knowledge Foundation and has spoken at hundreds of seminars, conferences, symposia, and meetings across the United States and in many other countries. He is the recipient of awards from the Educational Press Association of America, the National Association for Gifted Children, the National Alliance for Public Charter Schools, and the Education Writers Association. He holds three degrees from Harvard University and an honorary doctorate from Colgate University.

BRANDON L. WRIGHT is a managing editor and policy associate at the Thomas B. Fordham Institute, where he has worked since graduating from American University Washington College of Law in

2012 with a Juris Doctor. During law school, he clerked for an education law firm that advocates for students with special needs and was a senior staff member of the *Administrative Law Review*. He also holds a bachelor's degree in political science and philosophy from the University of Michigan.

Both authors are also products of gifted-education programs of very different kinds. Finn was able to accelerate in mathematics in the Dayton Public Schools and later graduated from Phillips Exeter Academy, a selective-admission private high school. Wright participated in a full-time gifted pull-out program from grades 4 through 8 in his Michigan public school system.

INDEX